# The New Social Worker ®
## the social work careers magazine

Winter 2014
Volume 21, Number 1

*Social work students from the University of Belize are involved in advocating and educating youths and communities on crime prevention. Crime Stoppers Belize recognized both their lecturer and the students in a yearly recognition day for the tremendous work they did in helping to make Belize a better place.*

# FEATURES

Turn Up the Tech in Social Work

Making the Tough Call: Mandated Reporting, Parts V & VI

Social Work Goes to the Movies

Reviews

Student Role Model: Erick Fugett

# In This Issue

- Ethics in Private Practice
- Becoming a Successful Field Supervisor
- What Every New Social Worker Needs To Know About the DSM-5
- Social Work Reinvestment Act (SWRA)

...and much more!

# CONTENTS

THE NEW SOCIAL WORKER®
Winter 2014
Volume 21, Number 1

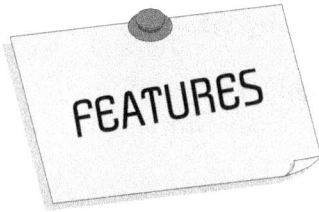

## FEATURES

## DEPARTMENTS

# Publisher's Thoughts

Dear Reader,

Happy New Year! I am very excited, because we have some great things in store for 2014 at THE NEW SOCIAL WORKER. Will you help us in our planning by participating in our 2014 Reader Survey? It will take about 5-10 minutes of your time. Go to *http://www.socialworker.com/2014-reader-survey* to get started. Thanks!

We are starting the new year with our ALL-NEW (and improved) website! In October 2013, we launched the first major overhaul of our site in several years. Please go to *http://www.socialworker.com* and check it out. It can be accessed on your computer, mobile phone, tablet, and other devices. Please note that the site is still at *http://www.socialworker.com*.

*The publisher/editor*

However, other pages within the site have changed, so if you have linked to any of our pages, please update your links! Also, the process for downloading the magazine has changed. Click on the "magazine" link on the site for details.

We are adding more creative work of social workers, both to the website and the magazine. This includes poetry, audio, and video features. In this issue, we have all three. See page 21, and then go to our website to access the video and audio.

In the Fall 2013 issue, we featured an article that responded to some concerns about the DSM-5. In this issue, on page 8, we look at some of the specific changes in the DSM that have social workers scratching their heads, to help you in your thinking about preparing for the implementation of the new manual.

Cultural competence helps us to best meet the needs of the diverse populations we serve as social workers. Janice Hawkins writes on page 12 about the imporance of a culturally sensitive approach to working with African American clients.

We continue with our series on mandated reporting. Parts V and VI in this issue look at questions about what to do if you are not sure about reporting suspected child abuse or neglect, and what happens if you are wrong in your decision.

In this issue, we are happy to begin a new collaboration with Social Justice Solutions (SJS). SJS focuses on all aspects of social justice and will be contributing articles to *THE NEW SOCIAL WORKER* on a variety of issues. We are starting with an introduction to the Social Work Reinvestment Act. See page 35.

I am encouraging all social workers to read Ogden Rogers' book, *Beginnings, Middles, & Ends,* which we published in October. It is a book that will make you laugh, cry, smile, and think a little differently about social work. It is available in print and Kindle editions at Amazon.com.

To subscribe to THE NEW SOCIAL WORKER's Social Work E-News and notifications of new issues of the magazine, go to the "Subscribe" link on our website at *http://www.socialworker.com.* (It's free!)

Until next time—happy reading!

*Linda M. Grobman*

# Write for The New Social Worker

We are looking for articles from social work practitioners, students, and educators.

Some areas of particular interest are: social work ethics; student field placement; practice specialties; social work careers/job search; technology; "what every new social worker needs to know;" and news of unusual, creative, or nontraditional social work.

Feature articles run 1,500-2,000 words in length. News articles are typically 100-150 words. Our style is conversational, practical, and educational. Write as if you are having a conversation with a student or colleague. What do you want him or her to know about the topic? What would you want to know? Use examples.

The best articles have a specific focus. If you are writing an ethics article, focus on a particular aspect of ethics. For example, analyze a specific portion of the NASW *Code of Ethics* (including examples), or talk about ethical issues unique to a particular practice setting. When possible, include one or two resources at the end of your article—books, additional reading materials, and/or websites.

We also want photos of social workers and social work students "in action" for our cover, and photos to accompany your news articles!

Send submissions to lindagrobman@socialworker.com.

## The New Social Worker®
*the social work careers magazine*

## Winter 2014
## Vol. 21, Number 1

### Publisher/Editor
Linda May Grobman, MSW, ACSW, LSW

### Contributing Writers
Barbara Trainin Blank
Allan Barsky, JD, MSW, Ph.D.
Addison Cooper, LCSW
Ellen Belluomini, LCSW
Kathryn A. Krase, Ph.D., J.D., MSW

THE NEW SOCIAL WORKER® (ISSN 1073-7871) is published four times a year by White Hat Communications, P.O. Box 5390, Harrisburg, PA 17110-0390. Phone: (717) 238-3787. Fax: (717) 238-2090. Send address corrections to: lindagrobman@socialworker.com

Advertising rates available on request.

Photo/art credits: Image from BigStockPhoto.com © Iqoncept (pages 4 & 6), Almagami (page 8), Olly2 (page 9), Mocker (page 12), Jackmicro (page 14), Yarndoll (page 16), Savannah 1969 (page 18), Pat Hastings (page 20), Gajus (page 24), Firstpentuer (page 27).

Send all editorial, advertising, subscription, and other correspondence to:

**THE NEW SOCIAL WORKER**
**White Hat Communications**
**P.O. Box 5390**
**Harrisburg, PA 17110-0390**
**(717) 238-3787 Phone**
**(717) 238-2090 Fax**

lindagrobman@socialworker.com
http://www.socialworker.com
http://www.facebook.com/newsocialworker
http://www.twitter.com/newsocialworker

**Print Edition:**
http://newsocialworker.magcloud.com

# Erick Fugett

*by Barbara Trainin Blank*

Erick Fugett's interest in social work began long before he knew what it was.

"I first realized there was social welfare injustice when I was a very young child," said Fugett, who just completed his BSW at Morehead State University in Ashland, Kentucky. "I grew up in a household with an alcoholic father and a younger brother who had been diagnosed with Duchennes muscular dystrophy. The combination of both was somewhat of a battlefield."

The family received no help from his father or from the "system." Fugett witnessed his mother struggling to handle all the "issues" alone, with support only from the immediate family but little or no community support. "At the time, in the early '90s, there was little or no help for a mother and her disabled child besides physical therapy (out of home), educational support, or institutionalization," he recalls.

His mother didn't know how to even inquire about home health, supported community living, respite services, medical transport, and the like.

"As I grew older, I realized that there are many other families right in our own community who are also suffering in vain," Fugett continues. "Yet, there are supports in place that could dramatically impact these individuals."

Eventually, he and his siblings left the home prematurely. Fugett dropped out of high school, overcome by all the family stresses and poverty. "It was truly a feat just to live and function on a day-to-day basis, even though I did secretly enjoy school, learning, and the socialization."

Fortunately, that was a temporary detour. With the support of family and friends, he returned to earn his GED at the Adult Education Learning Center in Ashland. "From that point on, education was first and foremost in my life's goals," Fugett says.

He singles out his grandparents Dora and Ken Conley, who "stepped up and became my impromptu parents in my time of need."

Fugett believes all the "struggle, conflict, and oppression" made him a stronger person. And because of the support his family had lacked, he decided to do something to help families and individuals with disabilities and to advocate against social welfare injustice.

After taking general and human services technology courses, Fugett transferred to Morehead State in 2011 for his BSW degree. In 2013, he was named Social Work Student of the Year for NASW-Kentucky.

"I was the first BSW student from Morehead to win the award," says the 32-year-old Kentucky native. "I'm so proud."

Fugett's dedication to education and "quiet leadership" were noted by Nancy Preston, regional campus director of Morehead, since the time he "wandered into her office" to talk about social work after arriving on campus.

"He still stops in and visits," says Preston, who taught Fugett in a policy class. "He is a wonderful student, a natural but quiet kind of leader. Other students gravitate toward Erick because of his friendliness and enthusiasm. He's always full of compassion and open."

Fugett was an officer/media specialist for the Student Association of Social

*Erick Fugett*

Workers and has done volunteer work for NASW-KY. He is also active in NASW and has volunteered with the Kentucky Chapter on a few different occasions.

Fugett himself says he finds little time for anything outside of work and school. But he is proud of having been the co-founder of "Bobcat 4 a Day" at Ohio University Southern, alongside his sister, Elizabeth Stevens.

The program served juvenile offenders from the county, who would go to the college for an entire day to experience campus life. By going to classes, eating lunch, meeting professors, filling out admissions paperwork, gathering information about obtaining a GED, and enrolling for classes, the young people learn about the benefits of higher education.

Although Fugett no longer volunteers with Bobcat, he keeps in contact. "I make sure if they ever need anything, they know where to call. We saw the need and planted the seed."

He continues to work at A Brighter Future, which provides support to clients with intellectual, developmental, and/or behavior disorders or issues. As the adult day training supervisor at the

*Fugett—continued on page 22*

# Ethics in Private Practice
## by Allan Barsky, JD, MSW, Ph.D.

A number of students entering the field of social work express interest in pursuing private practice. Perhaps, these students enjoy the thought of independent practice–being one's own boss, being able to set one's own policies and expectations, being accountable to nobody but oneself, and perhaps being able to earn more than one might expect in an agency-based position. There may also be tax advantages to private practice, including the ability to write off expenses that one cannot write off regarding employment income. So, given the allure of private practice, what does the *NASW Code of Ethics* (2008) say about private practice, and what are the main ethical concerns?

The *NASW Code of Ethics* does not mention private practice, per se...it does not specifically condone or support private practice, and it does not reject or warn against private practice. It does, however, include a number of relevant ethical standards, including competence (s.1.04), abandonment of clients (s.1.16(b)), supervision and consultation (s. 3.01), and fees (1.13(a)).

In most jurisdictions, social workers need licensure to provide independent, clinical services. Licensure, however, does not ensure competence to provide clinical services. Although clinical licensure typically requires completion of an MSW and two years of supervised, post-MSW experience, a social worker may or may not be ready for private practice–particularly if the social worker is not using appropriate supervision or peer consultation. Thus, just because one possesses the minimum legal prerequisite to engage in private clinical practice, this does not mean one is actually competent and ready for such practice.

Before engaging in private practice, consider the knowledge and skills you will need. Consider the challenges that may arise in practice, including issues of safety for suicidal, homicidal, mentally ill, and other vulnerable clients you may be serving. Consider what sort of legal liability you may be incurring.

Even if you do decide to enter private practice, consider restricting your areas of practice to those within your areas of competence, and consider which types of services may require further training, education, and supervision. Two years after completing an MSW, for instance, you may be ready to provide cognitive-behavioral counseling to clients dealing with parenting issues and child discipline. At the same time, you may not be ready to provide forensic assessments or parenting coordination for high conflict cases referred by the courts.

Supervision or consultation need not stop when one goes into private practice. In fact, it is generally good social work practice to continue supervision or consultation throughout one's career, regardless of the context of practice. For some social workers, cost may seem like a barrier to securing ongoing supervision or consultation. Consider, however, the cost of supervision in relation to one malpractice lawsuit that might be avoided. Also, consider ways to reduce costs of supervision or consultation. Some supervisors offer group supervision or supervision over the telephone to reduce costs.

Some social workers meet periodically with a group of peer consultants to offer each other guidance and support. Still, note that you may need individualized, face-to-face supervision for particularly challenging situations. Private practice can feel isolating. Social work is all about human relationships...not just with clients, but with professional peers.

If one is a sole practitioner, an important consideration is how to ensure continuity of services if you are not able to serve clients–for instance, when you go on vacation, when you are sick, if you have an accident, and if you become incapacitated or die. All social workers should have a back-up plan for clients. In agencies, the back-up plan may be easy because other workers are available. For sole practitioners, finding a colleague to provide back-up is also very important.

Some social workers eschew private practice because it goes against social work's historic mission of serving the most vulnerable in society (See Specht and Courtney's book, *Unfaithful Angels: How Social Work Has Abandoned its Mission,* for a thoughtful analysis of this issue). In private practice, clinicians may tend toward working with the more advantaged people in society. It makes sense–financially: people with money or with mental health insurance provide the clinician with a valued source of income. If one is in private practice, one's pay depends on the fees one earns.

So, does private practice go against the social work value of social justice? Perhaps not. Social workers are not obligated to promote social justice or serve the most vulnerable in society at all times. However, ethically, they should do so at least some of the time. The *NASW Code of Ethics* suggests that fees should be fair and reasonable. Perhaps a social worker in private practice could offer some services to people in need on a sliding scale, reduced rate, or even for free. Perhaps the social worker could help the client find a sponsor or scholarship to pay for services. Further, the social worker in private practice could donate some of his or her time to volunteer at a social agency or charitable organization. Supervising BSW or MSW students during their field placements is also a way of giving back–or paying forward–the help that the social worker has received earlier in his or her career.

Private practice is not necessarily an either/or decision. One could have a job with a social agency and also have a part-time private practice. Of course, the worker should advise the employer and discuss any potential conflicts of interest (e.g., to make sure the worker is not taking clients from the agency, and to make sure the worker's private practice obligations do not conflict with the worker's agency obligations). A private practice social worker may also engage in social advocacy–promoting social justice, advancing social policy, or redressing concerns related to the worker's own clinical practice. One challenge for the private practitioner is time. How does one balance time needed to provide service to clients (and bring in a source of income) with time to participate in social advocacy, policy, or charity work (which does not come with income)? Although it is a challenge, it is certainly a challenge that social workers in private practice should accept. Advancing social justice and serving those in need are the core aspects of who we are as social workers.

If you decide to pursue private practice, make sure you do so in an ethically-minded manner. You may want to develop your knowledge and skills in an agency setting, beyond two years post-MSW. And finally, when you develop a strategic plan for private practice, make sure you consider how you can implement the values of service, competence, social justice, respect for the

dignity of worth of all people, integrity, and human relationships. These values apply whether one is in private or agency-based practice.

*Dr. Allan Barsky is Professor of Social Work at Florida Atlantic University and Chair of the National Ethics Committee of the National Association of Social Workers. He is the author of Ethics and Values in Social Work (Oxford University Press), Conflict Resolution for the Helping Professions (Brooks/Cole), and Clinicians in Court (Guilford Press). The views expressed in this article do not necessarily reflect the view of any of the organizations with which Dr. Barsky is affiliated.*

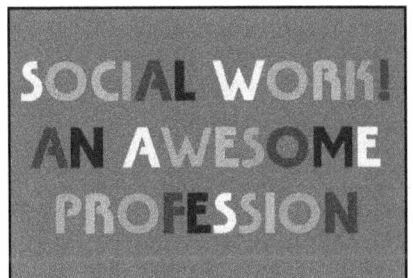

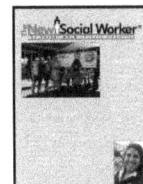

# The Whos, Whats, and Hows of Being a Successful Social Work Field Supervisor

### by Alyssa Lotmore, LMSW

The first day of field can bring anxiety and excitement. You may ask yourself a lot of questions. Am I cut out for this role? How do I make a good first impression? How can I define my role? Do I have enough experience and knowledge to even do this?

After reading those few sentences, you may think this article is going to be about a social work student's first day of field. This segment will actually be discussing the role of the field supervisor. When I first began supervising students a few years ago, I asked myself those questions. I had a wonderful supervisor when I was a student, and I wanted to have the same positive impact on current students.

Just like students, as a field supervisor I had anxiety and excitement. I was nervous about not possessing the knowledge, skills, and teaching ability to help shape a bright-eyed student just entering the field. At the same time, I was excited about this new role that I was taking on.

A survey of longtime supervisors found that the greatest aspects interns bring to placements are a sense of optimism and enthusiasm. They believe that interns bring a new perspective, and many supervisors value the opportunity to be a part of training future professionals (Baird, 2008). Those reasons are what led me to sign up for this new role.

Despite my willingness to accept interns, I still had nerves. Only being in my mid-20s, and somewhat new to the field myself, I questioned my ability. I forgot about my high GPA during college, or that I did well at my job. I now felt this added pressure of being a role model to future social work professionals. How do I ensure that I give them the best learning opportunities and make their experience worthwhile?

I went straight to the Internet and began looking up articles about being a field supervisor. There were a few articles written over the last few years, but it all was similar, as they just went over the how-to's to providing supervision.

As important as supervision is, there is so much more that makes an internship a great learning opportunity than simply the hour of face-to-face supervision each week. I decided to revise my search and look for what students want in a field supervisor. Bingo! I found pages and pages of results ranging from articles to blogs to message boards. After some hefty reading, I discovered what I needed to do.

*"Mini-Curriculum."* I took a step back from anxiety and reflected on all that I have done in my schooling and career. I knew that I was qualified to take on this role. I needed to develop my own mini-curriculum to be able to share with my interns my knowledge and what they would find valuable. I looked at all the possible learning opportunities–diversity among clients, trainings, opportunities for home visits, macro work. I laid everything out, so I could discuss with my interns what interested them and what could be used to challenge them to develop new skills.

*Resources.* Students are in college to learn. There is only so much a student learns in the classroom. After I graduated, the professional development trainings I attended really helped me take my ability to practice to the next level. I took to my office my binders of information and PowerPoint slides from trainings I had attended. I placed them on my bookshelf specifically for my interns to have access to. I wanted them to be able to go through the binders and see all the various training models and types of interventions that could be used. They could discuss what they were interested in with me during supervision. As much as field is a place to get hands-on learning experience, it can also be a place where educational and academic resources are available.

*Open Communication.* From my Google search, I found that several interns stated they were not being chal-

lenged enough. My first day with my interns, I sat down individually with each of them and asked them about their experience, their goals for this placement, and their expectations from me. I also went over my experience, my goals for them while here, and my expectations from them (and the consequences for not meeting some of the mandatory expectations). I found that sitting down and having open conversations in which we both talked and listened to each other was the most beneficial. It not only helped build our relationship, but it conveyed that I was a person who could be easily approached, even though I had authority. I also discussed advocacy with them. If they are not feeling challenged, or are not getting the experience they hoped to get, they have to speak up in a professional way. Letting your interns know that you want feedback from them helps make the students more comfortable to advocate for their needs.

*Student's View of Supervision.* Research has shown that during supervision sessions, areas associated with student satisfaction are mainly issues concerning students' practice experience. Examples of these include the practice skills used by students, types of cases and clients, ongoing performance issues, and personal strengths and limitations. The topics that were not associated with student satisfaction were discussions about administrative issues, community issues, and career plans. Students want the "direct and practical information that is going to help them become ethical and effective social workers" (Dettlaff, 2003). Topics such as career plans are wonderful to discuss, but not during supervision. Leave supervision as a time for students to discuss their practice, work in the field, and areas that need improvement.

*Allow Practice Time.* Much is discussed in supervision. Allow students time to practice. A supervisor must monitor interns, but being too directive hinders their ability to learn and grow. Internships can always be a learning opportunity. Some days at an internship can be uneventful in regard to clients, yet that is not a reason to assign new tasks to interns that do not meet the learning needs of the student (such as photocopying). This is another reason why I have the bookshelf with educational materials for my interns to have at their disposal when they have free time. No student wants to be bored at his or her placement. There is always a way to enhance the learning experience.

There is no start and end-point when in the professional work world. There is no minimum grade you need to achieve to pass. For interns and eventual social workers, learning is on-going, and the demand for high standards and continued learning will continue throughout your professional career. As a field supervisor, I have the opportunity to prepare the future of our profession. As with our clients, we need to empower our interns by acknowledging all the great skills they are developing and practicing. As interns, they are still learning (as we all are), so it is critical to provide feedback and discuss areas they need to work on. Being too nice and always saying that they are doing a "good job" is just as harmful as not recognizing the areas in which they are excelling.

Field supervisors have the privileged role of shaping the next generation of social workers. As graduates ourselves, we should want to give back to our college by taking on this privileged opportunity. We should come together as supervisors and share advice, resources, and experiences to gain in our own learning and continued development in this role.

Have confidence in yourself and do your best to listen to your interns and provide them with an opportunity to learn, practice, and grow. Be the supervisor that you yourself would have wanted to have when you were that bright-eyed, eager student.

## References

Baird, B. N. (2008). *The internship practicum and field placement handbook: A guide for the helping professionals* (5th ed.). Upper Saddle River, NJ: Pearson Prentice Hall.

Dettlaff, A. J. (2003). *From mission to evaluation: A field instructor training program.* Alexandria, VA: Council on Social Work Education.

*Alyssa Lotmore, LMSW, is a graduate of the State University of New York at Albany School of Social Welfare. Her focus is on social work in the educational setting.*

# What Every New Social Worker Needs To Know About...DSM-5

## by Martha Teater, M.A., LMFT

There are a lot of changes in the Fifth Edition of the *Diagnostic and Statistical Manual of Mental Disorders (DSM-5)* that have social workers talking. Some of the revisions are seen as positive. However, there are several that are raising concern among clinicians.

I have presented dozens of workshops on the *DSM-5* and have trained thousands of clinicians in its use. In these workshops, I've been able to pick up on a few changes that have raised some eyebrows among participants.

People have told me that they are overwhelmed, confused, and even a bit disoriented by all the changes. They have some anxiety with the upcoming conversion to the *DSM-5* and the many ways it will affect them as they diagnose people, and the major adjustments that agencies will need to make to adapt.

I'll share with you three of the areas that arouse the most passionate responses from people.

## No More Multiaxial System

The change that has been universally upsetting to people in my workshops is the loss of the multiaxial system.

We started using five axes to formulate a diagnosis when the *DSM-III-R* came out in 1987. Ever since then, we've had five main pieces of information that made up our diagnostic impression.

Axis I listed clinical disorders. Axis II included personality disorders and mental retardation. Axis III was where we listed general medical conditions. Axis IV was where we described psychosocial and environmental problems. Axis V was the place to put the Global Assessment of Functioning (the GAF), which summarized how severely a person was affected by his or her mental health condition.

Those five aspects of a diagnosis are no longer going to be listed in the diagnostic description. Instead, diagnoses will just be recorded in a list, with the principle diagnosis being listed first, and others following in order of importance to treatment.

We can reflect contributing factors by using appropriate V codes, and these factors will be reflected in the body of the assessment information (as always), but they will no longer be part of the diagnosis. We will document those factors in our notes, but as one workshop participant lamented, "But nobody reads my assessment!"

Another participant shared her observation, "It seems like we're losing something important by taking that information away from being front and center in terms of importance. I really like being able to look at the five axes of a diagnosis and being able to get a feel for the person. It's like seeing a snapshot of the person being treated, and it gives a much fuller picture of someone."

Let's look at an example of what a diagnosis would look like now.

Shannon comes in to see you for an initial appointment. She's 41 years old and reports that she's been irritable, short-tempered, and tired for the past couple of months. She has been less patient and engaged with her friends and family. She's not sleeping well, waking up several times at night, and she's tired when she gets up. She's gained weight and has stopped exercising. Shannon doesn't know what's wrong and has a hard time imagining that she'll ever feel like herself again.

She has a long history of disrupted relationships, beginning in early adulthood. She often feels that other people aren't there for her, even though she reports that she is always supportive and there for her friends. She struggles with feeling alone and worries that she'll be abandoned. She has had several jobs and can't decide on a direction for her life. Shannon often struggles with her identity and seems to reinvent herself periodically. Sometimes when the stress is too much, she ends up cutting herself, not in a suicide attempt, but to stop her emotional pain.

Unfortunately, Shannon has developed multiple sclerosis. She is still able to be independent, but has balance problems and needs to make some decisions about treatment options.

Along with a recent job loss, her financial situation has gotten desperate. She has been evicted from her apartment because she was so behind in her rent, and she is now staying with various friends.

Here's how you might write up your diagnosis under *DSM-IV*:

*Axis I: 296.22 Major depressive disorder, single episode, moderate*
*Axis II: 301.83 Borderline personality disorder*
*Axis III: 340 Multiple sclerosis*
*Axis IV: Unemployment, homelessness*
*Axis V: GAF=40*

And here's how it might look under *DSM-5*:

*296.22 Major depressive disorder, single episode, moderate*
*301.83 Borderline personality disorder*
*340     Multiple sclerosis*

## Asperger's Disorder Is Gone

By now, most clinicians have heard that Asperger's disorder is gone from the *DSM-5*.

There is no diagnosis of Asperger's disorder in the manual. The term Asperger's disorder is not even used anywhere in the content. This is now considered high-functioning autism, and will be incorporated as part of autism spectrum disorder.

This change has been one of the most controversial of the whole revision. People with Asperger's, parents of children with Asperger's, and advocacy groups have been vocal in their frustration with this omission. They see Asperger's as a different condition from autism, and they disagree with the decision to eliminate it as a separate disorder.

People are apprehensive about the ability of folks with a *DSM-IV* diagnosis of Asperger's to retain a diagnosis and continue to qualify for supportive services. The *DSM-5* task force has said that most people with a well-established *DSM-IV* diagnosis of Asperger's should meet the criteria for autism spectrum disorder in the *DSM-5*. If they don't, we are to evaluate them for social (pragmatic) communication disorder.

This has done little to allay the concerns of people with Asperger's and their advocates. Many feel that their condition, which they may have come to accept, is being replaced with a term that they are less than enthusiastic about.

This is a controversy that I don't think we've heard the end of, although it's too late to make a change in time for this revision of the manual.

Let's take a look at how you might assess someone with Asperger's symptoms:

Noah is a 15-year-old whose parents bring him to see you. They have often wondered why he seems so different from their other two children. Noah has few friends, makes little eye contact, and spends a lot of time alone. He does okay in school and isn't a behavior problem for his parents or teachers. Noah has a keen interest in movies and superheroes. He can quote long pieces of dialogue from his favorite movies, which he has watched many times. He collects superhero action figures and calls his room his "fortress of solitude," because he feels peaceful in his room.

To fall asleep at night Noah usually bounces on his bed enough to make the mattress jiggle a bit. His parents sometimes notice that he rocks himself gently, especially when he is feeling a lot of stress.

Noah likes to write stories about superheroes that he creates, and he is interested in clocks and lamps.

You may be thinking that Noah might fit a diagnosis of Asperger's disorder, and you'd be right. But with implementation of the *DSM-5,* you won't have that as an option. You would diagnosis him with autism spectrum disorder, and you would indicate the severity of that.

For autism spectrum disorder, you would gauge severity in two different areas: social/communication deficits and restrictive, repetitive behaviors (RRBs). For each of those domains, you can select a severity level of 1, 2, or 3, indicating the level of support that's needed. Most people with an Asperger's-looking presentation will end up with both severity indicators being a level 1.

## Dramatic Changes in Substance Use Disorders

There are a lot of revisions to the substance use disorders category that have people talking. Some practitioners are complaining that the symptom threshold is too low, and it will be too easy to tag someone with a diagnosis. Others don't like the loss of the abuse and dependence distinctions. Some people don't like the fact that gambling is the only behavioral addiction in the manual.

Let's start with the change in the symptom threshold. Substance use disorders have 11 symptoms to choose from. Severity is determined by the number of symptoms that are endorsed: mild is two to three symptoms, moderate is four to five symptoms, and severe is six or more symptoms being endorsed.

Someone could have two symptoms and end up with a substance use disorder. Some clinicians fear that this could too easily burden a person with a substance use disorder diagnosis prematurely.

I've been asked whether or not insurance companies will pay for treatment for a mild substance use disorder. I haven't heard anything definitive about that, but I suppose payers could decide not to cover such disorders if they want to save reimbursement for people who have moderate or severe substance use disorders.

There are some practitioners who like the descriptors of abuse or dependence to define the extent of a person's substance use. Those terms are gone from the manual, replaced by the severity scale related to each substance that a person uses problematically.

One question comes up at every training I've done on the *DSM-5*. A participant will raise a hand and ask where sexual addiction is listed. Someone else may then ask about pornography addiction. People are usually surprised and disappointed to learn that there are no behavioral addictions or compulsive behaviors in the manual other than gambling.

The task force maintains that the body of research doesn't yet support inclusion of those compulsive behaviors

in the manual. The research evidence appears stronger for gambling, so it's still in the manual. Problem gambling is now grouped in the substance use and addictive disorders category. It's no longer in the disruptive, impulse control, and conduct disorders section.

Here's an example of one person's presentation with a substance use disorder:

Ron is 37 years old and was referred to you by the court system following a recent DUI conviction. He says he was at a friend's birthday party and thought he could safely drive home after drinking "a few" beers. He's really upset about the DUI and feels a lot of embarrassment. He's worried about the financial expense and loss of his license for a year. He's had a hard time sleeping because of the worry and depressed reaction he's experienced since the DUI.

Upon further investigation, you find that Ron drinks "several" beers most nights of the week. He estimates that he drinks 6-8 beers a day, "sometimes more, sometimes less." He has tried to cut back, but has been unsuccessful in those efforts. He used to "feel a buzz" after drinking 3-4 beers, but now it takes 6-8 to get the same feeling.

He smokes pot with his work friends, but doesn't like to do that regularly because of his fear of failing a random drug test at work. He smokes pot 3-4 times monthly. When he tries to cut back, he finds himself feeling strong urges to smoke pot.

He is a cigarette smoker, smoking about a pack a day.

If you were going to diagnose Ron, it might look something like this:

309.0   Adjustment disorder with mixed anxiety and depressed mood
305.00 Alcohol use disorder, mild
305.20 Cannibas use disorder, mild
305.1   Tobacco use disorder, mild

## More to Think About

I do want to emphasize that not all of the changes in the new manual are causing angst and woe among clinicians. I've highlighted the top three modifications that people are finding frustrating.

There are some changes that people are feeling good about. They seem to like the severity scales being specifically tailored to many different diagnoses. For example, anorexia severity is determined by a person's BMI (body mass index). Bulimia severity is based on the number of inappropriate compensatory behaviors weekly (vomiting, laxative use, over-exercising, and so forth). Oppositional defiant disorder severity is based on the number of settings in which symptoms are present.

People also seem excited about the new symptom cluster for PTSD, which is negative alterations in mood and cognitions. They feel that these cognitive changes reflect ways that people with PTSD often feel most affected by their trauma exposure.

A couple of things that leave folks scratching their heads are some of the changes in gender dysphoria and caffeine-related issues. These issues don't seem to get a resounding positive or negative reaction, but they are causing people to think.

Changes in the language of gender dysphoria include wording that indicates that we are now looking at gender as being on a spectrum, not just as the two choices of either male or female, but some alternative gender. This is a departure from the way most people have conceptualized gender until this point.

The confusion in the area of caffeine use comes from the fact that we have choices of caffeine intoxication or caffeine withdrawal, but there is no option of caffeine use disorder. People have wondered why we have intoxication and withdrawal, but not a use disorder.

You've asked a good question, and now's the time to become familiar with the changes that are part of the *DSM-5*. I encourage you to read up on the revisions and prepare yourself well for this dramatically different way to diagnose people.

*Martha Teater is a licensed marriage and family therapist in Waynesville, NC. She was a collaborating clinical investigator for the DSM-5 field trials for routine clinical practice. She can be contacted at martha@marthateater.com or http://www. marthateater.com.*

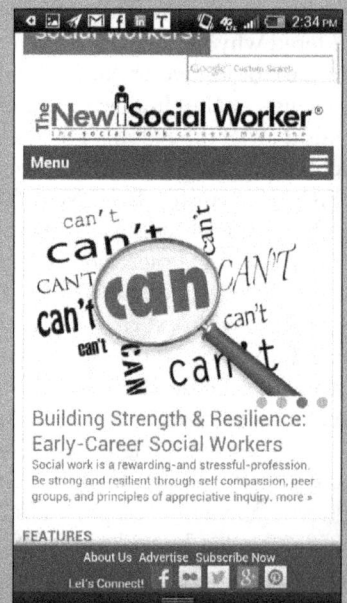

# Why Develop a Culturally Sensitive Approach to Work With African American Clients?

## by Janice Hawkins, Ph.D., LMSW

Being an Afro-Caribbean American social worker, I have always found it personally difficult to be receptive to therapy. I am by no means exempt from the vicissitudes of life and have entered therapy several times with varying degrees of success. I always start with good intentions, but I am the ultimate resistant client with attitude and too much information. As a black woman, I learned early that authority figures generally could not be trusted. I learned to distract them from focusing on my issues with my sense of humor and an outgoing attitude. I

knew instinctively that it was important to look okay so "they" left me alone.

Growing up in a household with Afro-Caribbean parents, I was brought up to neither share confidences nor admit emotional pain to outsiders. The personal disclosure and behavioral changes that therapists typically suggest were often embarrassing and totally unimaginable to me even from a cultural point of view. Most women from my background would rather "handle their own business" than seek outside help from a stranger. It was considered an embarrassment to one's family and upbringing to admit that any issue is so severe that only a "head doctor" could help.

As a social worker for a city agency, I was called in by a coordinator of a teen mother program to interview a teenage mother. According to the coordinator (who was Black American) and the social worker (who was Latino), there was "something wrong" with the girl. She would not carry through on instructions although she was a pleasant quiet girl who never said "no." When I spoke

to her, I recognized that as the youngest member of her household, she could not make decisions. Her grandmother would have to be consulted, as she was the family matriarch. Despite the teen mother's age (18) and her motherhood, she was still considered a child in her culture (Guyana) and behaved as such. The program coordinator remained resistant, stating she had to change because "she is in America now." Disclosing personal problems to a counselor ("stranger") could not only be seen as a sign of weakness, but also as leaking family secrets. Personal matters that cause pain or discomfort are only discussed with family members and very close friends. As an indirect result, parents and other extended family members exert considerable influence on important decisions, such as career choices and choice of marriage partners, assuming an unusually strong role in structuring and directing response to stress and stressful situations.

Culture and ethnicity have been well documented as key factors in the psychotherapeutic process. Even if therapists are aware of the variations of African diasporic cultures, they can mistakenly think that individuals from those cultures prefer to be called "African American." The term "African American" is commonly used to refer to individuals who share historical ties to the west coast of Africa, and to experiences of slavery. African Americans are diverse with respect to appearance, religious affiliation, socioeconomic status, sexual orientation, cultural expressions, family composition, and geographical origin. But black people from the Caribbean, South and Central America, and Canada speak different languages and/or different versions of English and may consider themselves to be black but not African American because of vastly different historical and cultural experiences (Liggan & Kay, 1999).

Generally speaking, in family systems of African descendants, family members assist each other with child care, finances, emotional support, housing, counsel, and so forth, particularly in times of trouble or stress. Families are considered to extend to non-blood

related relatives, such as neighbors, babysitters, friends, ministers, ministers' spouses, and church family, with ties as well as bio-family members (Evans & Davies, 1996).

## Standard Therapeutic Beliefs About Counseling and Family

Cultural consideration must be part of the therapy, as cultural issues will emerge under pressure of the process. The lack of knowledge of a particular client's culture and family dynamics could delay or harm the therapeutic process. A client's behavior that is labeled resistant may simply be a lack of recognition of the client's world view. Part of our job as social workers is to understand the client's world to the degree that we see their behavior for what it is.

Many standard therapeutic paradigms discourage developing a personal relationship with a client, because of the possibility of transference of feelings from the therapist to the client and vice versa (*NASW Code of Ethics,* Sec. 1.06c). This approach to therapy appears to be based on an assumption that all people, regardless of race, ethnicity, or culture, develop along uniform psychological dimensions and respond in similar ways to interactions. This assumes that there are no cultural biases in outcome between dissimilar analysts and clients.

The lack of understanding of a culturally different client's values and motivations, or the assumption that they are the same as one's own, can be a chief cause of resistance in the client (Comas-Diaz & Jacobsen, 1991). Studies of treatment outcomes seem to substantiate an assumption that therapy is often ineffective with black clients because their self identified view is crisis-oriented and non-introspective, valuing environmental change rather than personal change, independence, and self-actualization (Liggan &Kay, 1999).

In many cases, when clients come to the attention of government agencies and are judicially mandated to therapy or other programs, it is easy to forget they neither asked for nor wanted help. Part of the initial negotiation becomes to convince them that they need help and that we are the ones to give it. As humans who are also clinicians, we tend to see—based on our training and personal viewpoints—what we expect to see and behave toward other people as though they are the people we expect them to be. We project a mental model on the client and may behave in a way that is appropriate for our internal model, but inappropriate to the reality (Hughes & Kerr, 2000). In interracial or intra-cultural therapy, our internal preconceptions about the client can be devastating to the therapeutic relationship.

## Racism

It is not possible to discuss intercultural and/or interracial therapy situations without discussing racism. Racial discrimination is a phenomenon that African Americans experience in both blatant and subtle ways almost daily. Counseling is no exception to this phenomenon, despite the well-meaning intentions and efforts of therapists who believe they would never deliberately act in such a manner toward their clients. Even when therapists receive extensive multicultural training, racism can still be manifested unconsciously in the counseling process (Constantine 2007).

Social scientists describe it as the "illusion of color blindness," in which a therapist may assume that the black patient's culture is the same as that of the therapist's own culture, disregarding the importance the patient's blackness has for him or her. This can also ignore the impact of the therapist's culture on the patient, detracting from the patient's sense of the social realities of his or her experiences (Liggan & Kay, 1999). A less obvious form of racism, known as aversive racism, is characterized by the harboring of unconscious negative racial feelings and beliefs toward people of color, despite the fact that the person may perceive him- or herself as egalitarian, fair, and nonracist. Aversive racism is expressed via subtle, commonplace exchanges that somehow convey insulting or demeaning messages to people of color (Constantine, 2007).

## Conclusions

It is vitally important that therapists who work with African Americans be self-aware. In addition to taking courses to learn about the African American experience, therapists should identify any sources of uncertainty, discomfort, anxiety, bias, or cultural baggage that they might have (Comas-Diaz & Jacobsen, 1991).

African Americans are very cautious about seeking mental health services. Historically, those individuals who sought services were pathologized, overmedicated, given long-term and inpatient treatment rather than outpatient treatment, and were exposed to insensitive therapists who did not believe African Americans could benefit from verbal therapy. When African Americans obtain assistance and meet with a white therapist, they are often fearful that these therapists will be biased, use stereotypes, minimize the clients' experiences of discrimination, and not understand cultural traditions (Comas-Diaz & Jacobsen, 1991)

Today, non-Hispanic whites make up approximately 90% of mental health providers in the United States, whereas racial and ethnic minorities are projected to make up 40% of the U.S. population by 2025 (Ida, 2007). Regardless of race, 40% of clients attend one session and drop out, and the remainder typically end therapy after four or five meetings. African Americans drop out at rates higher than 40% (Liggan & Kay, 1999).

It is important for social workers to connect with clients on the basis of the client's reality rather than the social worker's agenda. When the social worker connects with the client's perceptions in the beginning of the counseling process, the social worker might lessen client resistance. Also important is to have mutually agreed-upon goals. It's all too easy for social workers to establish a goal for the client that the client either isn't aware of or doesn't agree with (Shallcross, 2010).

Most current training programs do not integrate exploration of therapists' attitudes regarding race, class, and [their] personal bias/discrimination into the curriculum. If future therapists had to examine and confront their views regarding racism and discrimination early on in their training, and reflect on evidence about how such attitudes affect the development of the therapeutic alliance and client outcomes, training programs might generate practitioners more in tune with the realities and perspectives of minority clients. Initiatives to make training programs more accessible to non-white populations and increase diversity within the mental health field can provide a long term solution to facilitating dialogue about techniques to best establish trust and understanding between therapists and clients from different racial and ethnic backgrounds (Cabral & Smith, 2011).

## References

Cabral, R., & Smith, T. (2011). Racial/ethnic matching of clients and therapists in mental health services: A meta-analytic review of preferences, perceptions and outcomes. *Journal of Counseling Psychology*, DOI: 10.1037/a0025266.

Comas-Diaz, L, & Jacobsen, F. (1991). Ethnocultural transference and countertransference in the therapeutic dyad. *American Journal of Orthopsychiatry, 61* (3), 392-402.

Constantine, M. G. (2007). Racial microaggressions against African American clients in cross-racial counseling relationships. *Journal of Counseling Psychology, 54* (1), 1-16.

Evans, H., & Davies, R. (1996). Overview issues in child socialization in the Caribbean. In *Caribbean families: Diversity among ethnic groups*, ed. J. L. Roopnarine and J. Brown. Greenwich, CT: Ablex.

Hughes, P. & Kerr, I. (2000). Transference and countertransference in communication between doctor and patient. *Advances in Psychiatric Treatment, 6*, 57–64.

Ida, D. J. (2007). Cultural competency and recovery within diverse populations. *Psychiatric Rehabilitation, 31* (1), 49-53.

Liggan, D., & Kay, J. (1999). Race in the room: Issues in the dynamic psychotherapy of African Americans. *Transcultural Psychiatry, 36* (2), 195–209.

Shallcross, L. (2010). Managing resistant clients. *Counseling Today*, February 14 2010.

*Janice Hawkins, Ph.D., LMSW, earned her master's degree in social work administration at Columbia University and her Ph.D. in public policy and administration from Walden University. Janice gained extensive experience during her tenure at ACS through several administrative roles, including direct casework on high-risk cases, development of training for staff, and assisting in creating ACS' first federal cost allocation plan. She lectures nationally on child abuse and neglect, ethical social work practice, and recognizing the importance of spirituality and ethnicity in social work intervention. She is a former recipient of National Association Social Workers, Black History Month Outstanding African American Social Worker, 2009/2011.*

# Media Multi-Tasking and the Learning/Developing Child

*by Anna Montana Cirell, MSW*

In today's digital age, multiple streams of competing information are exchanged rapidly through communication technology that has become more affordable, accessible, and available than ever before. Recent studies have shown that while the number of hours children are exposed to media (including printed material, television, websites, music) has remained constant at about 7.5 hours a day, the amount of media that many children are consuming has increased to 10.5 hours a day. Through media-multitasking, a significant number of children have increased their absorption of media as they text while surfing the Internet, listen to music while reading, and watch television while doing homework (Roberts, Foehr, & Rideout, 2005). Advances in digital technology tools, which make it easier for young people to consume an ever-increasing amount of media, are strongly affecting children's healthy development and learning.

Social workers, invested in the healthy socio-emotional wellness of our millennial generation, should attend to the effects of this emerging media trend on the developing child (Rideout, Foehr & Roberts, 2010). Furthermore, social work professionals, trained in a person-in-environment approach, may contribute valuable scholarly insights into the complex, mutually shaping ecological interactions influencing a child's behaviors, relationships, and social systems (Hutchinson, 2007).

The purpose of this article is severalfold. First, a background introduction will define the scope and implications of children's media usage and media-multitasking. Second, media usage factors will highlight salient differences across age, race, socio-economic status, and parental media limit-setting. Third, the positive impact of digital literacy on learning and creativity will be discussed in terms of the digital divide. Last, a conclusion will offer ways in which social workers can empower families to use discretion when accepting technology into their homes.

## Scope of Media-Multitasking and Healthy Development of Children

Children are spending around 53 hours a week (more than a full-time work week) absorbing media, and the boom in digital technologies has brought sweeping changes in the format and amount of media fighting for the attention of youth. (Roberts, Foehr, & Rideout, 2005). The phenomenon of "media-multitasking" and its inherent mental habits of dividing attention, switching attention, and keeping multiple trains of thought open have significant implications for young people's ability to attend, to plan, to relate to other people, and to understand the world.

Research on the information processing capabilities of youth has disproved the common myth that the newer generations of "TV babies" have developed an effective survivor-skill strategy for attention-dividing (Bergen, Grimes & Potter, 2005; Pittman, 1990). Multiple studies have found that the brain, regardless of the generation to which it belongs, cannot parallel process multiple streams of information efficiently (Armstrong & Chung, 2000; Bergen, Grimes & Potter, 2005).

The brain has the capacity to switch back and forth rapidly between various tasks, but something is always lost in the process (Rideout, Foehr & Roberts, 2010). Empirical findings indicate a disconnect between learning and media multitasking, as heavy media users report the lowest grades (Armstrong & Chung, 2000; Rideout, Foehr, & Roberts, 2010).

Recent studies report negative effects of media consumption on the very young (Christakis et al., 2009). When researchers began to explore the implications of television-as-"electronic babysitter," they found that infant television exposure correlates highly with delayed language development (Christakis et al., 2009). The American Academy of Pediatrics (2001), cognizant of the critical developmental task of language acquisition, cautions against television or video viewing before the age of two years; they believe that face-to-face interactive play between the parent and infant creates important opportunities for early communication. Furthermore, the audible and visual presence of the television significantly drowns out and, henceforth, reduces both infant and parental vocalizations (Christakis et al., 2009; Christakis & Zimmerman, 2006). These findings may alert parents to the false advertising claim of infant DVDs designed to foster quality parent-child interactions.

Social work advocates can acknowledge that most of children's media are directed from the business model's advertisement-driven platform and investigate the Federal Communications Commission's public policy efforts to regulate the amount of television advertising to children (Calvert & Kotler, 2003; Rideout, Foehr, & Roberts, 2010). Social work policy experts can explore the poor implementation and regulation of the Children's Television Act of 1990, and weigh the protests from broadcasters and owners of mass media corporations that "decent" educational programs are costly and do not draw in enough viewers to justify the effort to design them (Calvert & Kotler, 2003; Consumer Federation of America, 2000).

## Factors Contributing to High Media Consumption

In the average family home, there are three TV sets, three video players, three radios, three personal digital media players (iPod, MP3 player), two video game consoles, and one personal computer. Within this ecology of technology, the average child is spending more time with media than any other activity other than sleeping (Roberts & Foehr, 2008). Yet, not all children media-multitask. Research has shown that certain contextual factors (e.g., bedroom media and lack of parental regulation) and individual factors (e.g., pre-teen age range, minority race, and low socio-

economic status) influence the heaviest media usage patterns in children (Rideout, Foehr, & Roberts, 2010; Roberts & Foehr, 2008).

Children consume significantly higher levels of media in homes that indiscriminately embrace technology (Roberts & Foehr, 2008). Parents who allow television sets or personal computers in their children's bedrooms, or who support their children's purchase of portable digital media such as handheld video games or cell phones, are more likely to hold positive attitudes toward media. Recent work comparing media exposure times of children and adolescents with and without a television set in their bedroom reveals that easy access substantially increases exposure, even among very young children (Rideout, Foehr, & Roberts, 2010). Furthermore, children raised in families that set rules on media usage view television less. Changes in children's available time, driven by school or school-based extracurricular activities, results in different age-related patterns of media consumption (Roberts & Foehr, 2008). Children from two to five years of age absorb just under five hours of media daily, but once they enter preschool or kindergarten, media usage

decreases slightly. As children adjust to the demands of school and their bedtime hour is extended, their media exposure climbs until it reaches its peak at around eight hours daily during the "tween" years of 11 to 13. During later adolescence, as middle school segues into the advanced level of high school homework and extracurricular responsibilities, media usage gradually declines to about seven hours daily.

Differences in media usage patterns among race report that Hispanic and African American children are exposed to more media overall (4.5 hours more daily) than White children (Roberts & Foehr, 2008). Moreover, the racial disparity in media use has grown substantially over the past five years: for example, the gap between White and minority youth was just over two hours in 2004, and has grown to more than four hours today. African American and Hispanic children view more hours of screen media (television, movies, and videos) than White children, whereas White children report spending more time with computer media.

Screen media consumption has long been explained as resulting from differences in socio-economic status, as children raised in households earning less than

$20,000 a year view more television than children in households earning $75,000 or more (Roberts & Foehr, 2008).

## The Impact of the Digital Divide on Learning

Despite the high media usage of minority children, digital inequality exists across races. The next generation of digital natives is far from uniformly wired, and this has serious implications for student achievement and learning (Robinson, 2009). Studies that compare the learning experiences of children with high-quality home Internet access to the experiences of children with no or low-quality home access find striking differ-

ences across learning attitudes, skills, and habits (Robinson, 2009). Children raised with constrained Internet access spend less time leisurely exploring the Internet and developing sophisticated knowledge acquisition skills. As a result, these learners find information-seeking activities more challenging and suffer more emotional frustration than do more privileged children. Therefore the sweeping belief that all media content is damaging to our children's development ignores the significant amount of educational digital activities and practices shown to improve scholastic achievement and promote creativity (Schmidt & Vandewater, 2008; Weingerger, 2007).

## The Social Worker's Role in Technology and Learning

In sum, through media-multitasking, children's media consumption has increased significantly in the past years, and studies indicate that this behavior can affect their learning and development. Research has shown that high media usage correlates with poor grades, and infant media viewing may result in delayed lan-

guage acquisition. Factors that contribute to high media usage include the pre-teen years, minority and low socio-economic status, a television in the bedroom, and a lack of parental regulation on media viewing. Yet, access to high quality technology may enhance learning and creativity and narrow the student achievement gap.

Social workers working in schools and with families can consider the factors that may contribute to high media use and teach concerned parents how to accept technology into their homes. They can coach parents and families to set limits on infant television viewing and their children's media usage during homework hours. Last, social workers can embrace a sustainable approach to media literacy and empower both parents and their children to scrutinize both the content of media and the context of its use.

Practicing from an ecological perspective, social workers can acknowledge both the positive and negative impacts of media on youth, and understand that the goal is not to shut children's eyes to media, but to teach them to fine-tune their vision.

Today's children will grow up to be tomorrow's producers of media. The adult's place should not be to restrict, but to empower children to want better.

## References

American Academy of Pediatrics. (2001). Committee on Public Education. American Academy of Pediatrics: Children, adolescents, and television. *Pediatrics, 107* (2):423-426.

Armstrong, G.B., & Chung, L. (2000). Background television and reading memory in context: Assessing TV interference and facilitative context on encoding versus retrieval processes. *Communication Research, 2* (3), 327-352.

Bergen, L. ,Grimes, T., & Potter, D.. (2005). How attention partitions itself during simultaneous message presentations. *Human Communications Research, 31* (3) 311-336.

Calvert, S., & Kotler, J. (2003). Children's television act: Can policy make a difference. *Applied Developmental Psychology, 24,* 375–380.

Christakis, D.A., Gilkerson, J., Richards, J.A., Zimmerman, F.J., Garrison, M.M., Xu, D., Gray, S., & Yapanel, U. (2009). Audible television and decreased adult words, infant vocalizations, and conversational turns. *Archives of Pediatric and Adolescent Medicine, 163* (6), 554-558.

Christakis D. A., & Zimmerman, F. J. (2006). Media as a public health issue. *Archives of Pediatric and Adolescent Medicine, 160* (4):445-446.

Consumer Federation of America. (2000). Lessons from the 1996 telecommunications act: Deregulation before meaningful competition spells consumer disaster. *Consumers Union Report.* Retrieved from *http://www.consumersunion. org/telecom/lessondc201.htm.*

Hutchinson, E. D. (2007). Aspects of human behavior. *Dimensions of Human Behavior: Person and environment* (32d ed.). Thousand Oaks, CA: Sage Publications, p. 3-36.

Pittman, R. (1990, January 24). We're talking the wrong language to 'TV Babies.' *New York Times,* A15.

Rideout, V.J., Foehr, U. G., & Roberts, D. F. (2010). *Generation M2: Media in the lives of 8- to 18-year-olds.* Kaiser Family Foundation Report: Washington, D.C.

Roberts, D. F., & Foehr, U. G. (2008). Trends in media use. *The Future of Children, 18* (1),11-37.

Roberts, D. F., Foehr, U. G., & Rideout, V. J. (2005). *Generation M: Media in the lives of 8-18 year olds.* Menlo Park, CA: Kaiser Family Foundation. Available at: *http://www.kff.org/entmedia/ upload/Generation-M-Media-in-the-Lives-of-8-18-Year-olds-Report.pdf.*

Robinson, L. (2009): A taste for the necessary. Information, *Communication & Society, 12* (4), 488-507.

Schmidt, M. E., & Vandewater, E. A. (Spring 2008). Media and attention, cognition and school achievement. *The Future of children, 18* (1), 63-85. Available at *http://www.futureofchildren.org.*

Weingerger, D. (2007). *Everything is miscellaneous: the power of the new digital disorder.* New York, NY: Henry Holt and Company.

*Anna Montana Cirell, MSW, is a doctoral student at Arizona State University studying learning, literacies, and technology, with particular attention paid to sustainable digital initiatives affording all students the technological tools and thinking strategies to act as agents for social change. Previous experiences as an AmeriCorps Teaching Fellow in an under-funded New York City school and as a school social worker in an understaffed Florida school district inspired her to explore the intersection between learning and technology. She is a graduate of New College of Florida (B.A) and the University of South Florida (MSW).*

# Ageless Wisdom and the Booth Manor Theatre Group
### *by Brent Liebman, BSW*

A s I approached my senior year of intern placement, my social work professors (at Eastern University) and I explored agencies in which I could combine my passions for social work and theatre arts with youth. My goal for college (besides graduating), was to become trained and educated in both the field of social work and theatre.

My placement advisor found an agency that could possibly help bridge my educational goals with actual experience in the field. This agency, affiliated with the Salvation Army, was very excited about the prospect of an intern bringing in a theatre arts component. As my field placement advisor explained the prospects to me, she said the catch was that my target population would not be youth. I would be working with senior citizens.

After a slight pause, my inner social worker got a grip on what was being proposed. I grew inspired by the potential strengths in this equation. Although working with seniors would present some new challenges (such as physical limitations), this population could provide me with an experience rich in diversity and a means to test my ideas with a different population of people. This could allow for new discoveries, stretching me in new directions. Yes! It was on!

## Starting the Group

My placement site was a six-story apartment complex for low income seniors, located in downtown Philadelphia. The population was 100% African American, consisting of 95 residents. In addition to providing support and services for the residents, the mission of the agency was also to provide activities and a positive and encouraging social environment. In addition to leading a theatre group, I also had other responsibilities at the agency, such as doing assessments and connecting residents with outside services.

I'll admit, I was most excited (and humbled) at the prospect and opportunity of starting a theatre arts group. Realizing the importance and value of client self determination, I decided the group as a whole should determine the direction and focus of the theatre arts group. During my second week of internship, my supervisor and I arranged for a meet and greet with any residents interested in joining a theatre arts club. Around a dozen residents were in attendance. At this meeting, I explained my intention to start a theatre group, including some possible directions and examples of activities. I also handed out surveys, which allowed the residents to choose certain areas of interests. The survey included questions such as: *Would you be interested in reading a play? If so, what kind of play: comedy, drama, religious? Are you interested in creating original material? Are you interested in performance?*

The group's response to the surveys proved invaluable to the beginning of the process. In addition to an overwhelming request for "movie nights" (which our staff soon added to the schedule once a month, on Friday nights) and some requests for guitar lessons, the majority of residents expressed an interest in reading a religious play together. I consulted with my theatre director at Eastern as to what would be appropriate material, both developmentally and culturally, to fit the residents' preference. We decided on a play by James Weldon Johnson, the famous black poet, author, and playwright. (He also wrote the Negro national anthem.) The play was called *God's Trombones,* and it fit all the criteria for a first project together.

## The Next Phase

Soon after starting the group, I knew I had my work cut out for me. The eight residents who would come to represent the Booth Manor Theatre Group could not have been nicer and more welcoming. However, they did not hesitate to challenge me and test my leadership. I remember early on, when a 95-year-old member of the group was resisting a mirror exercise intended to build trust and collaboration between group members. He fought me to the bone, but he refused to walk away. In fact, that incident was a real turning point within the group. It was this struggle through resistance that the group's character began to emerge.

There were other tests as well, such as how well I could manage conflict between certain members of the group. In some respects, the group members showed amazing support for one another. Then again, every so often an argument would erupt. I definitely honed some mediation skills in those early weeks.

Leading this group demanded a focus and tuning in skills that would help me develop as a social worker in the months that followed. As I became more comfortable in front of the group, I began to find the balance of a demand for work and empathy. I also started to have fun. This unique group of individuals was shattering my stereotypes and perception of late adulthood. There was never a dull moment. The discussions we were engaging in were insightful, vibrant, and challenging. I was discovering an ageless wisdom that inspired me to push my own creative boundaries.

I remember one day when our group was discussing material for our next project, and a member of the group, Sharon, said to me: "You know Brent, we don't always have to work with black authors. There's other stuff out there, too." Here I am trying to be culturally sensitive as a white guy, and Sharon is challenging me to move beyond my comfort zone! I felt like more of a student than a

teacher, but we were working together and the group "buy in" was increasing with each session.

## The Turning Point

The group finally got its first opportunity to perform in front of a live audience at the Thanksgiving dinner, in front of the other 90 residents at the manor. We performed again a month later at Christmas time, adding music and singing to a narrative reading of the Christmas story. The night they performed at the Christmas dinner, everything changed. They received much affirmation and support from their peers. I could see an emerging pride in the work they had done. At our next meeting after the holidays, one member of the group spoke up about the group's commitment and how they needed to raise the bar in that area. There was a new energy in the room. They all had been afforded the sweet taste of performing live, and they wanted more. What's next? Let's perform for Black History Month!

For the Black History Month performance, the stakes were definitely raised. We settled on a project in which we would explore the poetry of Langston Hughes. It was up to me to find the material, so I found several of Hughes' poems that I thought would suit the group. The process of exploring this material with the group was an incredible experience. The discussions that resulted from the creative process were not only priceless in terms of substance and participation, but the group was really starting to open up and trust one another. The trust and vulnerability that was emerging was really quite beautiful. There is nothing more rewarding for a social worker than to see the members of a group trust each other enough to be vulnerable. They were opening up and making new discoveries every day. The project would far exceed my wildest expectations.

It was around this time that the "higher ups" at the Salvation Army began to take notice of what was emerging at the Booth Manor. They offered me a part-time job, extending my work through the summer. It was time to tackle a play. Up to this point in time, I had supplied material I felt would be safe and comfortable for the group. Now I wanted to go in the opposite direction and challenge them with something that would stretch them. I wanted them to play against type, in hopes they would discover something new about themselves.

It turns out that I did not have to look long and far for the right material. It sort of found me. My university, it turns out, was planning a fall production of Thornton Wilder's Pulitzer prize-winning play, *Our Town*. My own theatre director was interested in having me play a role and asked me to read the script. As soon as I read it, I realized it would be a perfect reader's theatre project for the Booth Manor group. Now I just had to convince them.

Our first reading of the material was both exciting and humbling for our group. We were on new terrain. This material was by far the most challenging the group had faced. They not only dealt with the characters' deep interactions with one another, but they also were playing against type, age, background, culture, time, place, and even gender in some cases. Nevertheless, the universal themes within the play conveyed their connection, understanding, and identification with the material through their wisdom, enthusiasm, and empathy.

## Collaboration

Not only was the August performance a great success and swan song for our theatre group, but my university theatre adopted us as a collaborative partner in its fall production. Our collaboration began with visits to the Booth Manor rehearsals from the Eastern Theatre production team. Then a month later, 18 cast and team members of Eastern's production caravanned to Booth Manor on September 10 to see a second performance of *Our Town*, followed by a meet and greet and conversation between the members of both student and senior citizen company.

A bond had clearly formed between the university students in the cast and the members of the Booth Manor theatre group. Then on November 10, our university held a special matinee engagement performance, followed by a dinner. At this time, the Booth Manor theatre group had the opportunity to experience a full length production of the play they had ushered in. I have to say that inviting the members of the Booth Manor group to my university to see me and the rest of the cast perform had to be one of the greatest highlights of my life. The bond I have shared with this amazing group of people has far outstretched my wildest dreams of collaborative theatre making.

Perhaps even more significant is the opportunity it has allowed me as a young social worker. Theatre making has allowed me a vehicle to connect with people and challenge them in ways few people in this age group are challenged. When I look back on this experience, the overwhelming highlight for me is in seeing how the groups' relationships with one another grew during these past months. The group members have shared an experience with one another that has developed them not only as artists, but also as a community.

I recall dropping them back off at their residence after the performance and dinner on November 10. I was struck by the amount of tolerance and patience they had with one another. They were not interrupting each other anymore. They were listening. The effort of unloading the group from the van was evident in their care for one other. The group's growth and trust in one another is more rewarding to me than any production I could ever conjure up. I set out to form a theatre group, but I ended up discovering an ageless wisdom that I will carry with me for the rest of my life.

*Brent Liebman was born and raised in Southern California (Los Angeles area). A summer internship with the organization Urban Promise, located in Camden, New Jersey, took Brent to the East Coast, where he has worked and been involved with the organization for more than fifteen years. In 2009, Brent enrolled at Eastern University in pursuit of a social work degree, combined with his passion for theatre arts. Brent is now in the process of developing a theatre program for Urban Promise, Camden, as well as coordinating the Urban Promise Arts program.*

## Single Adoptive Dads in Film
### by Addison Cooper, LCSW

Sitting in case conferences is a pretty quick way to learn what social workers really think. When advocating for the best outcome for a child, social workers draw from their own (sometimes unrealized) beliefs and assumptions. I wonder if the unrealized beliefs and assumptions make up some of what we call our "gut instinct." The conclusions reached aren't necessarily wrong. A social worker might advocate against a certain candidate for adoption, or advocate for a certain case plan. But are there certain categories of candidates that are always advocated against?

In my experience, single prospective adoptive fathers are viewed with much more suspicion than prospective adoptive couples or single prospective adoptive mothers. Maybe this resonates with you–but why? Maybe this surprises you, but again–why?

It's possible that the suspicion my colleagues feel toward single prospective adoptive fathers (as a category) might draw from societal expectations that men will be less nurturing and less emotionally-in-tune than women, and therefore less fit to be adoptive parents. If that's the case–and if those societal expectations are actually in the public consciousness– then it could be quite challenging for single men to pursue adoption, even if they want to. I can imagine one thinking,

"I feel like I have a heart to parent, but maybe I couldn't be nurturing enough." I can imagine another pursuing adoption but being met with resistance from peers and professionals. The path to adoption is an uphill climb for many applicants, and it might be even steeper for single adoptive fathers. But I recently stumbled across something that might help!

I recently wrote an article for *Foster Focus Magazine*. To celebrate National Adoption Month, I reviewed several of the year's best adoption-relevant films. As I was writing the first draft, I commended one movie for including a positive portrayal of a single adoptive father, "a rare feat for a movie," I noted. And then the next movie also included a positive portrayal of a single adoptive father. In fact, I've come across three films released in the past year with positive, single adoptive fathers. On quick reflection, two more come to mind.

Here are five examples to challenge preconceptions of prospective single adoptive fathers, and to encourage prospective single adoptive dads to view the healthy adoption they want to pursue as something attainable.

*1. Gru (Despicable Me 2).* Gru has left behind his life of super-villainy in exchange for a life of fighting crime. Although he wasn't a perfect parent in the past, he now dotes on and protects his daughters. He even dresses up in a tutu to make sure one of his daughters has a perfect princess party. Gru shows that dads can change and develop a sensitive side.

*2. John (Admission).* John has adopted Nelson from Uganda. John has helped Nelson develop a sense of understanding and acceptance of his adoption story. John is very mission-driven, but is able to put his drive to serve on hold in order to provide Nelson with a geographically stable home. John demonstrates that dads can listen to their kids and be not just empathic, but effective.

*3. Jean Valjean (Les Miserables).* Valjean rescues Cosette from an abusive foster home. He is completely devoted to her safety, and remembers her mother with love and kindness. Valjean demonstrates that dads can be protective, kind, and selfless.

*4. Mr. Ping (Kung Fu Panda).* Mr. Ping, a goose, adopted Po, a panda. Po came to Mr. Ping in a time of great need, and Mr. Ping met his needs. Later, Mr. Ping was able to share Po's adoption story with Po, and was able to help Po be both a full panda and part of Mr. Ping's heritage. Mr. Ping shows that dads can handle the difficult, nuanced identity issues in adoption.

*5. David Gordon (Martian Child).* Gordon, a widowed author, takes placement of a child some workers would call "difficult to place." Dennis has difficulty attaching, and his behaviors range from quirky to theft. Although some placements might have given up on Dennis, David draws support from his friends and family and persistently loves Dennis. David shows that adoptive dads can overcome adversity in their own lives and in their children's lives and still create a permanent, loving home.

With so many kids in foster care waiting for adoptive homes, it seems like a good idea to give full consideration to every category of people with love to spare.

*Addison Cooper, MSW, LCSW, is the creator of Adoption at the Movies adoption movie review website (www.adoptionlcsw. com). He is a foster care and adoption supervisor and therapist in Southern California. Find him on Facebook at http://www.facebook.com/AdoptionAtTheMovies and follow him on Twitter @AddisonCooper.*

# Labels and Dreams
## by Laura McBride, MSW

I have test anxiety. But I am more than the overwhelming fear that grips my heart in a vice when a teacher hands out a test or anyone mentions the word "licensure." I am more than the sleepless nights I've spent struggling, studying for exams I knew, knew, I would fail the next day. I am more than my lack of self-confidence.

I am "not smart enough." But I am more than the words of a teacher that didn't really know me: of a teacher that wanted to label me as not worthy of her time. I am more than an invented grade on a report card that merely compares me to others in my class. I am incomparable. I am the one and only me. I am more than the words you wish to label me with.

None of these labels defines me. None of them truly explain who I really am.

We constantly define ourselves with labels, as if that presents an accurate picture. I lived too much of my life buying into the labels others ascribed to me: not smart enough, not good enough, JUST athlete, untalented, dreamer.

Labels are meant to constrict, to bind us to someone else's way of seeing. I refuse to live by anyone else's standards anymore.

Tell me I'm not smart enough, not good enough, and I won't bother with the report card; I'll just prove you wrong in a battle of wits.

Tell me I'm just an athlete; I'll beat you first on the court, then in the classroom.

Tell me I'm untalented; I'll ask what you want to see first.

Tell me I'm a dreamer; I'll respond, "Yes, I am."

What's so wrong about being a dreamer?

The world has seen amazing dreamers. And we have praised them. Why do we talk down to children who dream big by calling them dreamers and telling them they'll never make it?

Dream. Do. Envision a world where labels belong only on clothing or boxes. Where people are defined by their actions and how they lived their life.

I am ME. I am a graduate student balancing work, internship, school, and life. I am a daughter, sister, and aunt, constantly trying to find more free time for my family. I am a friend, who seldom gets to see my friends. I am a reformed pessimist who constantly relapses. I see the beauty in nature but sometimes struggle to see it in the people around me.

I am a dreamer.

I dream of a world where everyone is treated equally. I dream of a day when petty arguments stop and honest discussions begin.

I dream of a day without labels. A day when I stop remembering the words of a teacher from long ago that didn't know me and listen to myself.

I dream of a day when I can stare down a test and not be afraid; a day when I believe in myself and my ability.

I dream of the day when I hold my doctoral diploma and I prove doubters wrong. I dream of the day I step back into a classroom–not as a student, but as a professor. A day when I can tell my students labels don't exist in my classroom but we have more dreams than we can count, and we are going to chase them.

So you can tell me I'm just not good enough or not smart enough. Tell me I'm not talented or tell me I'm just a dreamer. I'll tell you I am just. Just amazing. And I don't need your labels anymore.

*Laura McBride, MSW, is a recent graduate of Spalding University in Louisville, KY, where she earned her Master of Social Work degree. She works for her local community mental health center as a mental health outreach case manager.*

Watch the video of *Labels and Dreams* at:

http://www.socialworker.com /extras/video/poetry-labels-and-dreams/

# Audio Feature

## Merely a Man
## by Mozart Guerrier, MSW

Listen to the poem, *Merely a Man,* at:

http://www.socialworker.com/extras/audio/audio-feature-merely-a-man/

**About the Poem**

*Merely A Man* is a poem that explores and expands the biography and activism of Dr. Martin Luther King, Jr. It honors Dr. King as a man, father, husband, and friend and the long journey to justice that he walked.

**About the Poet**

Mozart Guerrier is a social worker and poet from Philadelphia. He has organized to solve social problems in cities, assisted families in finding safe and affordable housing, and served as a community engagement professional nationally. He's been asked to guest lecture at schools and cultural centers across the country, including, social innovation conferences at Brown University, MIT, the City of Syracuse Neighborhood Action Conference, the City of Corning, University of Rochester, Denver City School District, the New York State Fair, ABC and NBC television stations, and the nationally televised show, BETj Lyric Cafe. His work challenges and inspires. He can be reached at *mozartpoetry@gmail.com.*

## STUDENT SOCIAL WORK ORGANIZATIONS

Please send us a short **news** article about your group's activities. Also, send us **photos** of your club in action–we may even feature you on our front cover!

It's easy to share your club's activities with our readers. Send your news/photos to:

Linda Grobman, ACSW, LSW, Editor/Publisher
THE NEW SOCIAL WORKER
P.O. Box 5390, Harrisburg, PA 17110-0390
or to *lindagrobman@socialworker.com*

## Greetings From the Phi Alpha Honor Society for Social Work

The Phi Alpha Poster Board Presentation competition was held at the Council on Social Work Education Annual Program Meeting in Dallas, Texas in October/November 2013. Congratulations to the Phi Alpha Poster Board Presentation winners, listed below:

- Texas Woman's University
- Boise State University
- Loma Linda University
- Texas A&M University-Central Texas

Join the Phi Alpha listserv hosted by East Tennessee State University, and network with Phi Alpha members across the United States and Canada:

*Phialpha-subscribe-request@listserv.etsu.edu*

Happy Holidays!

Tammy Hamilton, Executive Secretary
*PhiAlphaInfo@etsu.edu*

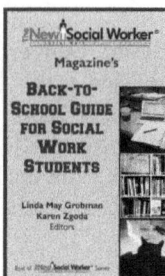

*Fugett–continued from page 3*
home office, Ashland site, Fugett supervises four to six staff, up to 16 clients, and student interns on a daily basis.

Previously, he did internships at a group and shelter home of a juvenile detention center and a child advocacy agency and provided direct care support at Crossroads of Hope, Inc. He also volunteered for the Ironton Lions Club for two years, to help raise money for community members in need to receive eyeglasses.

Fugett's main focus is on his family. He and his wife Sarah have two children, Ethan, 12, and Aidan, 7. He also enjoys spending time with his mother and siblings as well as with friends. "In my spare time, as if there is much for a social worker, I enjoy photography and the outdoors–including fishing, camping, and just hanging out with the people I love and care about," he says.

Despite Preston's assessment, Fugett sees himself as a mentor rather than a leader–"someone others can come to for help, in any capacity–whether it be staff, clients, friends, or family."

If he is a leader, Fugett insists, it's a "backseat one," who tries to let others make and learn from their own mistakes and see if they can correct those mistakes on their own before he steps in. "I found that people work more efficiently and more cohesively as a team if they can grow and learn on their own and be comfortable enough to come to a leader when they need guidance or assistance," Fugett says.

The next step for Fugett is obtaining his MSW and continuing to work for the foreseeable future at A Brighter Future.

Ten years from now, Fugett would like to have his Ph.D and eventually open up his own practice or center to serve the DDID and physically disabled community.

*Freelance writer Barbara Trainin Blank, formerly of Harrisburg, PA, now lives in the greater Washington, DC, area.*

## Home Together

On March 5, the Home Together Group from Shippensburg University conducted a silent auction and homelessness workshop. The homelessness workshop educated and brought awareness to the campus community about homelessness in the Shippensburg, PA, area. Scott Shewell from Safe Harbour Homeless Shelter provided stories and information about homelessness and how people can help. More than 50 people attended the workshop. The silent auction went from 10:00 a.m. to 5:00 p.m., and all the proceeds went to Safe Harbour. The group received more than 25 donations for the auction from various businesses and staff members. The Home Together Group raised $962.00 to benefit the Safe Harbour Homeless Shelter in Carlisle, PA.

## Life Beyond Natives

Social work students at USST Colleges Tarlac City Philippines held their rural camp/immersion with the Aeta community. The students had to walk across rivers to reach the place. According to one of the social work students, "I learned to appreciate a lot of things, that we are not better off than those who live in the mountains. Sometimes we look down onto them and even took advantage of their innocence. Many times we laugh at them for no reasons. Is that fair? They don't deserve that, because these people have also the same rights and privileges to live just like we do. They also have their principles and good values."

The Rural Camp is just one of the many activities of the BS Social Work Department of USST Colleges San Isidro Tarlac City Philippines with Marivic E. Manlutac, RSW, MSSW, Ph.D., as the Dean.

*Social work student Divine Carmela Olea with the Aetas.*

## Part V: Do I Have To Be Sure?

### by Kathryn S. Krase, Ph.D., J.D., MSW

*Editor's Note: These articles are part of an ongoing series.*

As a mandated reporter, the law requires that you make a report as soon as you have REASONABLE SUSPICION (or reasonable cause to suspect/believe) that child abuse or neglect is occurring or is about to occur. But what does reasonable suspicion mean, and how do you know you have it?

This confusion is completely understandable, especially because most reporters don't want to jump the gun and be wrong, while simultaneously wanting to do what is right and protect a child in harm's way. This article will help you by offering a process you can use to figure out if you have reasonable suspicion, thus requiring you to make a report to child protective services (CPS).

## Am I Suspicious Enough?

When a mandated reporter, based on his/her training and experience in combination with what the reporter has observed/been told, entertains the possibility that a child is being abused and/or neglected or is in imminent danger of abuse or neglect, she or he has "reasonable suspicion." It may be enough that explanations provided by a parent and/or child are inconsistent with your observations, experience, and/or knowledge. You do not need to be sure that child abuse or maltreatment has taken place, just reasonably suspicious (Lau, Krase, & Morse, 2009).

## How Does Reasonable Suspicion Measure Up to Other Legal Standards

One way to get a better understanding of "reasonable suspicion" is to compare this legal standard with others that may be more familiar to you. The legal system uses various levels of evidence (otherwise known as standards, burdens, or degrees of proof). The burden of proof required in a legal action is the threshold needed to convince the fact-finder (usually the judge or jury) that an allegation is true.

There are different burdens of proof applied in different kinds of cases. The level of proof required in a legal proceeding generally relates to the seriousness of the consequences that a person faces if the allegation is found to be true. For instance, charges that carry mild consequences, such as a fine for a traffic ticket, have a lower burden of proof and therefore are easier to prove than those that carry serious consequences, such as a jail or prison sentence for an assault charge.

The highest burden of proof is found in criminal cases. In most criminal cases, the prosecution must prove that the defendant committed the crime he or she is accused of "beyond a reasonable doubt." This means that a juror can only vote to convict when the juror has no reasonable doubt that the defendant is guilty. Any and all jurors can still have doubt, but that doubt cannot affect a reasonable person's belief that the defendant is still guilty (Kagehiro & Stanton, 1985). This means that before jury members can vote for conviction in a criminal case, they need to be close to 100% sure that the person committed the crime, based on the evidence presented to them.

For most cases in civil court, including family or juvenile courts, the standard most often used is "a fair preponderance of the evidence." Simply put, this standard means that the burden of proof is met when the fact-finder determines that there is more evidence supporting the truth of an allegation as compared to evidence that the allegation is untrue. The fact-finder has to be more than 50% sure that the allegations are true to uphold an allegation under the "preponderance of the evidence standard." This standard is most often used in Family Court when a judge determines whether a parent is abusive or neglectful.

Some states use "preponderance of the evidence" as the burden of proof for substantiating child protection cases after investigation. However, most states use a less rigorous standard of proof–"some credible evidence." Under this standard, the fact-finder has met the burden when he or she has secured some minimal amount of evidence that is credible, even if she or he has also found evidence that is "incredible." More simply put, the CPS worker can substantiate an allegation of abuse or neglect based on information from one person he or she deems reliable, even if there is information from one or more reliable people saying something different. Whereas the "preponderance of the evidence" standard requires at least a 50% likelihood of guilt, experts often measure "some credible evidence" at about 35%.

As compared with all the levels discussed above, reasonable suspicion is a lower burden of proof and could be quantified at around 10% to 15% likelihood of guilt. The reason lawmakers keep this standard so low is to encourage reports of suspicions, instead of discouraging them. This standard follows from the perspective that it is better to err on the side of protection of children.

At each stage of a CPS proceeding, a different burden of proof may be required to initiate action on behalf of the child and against the accused abuser. To summarize, if a social worker has reasonable suspicion of child abuse or neglect, he or she must make a report to alert the child protective authorities. At the conclusion of the investigation of that report, a "finding" or "indication" will be entered if "some credible evidence" or a "preponderance of the evidence" has been found (depending on the standard in the given state). If the degree of abuse and/or neglect is a major concern and the ongoing safety of the child is ques-

tionable, a petition against the parent may be filed in family court. In family court, the judge will examine the evidence against the parents and use the "preponderance of the evidence" standard to weigh the proof. If the allegations indicate a crime may have been committed, the parents may also be arrested and prosecuted in criminal court. In criminal court, the judge or jury would apply the "beyond a reasonable doubt" standard.

## I Think I'm a Reasonable Person... But How Do I Know That My Concerns Are "Reasonable"?

We use the word "reasonable" all the time when we're talking to each other, but the term "reasonable" has legal connotations that are important to understand. A belief or suspicion is reasonable if someone else with your education, training, and professional experience, would have the same suspicion. Reasonable suspicion can start with the feeling that something doesn't feel right, but such a gut feeling, without other concerns, is not "reasonable." You need to objectively identify and examine your biases and overcome those that might interfere with your ability to be reasonable. Supervision and consultation with supervisors and colleagues can be really helpful in this situation.

If you consult with a supervisor or colleague and that person agrees with you that your suspicions are reasonable and a report must be made, you have generally met the "reasonable suspicion"

standard, since someone with similar education, training, and experience knowing what you know is just as suspicious as you. However, there may be a time when a supervisor or colleague does not agree with you. Perhaps he or she points out how you may be processing your suspicions through your own biases. If, based on consultation, you no longer feel suspicious, then you do not need to make a report. However, if you disagree with your colleague, and believe that your suspicions are still valid, then you are required to make a report to CPS.

In practice, you will find that in some cases you will make the decision to report easily. In other cases, you may struggle trying to determine whether your suspicions reach the threshold to report. Remember, it is not your responsibility to know or prove that a child has been abused or neglected, but only to have reasonable suspicion that such abuse or neglect has occurred. A report is not an accusation, but rather a request for an investigation of a suspicious situation.

## References

Kagehiro, D. K., & Stanton, W. C. (1985). Legal vs. quantified definitions of standards of proof. *Law and Human Behavior, 9,* 159–178.

Lau, K., Krase, K., & Morse, R.H. (2009). *Mandated reporting of child abuse and neglect: A practical guide for social workers.* New York: Springer.

# Part VI: What Happens If I'm Wrong? The Immunity Provision
## *by Kathryn S. Krase, Ph.D., J.D., MSW*

When deciding whether to make a report, or not, mandated reporters often wonder, "What if I'm wrong?" "Can I be sued?" "Can I lose my license?"

After a mandated reporter logs his/her suspicions with child protective services (CPS), CPS conducts an investigation. At the end of that investigation, CPS makes a determination whether to substantiate the allegations. If the report is substantiated, there is nothing for the reporter to be worried about, because CPS confirmed the reported suspicions.

If the report is unsubstantiated, there are no repercussions to the reporter, as long as the report meets certain basic requirements–thanks to legal protection in the form of immunity. This article will outline immunity and how a reporter secures its benefits.

## Where Does Immunity Come From?

In 1974, the United States Congress passed the Child Abuse Prevention and

Treatment Act of 1974 (CAPTA), and President Richard Nixon signed it into law. This sweeping legislation required all states to add provisions to their laws that protect reporters from legal retaliation for making a report. This legal protection is called immunity. Without immunity, a reporter could be sued if the report was not substantiated after investigation. Immunity provisions were included in the law to encourage reports to be made, even when the reporter is unsure of whether abuse or neglect has occurred (Kalichman, 1999).

> **To assert the legal defense of immunity, the report must have been made in good faith.**

## How Do You Know If You're Covered by Immunity?

In most states, reporters are protected by immunity as long as the report was made in "good faith." Making a report in good faith means that the reporter believed that the information she or he was providing to CPS was true, to the best of his or her knowledge. The reporter does not have to be sure that the information is true. The reporter should not investigate his/her suspicions before making the report. As long as the reporter believes that the child in question may be the victim of abuse or neglect, a resulting report will be considered made in good faith.

In a few states, including California, the mandated reporter benefits from absolute immunity. (See Child Welfare Information Gateway at *https://www. childwelfare.gov/* for specific information about your state.) Absolute immunity means that the mandated reporter is protected from legal retaliation regardless of whether or not the report is made in good faith. In these states, however, absolute immunity is not provided for non-mandated reporters.

## So I'm Covered by Immunity. What Does That Mean?

Unfortunately, legal immunity does not mean that the mandated reporter cannot or will not be sued for making the report, although such lawsuits are very rare. However, mandated reporters will successfully defend themselves by asserting immunity. In some states, such as California, there are provisions in which mandated reporters can be reimbursed for expenses made to defend themselves in such suits.

To assert the legal defense of immunity, the report must have been made in good faith. In more than 15 states (and the District of Columbia), there is a "presumption of good faith" for reports made by all persons, not just mandated reporters. This means that the person suing the reporter has to show that the report was not made in good faith. This is a difficult

burden to meet. A presumption is a legal advantage for the reporter. The reporter does not have to defend him/herself unless the accuser has convinced the court the report was not made in good faith. In that case, the reporter will then have the opportunity to provide evidence to support him/herself.

Reporters are protected by immunity as long as they made the report in good faith. However, related behaviors outside the reporting of the suspected child abuse or neglect are not protected through immunity. For example, if a reporter makes a report to CPS, and then writes about the case on Facebook or Twitter (which in itself brings up ethical concerns regarding confidentiality), and the allegations are found to be untrue, the reporter may be liable for any damage to the person's reputation caused.

## What If I Was Wrong... On Purpose? (False Reports)

You are protected from legal repercussions when making a report in good faith. However, reporters who make reports in "bad faith" can be punished. The law provides civil and/or criminal liability for knowingly filing a false report. The reporter must have "willfully" or "intentionally" made a false report of child abuse or neglect to CPS. This means that the reporter knew that the report was false or knew that it was likely that the report was false.

Cases of false reporting by mandated reporters are few and far between. False reports are more often experienced in non-mandated reports. Disgruntled neighbors and ex-lovers might make a report to CPS seeking to disrupt and intentionally injure a family. A reporter who makes a false report is subject to criminal and civil action.

False reporting is usually classified as a low level misdemeanor, which is a crime. In some states, filing a false child abuse report is a higher-level crime—a felony. People who make false reports can be subject to fines ranging from $100 to $5,000 or sentences from 90 days to five years in jail or prison. Reporters who are found to have filed multiple false reports may be subject to even harsher penalties (See Child Welfare Information Gateway for information on your particular state).

Besides criminal penalties for making a false report, reporters can also be

subject to civil liability in the form of compensatory and/or punitive damages. Compensatory damages are meant to pay for any actual losses the family incurs as a result of the false report. Losses are not limited to the financial kind, but the damage award will generally be in the form of money. Compensatory damages can include damage to reputation, disruption caused by the investigative process, and even assault and battery for unwarranted physical examinations of children in response to a false report (Lau, Krase, & Morse, 2009). In addition to compensatory damages, punitive damages may be awarded for a false report. Punitive damages "punish" bad behavior, and usually involve a large monetary award, above and beyond the actual damages caused by the report.

## References

*Child Abuse Prevention and Treatment Act,* Public Law 93-247.

Kalichman, S. C. (1999). *Mandated reporting of suspected child abuse: Ethics, law & policy.* Washington: American Psychological Association.

Lau, K., Krase, K., & Morse, R. H. (2009). *Mandated reporting of child abuse and neglect: A practical guide for social workers.* New York: Springer.

## Resources

*Child Welfare Information Gateway (http://www.childwelfare.gov)*

A service of the Children's Bureau, Administration on Children and Families, United States Department of Health and Human Services. The Child Welfare Information Gateway connects child welfare and related professionals to information and resources to help protect children and strengthen families.

*Kathryn S. Krase, Ph.D., J.D., MSW, is an assistant professor of social work at Long Island University in Brooklyn, NY. She earned her Ph.D. in social work, her Juris Doctor, and her Master of Social Work from Fordham University. She has written and presented extensively on mandated reporting of suspected child abuse and neglect. She previously served as Associate Director of Fordham University's Interdisciplinary Center for Family and Child, as well as Clinical Social Work Supervisor for the Family Defense Clinic at New York University Law School.*

# What I Learned in Miss Martha's Preschool
## by Gina Maguire, MSW, LSW

Most of what I need to know as a healthy person, I learned in preschool... if only I had paid better attention. I went to preschool in a small, private, Jewish preschool on the first floor of one of the buildings in the projects where we lived. Living near Pelham Parkway in the Bronx, I was raised Catholic, but all of the three- and four-year-olds in the 2250 building went to this Jewish preschool. I can still remember my teacher, Miss Martha.

Looking back now, I realize that Miss Martha taught me most of what is important to know in life, and as a social worker. I'd like to share her lessons with you, in case you, like me, didn't pay close enough attention back then.

First, she taught us about colors. We had crayons and we had finger paint. When we used the finger paints, we wore smocks. When we used crayons, we didn't have to. We were always allowed to use all of the colors! Miss Martha never chose one color as "the best color," nor did she ever tell us that any colors were bad to use or have. In that class were children of several religions, races, and ethnicities. We were as colorful as our crayons, and we mixed as well as our finger paints.

Miss Martha taught us our shapes. We drew circles, triangles, squares, rectangles—well, you get the idea. We learned that circles had to have curves. Triangles never had curves, and squares had all equal sides. Again, all of the shapes were equally represented in examples, and equally desirable to draw. Why, then, do we look down upon the different shapes of our bodies, and the bodies of others, as we age? Why do we love the curves of a circle as a child, but turn our noses up at "curvy" women who do not fit the "norm" seen in magazines? Why do we look at the rectangular shapes of super models and aspire to that one shape? When did rectangles become the norm? If I remember correctly, Miss Martha showed us many shapes, not just rectangles. We liked them all.

We learned about numbers, too. Amazingly, when you put two numbers together, you get a new number. A number always represents a numerical value. That's what I remember. Amazingly, as I grew up, I was taught by others that this was not always the case. I learned that a woman who weighs 120 pounds and gains 30 pounds becomes fat. Shouldn't she just become 150 pounds? Why then does a high number for age equal a lower status in society? Who decides at which number we change from a number of pounds to "fat or skinny"? Who decides that 66 is old, not simply one year more than 65? I like the math Miss Martha taught me much better. I am 43. I will be 44, and so on. I will not be "old" until I DECIDE that I am old, and I want to act old. Until then, my age is only a number. It defines neither my personality nor my abilities.

Miss Martha taught us to do things in pairs. We always had a "partner" to work beside. Having a partner was nice. We shared the work and had someone to talk to. We were usually allowed to choose our partners. Usually, we chose the other preschooler to whom we were closest. For my birthday, I chose Christine G. to help me deliver my cupcakes and to be that day's helper. I know we held hands when doing our duties. Why was it okay in Miss Martha's class, but not in today's society, for me to hold another woman's hand? Holding hands is a sign of affection, something every person deserves and needs. Why do we now try to choose who should be more deserving of this affection than others? When I walk in a park and hold my husband's hand, people smile at us. I have some friends who are afraid to hold hands in public, because they have same sex partners. It's not fair. Miss Martha told us holding hands was fine. I think she was right.

I learned about these things: colors, shapes, numbers, and partners, in 1973 or 1974. The lessons Miss Martha taught me were not understood and appreciated until I began my master's degree in 2010. I had to "unlearn" 36 years of society's lessons. I have always tried to celebrate the fact that we are all equal, different colors, shapes, ages, weights and orientations, but I never applied this knowledge to my life. Accepting one's own differences, and celebrating diversity within, is more difficult to grasp.

If only I hadn't waited all of these years to apply this knowledge. If only I could remind others of the important lessons we learned as children. If only I could help others to "unlearn" society's unhealthy assumptions. Oh, I can! I am a social worker!

Thank you, Miss Martha, wherever you are!

*Gina Maguire, MSW, LSW, is an adjunct professor of gerontology at Stockton College, an adjunct professor of psychology/ human services at Brookdale Community College, and program assistant for the Stockton Center on Successful Aging. Gina has provided individual and couples counseling to older adults; organized and facilitated activity programs for older adults and a reminiscence autobiography group with older adults, which culminated in a published work; and provided research for several textbooks in areas of military, health, and mental health, social work advocacy, depression of older adults, and the anniversary reaction to death.*

# Looking at Change Through the Lens of Wraparound

## by Katherine Schwartz, LCSW

When I made the decision to go back to school and get a master's degree in social work, I had already been working in the field for several years. At the time, I was a Parent Aide in Lowell, a small city outside of Boston, and had begun to realize how hard it was to facilitate positive change effectively. I hoped that by continuing my education, I would learn more about how to best support the change process. After graduate school, I moved to California and got a job with Seneca Center. Now called the Seneca Family of Agencies, the social services nonprofit's mission is to sustain children and families through the most difficult times of their lives. For the majority of the 12 years I have been at Seneca, I have worked in or overseen wraparound programs. I feel lucky to have found what I believe is an effective way to approach helping people make positive change.

Wraparound is a goal-oriented, problem solving and skill building practice that uses "team" meetings as its central strategy. Teams are usually made up of a clinician, a mentor/behavioral coach, and a family partner (a peer parent), as well as the youth, family members, natural supports, and referring party. Teams work together to identify client (youth) and family needs and develop plans to meet those needs, so the client and his or her family increase success across all life domains and reduce formal county agency involvement.

All wraparound programs are comprised of these elements and are guided by the Wraparound Principles. I call programs that stick solely to this composition Traditional Wraparound. Seneca and some other agencies, however, provide a different version that I call "Treatment-Oriented Wraparound." This version of wraparound adds mental health services. It is the combination of traditional wraparound and mental health services together that I have found to work so well. In other words, emphasis on connecting relationships plus skilled intervention often equals success (no surprise there)!

We receive wraparound referrals from Children and Family Services, the Department of Juvenile Probation, and until recently, Community Mental Health. The referrals we receive cover a broad range of issues stemming largely from poverty and include issues from criminality on the part of the youth to extremely challenging family dynamics. For youth to meet criteria, they have to either be at risk of out-of-home placement or returning to a family after being placed in a group home. While the youth are technically our clients, we work from a systems perspective and bring the family as fully into the process as possible. It is the responsibility of the entire team, which is led by the master's level clinician, to assist the family in crafting a plan that identifies the steps needed to obtain the agreed upon goals. Although participation in the program is voluntary, because the referrals are made by the department of juvenile probation or children and family services, we assume that families often feel pressured to participate. So, as you can imagine, we find family members to be at different places on the change-readiness continuum with a wide range of motivations.

> **Wraparound is a goal-oriented, problem solving and skill building practice that uses "team" meetings as its central strategy.**

To illustrate the question of how best to facilitate change within a treatment-oriented wraparound model, I thought it might be helpful to use a couple of different case examples. I changed names and details to protect the clients and adhere to HIPAA regulations. I believe that these are fairly standard examples and typify the work being done in the wraparound field.

CASE EXAMPLE 1: John was referred for wraparound services by the Department of Juvenile Probation. John was a 14-year-old Caucasian male, was constantly breaking probation, and was at risk for out-of-home placement. He was initially placed on probation because of gang involvement, fighting at school, truancy, and stealing. He lived with his aunt because he and his mother were arguing so much. His father was not in the picture. His mother also had a history of gang involvement and domestic violence. Seneca's wraparound team was asked to work with the family to help John meet his probation requirements and get back on track. He was attending school only occasionally and continually came home after curfew. His gang involvement and experience witnessing domestic violence appeared to be driving a lot of his behavior.

The team was faced with a difficult situation, as John refused services when the team initially met with him and his aunt. His aunt and mother both agreed to participate, however, and signed him up. The question the team had to answer was how to engage John and his family in services and in the change process. The team ended up working with this young man and his family for almost a year, and it was only in the last three months that John began to fully engage in services. This is not an unusual case scenario. Social workers everywhere can probably identify with it.

In the end, the intervention that seemed to make a difference with John was the relationship his mentor was able to develop with him. His mentor's ability to listen without judgment to John talk about why he felt so loyal to his gang buddies played a big part in his being able to develop the relationship. This is such a basic intervention, but such an important one. His mentor was able to employ some motivational interviewing techniques and modeled for him that men can talk about feelings without being considered weak. In addition, John was suffering from depression and PTSD resulting from early trauma that occurred while he was still living with his mother and father. He also struggled with attachment issues and reported feeling as if he didn't belong anywhere or to anyone, but that changed when he entered the gang.

John's relationship with his mentor helped him feel safe enough to begin to explore his feelings of loneliness, fear, and rejection with the clinician involved, which in turn set the stage for him to be able to develop insight into his behavior. Validation, insight, and understanding slowly began to shift his behavior and opened him up to the possibility of change.

CASE EXAMPLE 2: Brandi, a 12-year-old Latina female, was referred from the Children and Family Services Agency. She was referred because her mother, a recovering drug addict, was struggling to find her footing as a parent now that her daughter, Brandi, had returned from group care. The county worker explained that the daughter was very angry at her mother for everything that had happened while the mother was using drugs. Brandi was having a hard time accepting limits her mother set and often stayed out for days at a time. Mom often resorted to yelling when she was feeling scared and powerless to protect her daughter and described feeling incredibly anxious all the time.

Seneca staff met with the mother and daughter, and they shared some of their history and ways that trust had been broken. When asked what they needed for things to get better and what that would look like, Brandi said she was sick of her mother yelling at her all the time. Brandi's mom was tired of trying to get Brandi to do what she was supposed to do. Helping Brandi and her mom learn how to communicate was the first step, but neither Brandi nor her mom seemed to know how to break out of the cycle. It

was ultimately the family partner, who was also a recovering drug addict, who was able to connect with the mom and help her think about what was underlying her feelings and behavior toward her daughter. Brandi's mom felt supported through this relationship and was able to listen more to what her daughter was saying without shutting down. The family partner helped Brandi's mom also feel more comfortable with the idea of family therapy. Subsequently, the family therapist was able to work with Brandi and her mom on communication and on helping the mom set more consistent limits, despite the guilt she felt over the past. Brandi and her mom were able to rebuild trust slowly and things between them began to improve.

It seems clear that the program's capacity to build relationships and address the underlying mental health issues simultaneously ultimately resulted in good outcomes. It is my experience that assigning a skilled clinician to each family allows the wraparound service to go that extra mile and offer interventions that help foster greater functionality, which in turn helps the family take advantage of the wraparound service being offered. It is also clear that relationship and con-

nectedness are essential ingredients in the success of both of these cases. Hence, the combination of relationship and a strong support network propped up by an ability to patiently teach and model new skills, often through a therapeutic process, helps facilitate positive, sustainable change.

I believe that wraparound works because it is not limited to a prescribed methodology, but rather builds on these tenets and creates an individual map to success for each youth and family.

*Katherine Schwartz, LCSW, has more than 16 years of experience in the mental health field. Twelve years have been spent at the Seneca Family of Agencies providing intensive, community-based mental health and social services to severely emotionally disturbed youth and their families. While at Seneca, Ms. Schwartz has been the administrator in charge of the successful start-up and implementation of three wraparound programs in three different counties. She has also overseen Seneca's Intensive Treatment Foster Care, Therapeutic Behavioral Services, and Mobile Crisis programs. Through her extensive experience in the wraparound field, she has developed a deep appreciation for this particular kind of work and its efficacy.*

# Turn Up the Tech in Social Work

## Using Digital Self-Advocacy To Empower Social Work Populations

*by Ellen Belluomini, LCSW*

*March on the Republican National Convention in Minneapolis, MN, September 1, 2008.*

Advocacy is at the foundation of social work practice. One of the differentiating premises between social work and other fields of human services is the underlying need to work toward equality and social justice for every population. Traditional forms of advocacy range from organizing demonstrations and community education activities to changing local, state, and federal policies addressing social injustice. Advocacy for our client populations is needed in the political, economic, social, and environmental arenas. Digital self-advocacy is a way to involve and empower every client population toward change.

In the past, fewer options have been accessible to clients for self-advocacy. Demonstrations or organized events may be held during work hours, inaccessible, or overwhelm vulnerable participants. Writing letters of support or meeting with government officials may be intimidating. Digital advocacy creates a manageable way to connect to client interests with activism for their empowerment. If you want to understand more about effective digital advocacy, you can visit MoveOn.org, Heartland Alliance (heartlandalliance.org), Amnesty International (AmnestyUSA.org, check out activism tools), Change.org or the Human Rights Campaign (hrc.org). These sites can give social workers ideas about how they, and their clients, can advocate successfully.

Teaching digital self-advocacy can effect change within political, economic, social, and environmental systems. Social workers can help clients problem solve the most effective way to have a voice.

There are four steps in educating clients to choose self-advocacy methods. *Evaluation, identification, practice, and evaluation* are the four steps that provide the path to effective engagement. These steps develop critical thinking skills in the client's ability to voice concerns, traumas, or values.

*Step 1: Evaluate technology literacy with the client.* Demographics or client situations do not determine digital literacy. Some client populations may experience digital exclusion, which hinders their ability to advocate for themselves. Clients should minimally be able to understand multiple forms of digital communication, open programs on a computer, be proficient in word processing, effectively search for information on the Internet, fill out web forms, and be informed about digital etiquette and security. Everyone can be taught something new about technology. Clients can feel empowered by learning technological advancements that previously confused them. Those clients who are digitally literate can benefit by understanding how to use the power of technology to effectively advocate in their lives.

*Step 2: Identify which digital advocacy needs will empower the client.* Encourage the development of an outline by subject. Helping the client determine areas of concern is the most difficult step. Where do they want to effect change? A specific therapeutic issue is usually perfect for self-advocacy. The issue can be anything clients recognize as needing activism to heal or inspire their lives. Sometimes the client may need guidance in this area, but remember—the social worker's role is to teach to fish, not fish for them.

Once the needs are labeled, the second part of identification is discovering the appropriate advocacy tools. There are many digital alternatives for self-advocacy. I have a running list of appropriate blogs, websites, mailing lists, social media options, newsletters, and educational videos, as examples of self-advocacy. Apps in this area are limited, but the larger causes have the money to invest in these resources. Coupled with strategies on how to delve into each format, the client reviews options for involvement. We start with one route best fitting the client's situation, drive, and digital literacy. Small steps in the beginning help clients to feel empowered when they succeed.

*Step 3: Have the client practice with the digital tools he or she can identify.* This can be done in session to develop a better understanding of the process. Practice with the tool can involve keeping a journal about the experience to use in the evaluation stage. Self-advocacy may be a new concept. Homework can be tailored to the area where empowerment is needed. Even digitally literate individuals need help understanding avenues for championing themselves.

*Step 4: Engage the client in a process of evaluating effectiveness.* Evaluation develops critical thinking and problem-solving skills that are transferable to their lives. The social worker communicates with the client on what works, what does not, and why. If a client is frustrated with the process, no matter how effective the tool, it will not help him or her to feel empowered. After mastery of the tool, clients can reflect on their thoughts, feelings, and actions in the empowerment process. Once a client grasps the skills of advocacy for one issue, he or she can work toward self-advocacy in any area.

On a micro level, I had a client who came to this country as an adult from Vietnam. During therapy, she disclosed that a doctor had inappropriately touched her and made derogatory comments about her ethnicity. This abuse of power left her unwilling to seek medical attention. We looked up the American Medical Association (AMA) Code of Ethics and information about filing complaints electronically. Through her healing process, she learned to voice her strength by going online and filing a complaint with the medical board, the AMA, the Office of Professional Regulation for the state, and she wrote a letter to the hospital. Her final ritual for healing came as she e-mailed a letter to the physician detailing the trauma inflicted by him and the steps she took for reporting.

Clients can feel powerful on a macro level by participation in demonstrations. Digital advocacy efforts coordinated 10,000 peaceful protestors in the demonstration pictured on page 30 through Facebook, websites, mass e-mails, and posts on mailing lists to concerned citizens. Walking city streets closed for the march, chanting messages, and speaking with others in the cause, can provide a strengths-based approach for self-advocacy. Clients using digital tools on a micro or macro level create experiences that stay with them as a foundation for future empowerment.

*Ellen M. Belluomini, LCSW, received her MSW from the University of Illinois, Jane Addams School of Social Work and is currently a doctoral student at Walden University. She is an educator at National Louis University and Harper College. She has developed online and blended curricula with an emphasis on integrating technology into human services practice. She writes a blog "Bridging the Digital Divide in Social Work Practice" to increase awareness about technology's uses. She presents and consults on various issues related to social services. Her clinical work has been in private practice, management of nonprofit agencies, and programming for vulnerable populations.*

# Accessing Apps: Advocacy
*by Ellen Belluomini, LCSW*

There are many different ways clients can be empowered to advocate for themselves or their causes. These apps give tools for both avenues of expression. Access the applications by placing the name of the app in a web browser.

## Apps by Population

### ALZ Advocacy
The Alzheimer's Association Advocacy Forum with talking points, social media engagement tools, legislative feedback forms, and advocacy videos.
Cost: Free Apple and Android

### Homeless Helper
This app helps people experiencing homelessness to find shelter, food, medical help, hotlines, legal assistance, employment, and social services within their area. We can advocate for our area to adopt the app.
Cost: Free Apple and Android

### HIV Connect
This HIV app helps people with this disease have conversations involving treatments, support, and what is new with advocacy for this population.
Cost: Free Android

### HRC Foundation Buying for Workplace Equality Guide
This is one of many apps by HRC. HRC identifies LGBT friendly brands and businesses by an easy-to-understand color coding system. There is a method to share purchases on social media.
Cost: Free   Apple

### Parkinson's Central
This app gives patients and caregivers access to local resources, recommendations for doctor's visits and disease management, information about insurance and caregiver issues.
Cost: Free, Apple and Android

### Pocket DACA
Deferred Action for Childhood Arrivals app is for immigrants to understand and participate in President Obama's non-deportation policy for dream immigrants.  There are prescreening tools, legal help, news, polls, and resources.
Cost: Free Apple and Android

## Advocacy Apps for Children

### Rule the School Self Advocacy Board Game
This app helps students with hearing loss learn how to advocate for their needs and ability to have equal access to their school's resources. Problem solving scenarios included.
Cost: Free Apple and Android

## General Advocacy

### The Extraordinaries
Choose an organization, cause, or person and then make a difference in people's lives.
Cost: Free Apple

### Facebook
I know, Facebook is not an app per se, but there are Facebook apps on smartphones. When a client "likes" an organization on Facebook, he or she will get updates from those organizations or causes. They can be a part of the revolutions this connection provides.
Cost: Free Apple and Android

### Super PAC App
Hold your phone to the television during ads for the presidential campaign and this app will tell you the accuracy of the information. This is bipartisan information.
Cost: Free   Apple

*Handbook of Military Social Work, edited by Allen Rubin, Eugenia L. Weiss, & Jose E. Coll. John Wiley & Sons, Inc., Hoboken, New Jersey, 2013. 608 pages, $65 hardcover, $45.99 e-book.*

*Handbook of Military Social Work* is a true handbook! This text is all-encompassing and contains everything needed in a handbook—resources, glossary of military terms, case vignettes, and content covering all aspects of the helping process and connecting to the core military social work competencies based on the Educational Policy and Accreditation Standards (EPAS) of the Council on Social Work Education (CSWE). Edited by Allen Rubin, Eugenia L. Weiss, and Jose E. Coll, included are 26 powerful chapters authored by civilian practitioners, military practitioners, and scholars covering aspects of social work with service members, veterans, as well as their associated family members. Beginning with the history of social work in the military, the text lays the foundation for social work with service members and veterans including unique challenges facing women in the military, as well as ethical dilemmas facing uniformed and civilian social workers—chapters useful for all, from military providers to students.

Considered important for educators, the editors have done an outstanding job of organizing the text—Part I: Foundations of Social Work With Service Members and Veterans; Part II: Interventions for the Behavioral Health Problems of Service Members and Veterans; Part III: Veterans and Systems of Care; and Part IV: Families Impacted by Military Service.

As a social work educator and uniformed military social worker, I am adding this text to my repertoire of resources. This is a desktop resource that students, educators, clinicians, clients, and those not in the field of social work can immediately use. This text scores high in readability, is easy to understand, and has applicability to almost any circumstance confronting social workers today. Nothing is omitted! The layout makes it practical for educators, allowing for the ability to design a curriculum appropriate for MSW and BSW programs. Several chapters contain case vignettes and discussion questions, making the text applicable and relevant.

Vignettes bring to life circumstances and varying experiences faced by clients and providers.

Key features are topics related to specific treatment modalities and therapeutic approaches used with families and veterans. An important chapter is *Psychopharmacology for PTSD and Co-Occurring Disorders*. The authors define various classes of medication and even address gender differences and medication side effects. The editors and authors have also made the *Handbook* relevant for clients in chapters such as *Cycle of Deployment and Family Well-Being* and *The Exceptional Family Member Program*.

Although the intended audience is social workers serving military members and veterans, military service members who are not social workers may avail themselves of the contents of the text. Those in leadership positions within the military, the chaplaincy, JAG corps, and other professions within the military will find this book helpful. Even the *Glossary of Military Terms and Veteran Organizations* and *Military Family Resources* sections are a great resource. I will definitely recommend this text to others and will use it in my Social Work in the Military course and in my role as a military social worker. The *Handbook of Military Social Work* is an awesome tool!

*Reviewed by Sonja V. Harry, PhD, LMSW, ACSW, Assistant Professor of Social Work, Winston-Salem State University.*

---

*Mindfulness-Oriented Recovery Enhancement for Addiction, Stress, and Pain by Eric L. Garland, PhD, LCSW, NASW Press, 214 pages, 2013, $37.99 paperback.*

From the first paragraphs, it is clear that author Eric L. Garland is both a well-researched author and a social worker. Although many amazing books for social workers are written by those in other professions, it benefits the reader that Garland is the developer of Mindfulness-Oriented Recovery Enhancement (MORE), assistant director of the Trinity Institute for the Addictions, and assistant professor at the Florida State University College of Social Work. The compilation of Garland's knowledge from both the classroom and the field lends to a book that is strong and easy to follow.

Written in a linear style, Garland begins by laying out how addiction, stress, and pain are cyclical. Next, he examines

how one leads to the next and the most common reasons a person struggling to overcome any of these may begin to struggle with the other two. It is at this point that the author introduces Mindfulness-Oriented Recovery Enhancement (MORE). This general explanation then becomes more specialized, as the author spells out how a person struggling with addiction, stress, and pain will benefit from each of MORE's steps.

The following section describes and guides a clinician through using this treatment model, including scripts and rationale for each of several client sessions. Most helpful is his inclusion of "clinician tips," tiny reminders or helpful hints for a clinician to keep in mind while following the laid out steps. As a social worker working to follow the book and utilize this treatment model for the first few times, these additional bits of information come across as being supported by the author as a social work colleague, a lovely emotional boost during what may be a stressful learning experience for a clinician new to MORE and focused on trying to get each step exactly right.

The closing of this book is full of helpful appendices, including a section on working with clients struggling with opiate addiction, multiple worksheets for use with clients, and information regarding how mindfulness integrates with physical activity and how it affects personal relationships.

Overall, author and MORE developer Eric L. Garland has created a wonderful training tool for social workers whose clients struggle with addiction, stress, and pain. Both clients and clinicians will benefit from what amounts to a written guided training of Mindfulness-Oriented Recovery Enhancement.

*Reviewed by Kristen Marie (Kryss) Shane, MSW, LSW, LMSW.*

---

*School Social Work: A Direct Practice Guide, by JoAnn Jarolmen, SAGE Publications, Inc., 2014, 438 pages, $75.00.*

Jarolmen's book is comprehensive and includes an exciting array of subjects. Some of the topics seem at first glance misplaced in a practice textbook. The subtitle may misdirect the reader to wonder whether the intended audience is social work students or practicing social workers. The lack of a preface or foreword reinforces the ambiguity of the intended audience. Jarolmen seems to tackle the issue by striving to address both micro and macro issues.

The beginning chapters focus on setting a theoretical foundation, establishing the experience of actual social workers in the school setting, and providing a basic overview of educational stakeholders. It is at chapter six that the shift begins and widens to a macro system approach. The remaining chapters identify social issues in society that have a direct impact on children in schools. These issues include homelessness and poverty. Inclusion of such a breadth of topics is intriguing and expands the practice relevance. However, one glaring omission is the subject of foster children. Since all foster children are required to attend school, they bring specific challenges and may need the services of a school social worker.

It was especially refreshing to read the chapter on cultural competence and inclusion of race, gender, religion, and socioeconomics as the foundation for the discussion on diversity. The chapter on global issues in schools is fascinating, but may not be of much use to the school social worker in an urban school setting, and is unrelated to the subtitle of direct practice. The macro perspective allows school social workers to intellectualize issues not directly related to their individual practice and offers a respite from their routine issues of concern. As a social work educator with a current focus on global issues of concern to children, I view this chapter as dynamic but with little appeal and no practicality to new or experienced school social workers in the field.

Six appendices constitute approximately 25% of the book and cover nearly 100 pages. The information is included for its pragmatism. It is here that Jarolmen's contribution to evidence-based practice is evident. For example, these appendices are templates for group formation, conflict resolution, and at-risk assessment. The level of detail in the appendices is highly proscriptive but can be somewhat confusing and difficult to follow. The references are robust, and a sampling of the first 50 citations revealed that Jarolmen's research met the 15-10 rule, with 25 of the first 50 sources having been published within the last 10 years.

Case studies and analyses are included in many chapters, along with a summary of the key concepts. The class discussion questions stimulate critical thinking and problem solving. The practice aspect is reinforced by activities and self-reflection questions. Since the book is anchored with the theoretical overview, it seems most appropriate for use with future school social workers.

*Reviewed by Vanessa Brooks Herd, Ed.D., LMSW, ACSW, former school social worker, Associate Professor and Project Manager for Youth in Transition Program, Department of Social Work, Saginaw Valley State University, Saginaw, Michigan.*

---

*Exploiting Childhood: How Fast Food, Material Obsession and Porn Culture are Creating New Forms of Child Abuse, edited by Jim Wild, Jessica Kingsley Publishing; Philadelphia, PA, 2013, 206 pages, $23.95.*

This captivating book is a must read for parents, teachers, ministers, counselors, social workers, and pediatricians. Jim Wild, the editor, has skillfully found a way to link the new culture of children's addiction back to the family, or lack of family guidance, and more interesting, the community. The book details the many ways that corporate America has preyed upon the innocence and gullibility of children as well as parents. These corporations, assembling multi-billion dollar marketing teams, have successfully found a way to increase the public's thirst for platonic, superficial materialism.

Prior to reading this book, I never truly comprehended the massive, macro abuse that is happening to children, teens, and young adults. Fast food marketing campaigns aimed primarily at young children and teens are one of the largest perpetrators of this physical abuse, as more young children are consuming fast foods and are becoming overweight, obese, and are being diagnosed with early onset diabetes at staggering rates. Nipping at the heels of the fast food marketing are the clothing and electronic marketing abusers, specifically targeting young children and teens to buy the skimpiest clothing and the latest electronics, and when they don't, they are marketed as being "uncool," "unhip," and losers. Only "winners" buy these electronics and only "winners" wear these styles.

This book was enlightening, frightening, and infuriating, as adults are allowing this abuse to take place, often condoning it to assuage the child. This placation to children, with videogames, and iPods, and PlayStations, is keeping children indoors, unable to remember to play, create, recreate, run, scream, climb trees, run on the grass. And the more we keep our children inside, the more obese, apathetic, lethargic, and sickly they are becoming.

The book is an easy-to-read collection of well written, short, concise, and very clear chapters, focusing on material and sexual exploitation. There are 15 chapters in the book, detailing the amounts and types of abuse our nation's children are suffering, without even knowing it. The financial gain associated with the exploitation of children is sickening and will only continue to decimate, slaughter, and destroy our children as long as social workers, teachers, pediatricians, psychologists, psychiatrists, mothers, fathers, churches, and communities passively sit by and wait for someone else to take the lead and fight this battle.

This book outraged me, as I hope it does every single other reader. I hope, however, the outrage turns into action, as this book draws a straight line from corporate America greed to physical, emotional, and psychological abuse.

*Reviewed by Marian Swindell, PhD, MSW, Associate Professor of Social Work, Mississippi State University.*

---

*Witness to Resilience: Stories of Intimate Violence, by Jane Seskin. CreateSpace, 2013, 68 pages, $10.95.*

A precious collection of poems that leads the reader through the hallways and corridors of intimate violence. Each poem is beautifully crafted out of the story of each surviving poet-artist. The reader will experience a feast of emotions with the turning of each page: sadness, sympathy, empathy, longing, panic, happiness, joy, fear, relief, and anger. The poems range from upbeat and happy to dark and hollow, reflecting the unknowing and ever shifting life of the survivor.

*Reviewed by Marian Swindell, Ph.D., MSW, Associate Professor of Social Work, Mississippi State University.*

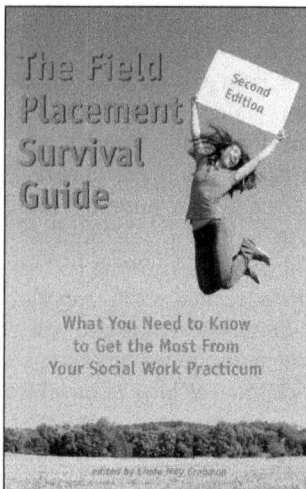

# THE FIELD PLACEMENT SURVIVAL GUIDE
## What You Need To Know To Get the Most From Your Social Work Practicum
## 2nd Edition

Field placement is one of the most exciting and exhilarating parts of a formal social work education. It is also one of the most challenging. This collection addresses the multitude of issues that social work students in field placement encounter, including choosing a placement, getting prepared, using supervision effectively, working with clients, coping with challenges, and moving on to a successful social work career.

This collection is a goldmine of practical information that will help social work students take advantage of all the field placement experience has to offer. Each chapter (many written by seasoned experts in field education; others by students) presents a different aspect of the practicum and offers students insight into the importance of both the challenges and the joys of this unique learning experience.

This book brings together in one volume the best field placement articles from THE NEW SOCIAL WORKER. Packed with practical, essential information for every student in field placement!

*"As an older (52), non-traditional student working my internship for my B.A. in social work, I ordered your book. It was so reassuring that others had survived and gone on to successful careers!"*

*Linda Chamberlain*

Edited by Linda May Grobman, ACSW, LSW
Founder, publisher, and editor of *THE NEW SOCIAL WORKER*.

ISBN: 978-1-929109-26-5  2011  Price: $22.95  284 pages

Shipping/Handling: add $8.50/first book, $1.50/each additional book in U.S.
Canadian orders: add $14.00 first book, $4 each add'l book. Other orders: contact us. If ordering from Pennsylvania, add 6% sales tax.
Order from White Hat Communications, PO Box 5390, Harrisburg, PA 17110-0390
http://shop.whitehatcommunications.com  717-238-3787 (phone)  717-238-2090 (fax)

# IS IT ETHICAL? 101 Scenarios In Everyday Social Work Practice
## A Discussion Workbook
### by Thomas Horn, MSW, RSW

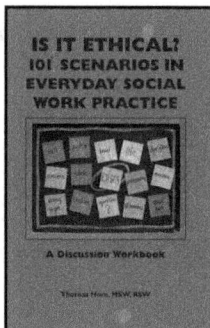

What would you do if you were asked to be your hairdresser's social worker? How about if you developed a crush on a client? Or if you unexpectedly received a $100 check in the mail from an agency to whom you had referred a client?

Social work is filled with these kinds of questions. They come up every day in professional life. Will your students be prepared to make the ethical decision?

Very few social workers go to work looking for ways to exploit, manipulate, or mislead the people with whom they work—clients, colleagues, managers, the government, or the general public. Yet, it is possible to cross into unethical behavior unintentionally, often as a result of poor decisions that are misguided. The line between ethical and unethical can become blurred.

This workbook provides students with 101 different everyday scenarios and challenges them to think about what the ethical and unethical choices might be in each situation. Through examining these scenarios on their own and in discussion with classmates and others, they will become more familiar with how to apply the ethical guidelines and standards that they will be required to follow as professional social workers.

Space is provided after each scenario for readers to write their own responses as they prepare to discuss the scenario with classmates, supervisors, and others. There is space for students to write their own scenarios, as well.

Resources are listed, including Code of Ethics Web addresses for nine different social work associations, as well as ethics journals.

*"...if you need a resource to begin a discussion of ethics in a classroom or agency in-service, this workbook qualifies for Social Work Ethics 101."* Paul Dovyak, ACSW, LISW-S, University of Rio Grande, Journal of Social Work Values and Ethics

## ABOUT THE AUTHOR

Thomas Horn, MSW, RSW, is a Registered Social Worker (RSW) with both the Ontario College of Social Workers and Social Service Workers (OCSWSSW) in Ontario, Canada, and the General Social Care Council (GSCC) in England. Tom is also a graduate member of the British Psychological Society. He has worked in the social services field for more than 20 years in a variety of settings, including residential developmental care, residential and outpatient child and adolescent mental health, residential drug/alcohol treatment, and inpatient psychiatry. Currently, Tom works with an inpatient forensic mental health team at a large psychiatric hospital in Ontario. He routinely provides field supervision to social work students at the undergraduate and graduate levels.

2011 • ISBN: 978-1-929109-29-6 • 118 pages, 5½ by 8½ • $14.95 plus shipping
White Hat Communications, P.O. Box 5390, Harrisburg, PA 17110-0390 Phone: 717-238-3787 Fax: 717-238-2090  shop.whitehatcommunications.com

# Social Work's Watershed Moment: The Social Work Reinvestment Act (SWRA)

## by Courtney Kidd, LMSW

Social work is facing its watershed moment–the crucial turning point that will define our future. Six years ago, the Social Work Reinvestment Act (SWRA) was brought before Capitol Hill in an attempt to promote the need for social workers, and to address many of the concerns the profession faces. With the rejuvenated efforts of Congresswoman Barbara Lee and Senator Barbara Mikulski, as well as support from the Congressional Social Work Caucus, the SWRA is once again making its way to the hill. This time, it has some help. The Social Work Caucus, founded in 2011 by Congressman Edolphus Towns, acts as the representative for the interests of social workers on Capitol Hill. Together, these social workers on the hill are looking to help social work become a sustainable work force.

Petition available at
www.socialworkpetition.com

The SWRA attempts to identify and address the ongoing concerns in the social work profession, including competitive and fair wages, research, tuition assistance, and national licensing. Social workers face many challenges in the workforce, with almost 75% of graduates beginning their careers with more than $35,000 in debt, while the national mean salary for social workers is $52,000. The SWRA identifies the national shortage of trained social workers in the workforce, and addresses the direct implications that has on the population. The bill intends on launching a commission to study recruitment and retention techniques to promote the profession, relying on areas such as grants, workplace improvements, education about the profession, and perhaps most importantly, continued Congressional advocacy for social workers.

The goal is to not only reinvest in social work, but to rejuvenate it. We, at Social Justice Solutions, strive to support these first steps in promoting social workers by hosting a social worker driven petition. It is our belief that social workers hold a unique skill set that provides a vital role. In few other professions can you use these skills, combined with a code of ethics, to provide direct practice, community organizing, policy making–the list is endless to what social workers can do, but we limit ourselves by not advocating for our own needs. The social work petition provides a way for every social worker to help the efforts of the Social Work Caucus, and the SWRA. Each signature is another voice supporting the advancement of the profession.

The challenge we face is to demonstrate the need for social workers in our roles, and in turn, receive support from the community. Social workers must be at the decision-making table to be effective change agents. The SWRA Petition looks to connect our profession together in pursuing this goal. The SWRA bill is the first step for social workers to advocate for ourselves. Together, with our partners in the Congressional Research Institute of Social Work and Policy (CRISP), we hope to see social workers benefit from an increase of support within society. We look to you for aid in our venture. We look to you to make a difference. You can sign the petition at *http://www.SocialWorkPetition.com*.

*Courtney Kidd, LMSW, is Social Justice Solutions Co-Founder and Chief Operating Officer. Courtney graduated SUNY Stony Brook with her Master's in Social Welfare, and Dowling College with a B.A. in psychology. She is currently working for the Department of Veteran Affairs, with a strong interest in military/veteran mental health. Courtney continues to work for the promotion of the social work profession and is actively involved in the NASW as the Veteran Steering Committee Chair. Her other areas of interest include policy, program development, advocacy, and systems work. Courtney can be reached at: Courtney@ Socialjusticesolutions.org.*

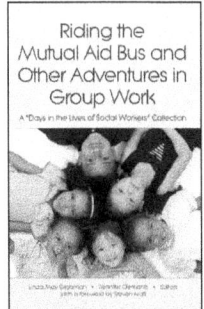

# NEW!

# Beginnings, Middles, & Ends
## Sideways Stories on the Art & Soul of Social Work
### Ogden W. Rogers, Ph.D., LCSW, ACSW

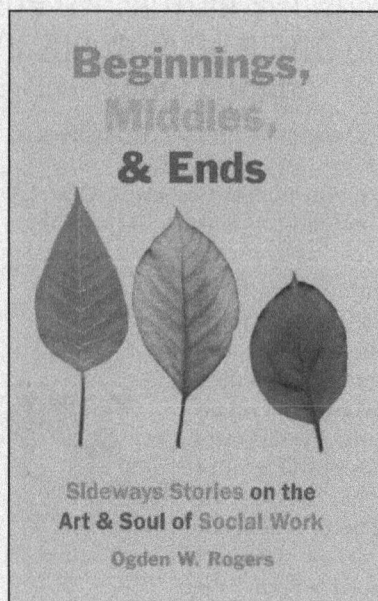

A sideways story is some moment in life when you thought you were doing one thing, but you ended up learning another. A sideways story can also be a poem, or prose, that, because of the way it is written, may not be all that direct in its meaning. What's nice about both clouds, and art, is that you can look at them and just resonate. That can be good for both the heart and the mind.

Many of the moments of this book have grown from experiences the author has had or stories he used in his lectures with students or told in his office with clients. Some of them have grown from essays written for others, for personal or professional reasons. They are moments on a path through the discovery of social work, a journey of beginnings, middles, and ends.

With just the right blend of humor and candor, each of these stories contains nuggets of wisdom that you will not find in a traditional textbook. They capture the essence and the art and soul of social work. In a world rushed with the illusion of technique and rank empiricism, it is the author's hope that some of the things here might make some moment in your thinking or feeling grow as a social worker. If they provoke a smile, or a tear, or a critical question, it's worth it. Everyone makes a different journey in a life of social work. These stories are one social worker's travelogue along the way.

## PRAISE FOR THE BOOK

"As someone near the end of a long career in social work and social work education, I found the stories of Ogden Rogers in his collection, Beginnings. Middles, and Ends, to reflect so much of my own experience that I literally moved back and forth between tears of soulful recognition and laugh-out-loud moments of wonderful remembrances. There is something truthful and powerful about the artist who is willing to put a masterpiece together and leave the telltale signs of failed attempts. Too many who reflect on their past do so to minimize imperfection, setting standards unreachable by others. Ogden Rogers has charted a course of professionalism that encourages creativity, allowing for errors, and guided by honest reflection and dedication to those whom he would serve. This read is a gift to all, whether they are starting or ending their journey of service to others."
Terry L. Singer, Ph.D., Dean, Kent School of Social Work, University of Louisville

"I found the stories humorous, sometimes painful, and incredibly honest and real. There is really nothing else out in our literature that is quite like this. It reminds me of when we teach the art and science of social work practice—this is the art."
Jennifer Clements, Ph.D., LCSW, Associate Professor, Shippensburg University

"...a profound piece of creative literature that will reinstill idealism within senior social workers who are on the threshold of being cynical about their work."
Stephen M. Marson, Ph.D., Professor, University of North Carolina Pembroke

"Recommended reading for new social workers, experienced social workers, friends and families of social workers, and future social workers because of the variety of anecdotal case presentations and personal perceptions. Truly open and honest portrayals of social work and the helping professions with touching, easy-to-read entries fit within the beginning, middle, and ending framework. This book is suggested for both public and academic libraries to support the career services and/or professional development collections."
Rebecca S. Traub, M.L.S., Library Specialist, Temple University Harrisburg

For the complete
Table of Contents of
Ogden Rogers'
***Beginnings, Middles, & Ends***

and other information
about this book, see:

***beginningsmiddlesandends.com***

Available directly from the publisher now! Available in print and Kindle editions at Amazon.com.

## ABOUT THE AUTHOR

**Ogden W. Rogers, Ph.D., LCSW, ACSW,** is Professor and Chair of the Department of Social Work at The University of Wisconsin-River Falls. He has been a clinician, consultant, educator, and storyteller.

ISBN: 978-1-929109-35-7 • 2013 • 5.5 x 8.5 • 249 pages • $19.95 plus shipping  Order from White Hat Communications, PO Box 5390, Harrisburg, PA 17110-0390
http://shop.whitehatcommunications.com  717-238-3787 (phone)  717-238-2090 (fax)

20th Anniversary Issue!

# The New Social Worker ®
## the social work careers magazine

Spring 2014
Volume 21, Number 2

*BSW students from Park University in Parkville, MO, show off their "got strengths?" t-shirts. Shown at the recent Association of Baccalaureate Social Work Program Directors conference in Louisville, KY, are (left to right): Andrea Kesler, Afton Salas, and Jessica Caudillo. The t-shirts were inspired by Park's focus on the strengths perspective (BSW program chair Walter Kisthardt was a contributor to early published works on the strengths perspective in social work practice) and the program's social work club advisor, Gary Bachman. Students sold the t-shirts to raise money to adopt families at Thanksgiving and Christmas.*

# FEATURES

Turn Up the Tech in Social Work

Making the Tough Call: Mandated Reporting, Part VII

Social Work Goes to the Movies—The Oscars

Reviews

Student Role Model: Susan Vanino

# CONTENTS

THE NEW SOCIAL WORKER®
Spring 2014
Volume 21, Number 2

## FEATURES

## DEPARTMENTS

# Publisher's Thoughts

Dear Reader,

Well, as the song goes, "It might as well be spring!" And it IS spring here in the eastern U.S., where *THE NEW SOCIAL WORKER* is based. We are celebrating here, because in addition to welcoming the arrival of spring, we have just completed National Social Work Month, AND this is our 20th Anniversary Issue!

During Social Work Month (March), we published a series of essays, poetry, artwork, video, audio, and other creative works about the profession of social work. Did you see it? You can still access these inspiring and creative items at: *http://www.socialworker.com/topics/social-work-month-2014*

*The publisher/editor*

I've been looking through our 20+ years of past issues. Technology, field placement, ethics, and book reviews have been staples of our pages since the earliest issues. We have had a focus on social work careers all along, too. More recently, we added a movie column and a series on mandated reporting. We are working on creating a searchable index of the first 20+ years of publication. Also, in this anniversary issue, we wanted to honor the many student role models we have featured over the years. See page 20 for a complete list of them. Where are they now? Some have gone on to get more advanced degrees and become social work professors and leaders in the profession. The role models have represented social work in a wide variety of settings at the micro, mezzo, and macro levels. They are a widely diverse group, as is the profession as a whole.

In this issue, we have focused on adoption, with two related articles, and on involuntary clients' self determination, also with two articles. In addition, Melinda Pilkinton's article on Bayard Rustin (page 26), which appeared on our website during Black History Month, provides insight into why this leader in the Civil Rights Movement was relegated to the background. Marian Swindell (page 32) urges social workers to go beyond cultural competence to a new model of *compassionate competence*. And D.J. Williams (page 8) invites students and new social workers to GO FAR! in their careers. Microaggressions are the focus of Ellen's tech column (page 30), and Addison looks at the Oscars (page 18). We continue with our series on mandated reporting with a look at what happens after you make a report. A student's first-year field reflections and an article on an art expression group round out this issue.

Have you taken our Reader Survey? It will take about 5-10 minutes of your time. Go to *http://www.socialworker.com/2014-reader-survey* to get started. Thanks!

To subscribe to THE NEW SOCIAL WORKER's Social Work E-News and notifications of new issues of the magazine, go to the "Subscribe" link on our website at *http://www.socialworker.com*. (It's free!)

Until next time—happy reading!

*Linda M. Grobman*

# The New Social Worker

## Spring 2014
## Vol. 21, Number 2

*Publisher/Editor*
Linda May Grobman, MSW, ACSW, LSW

*Contributing Writers*
Barbara Trainin Blank
Allan Barsky, JD, MSW, Ph.D.
Addison Cooper, LCSW
Ellen Belluomini, LCSW
Kathryn A. Krase, Ph.D., J.D., MSW

THE NEW SOCIAL WORKER® (ISSN 1073-7871) is published four times a year by White Hat Communications, P.O. Box 5390, Harrisburg, PA 17110-0390. Phone: (717) 238-3787. Fax: (717) 238-2090. Send address corrections to: lindagrobman@socialworker.com

Advertising rates available on request.

Copyright © 2014 White Hat Communications. All rights reserved. No part of this publication may be reproduced in any form without the express written permission of the publisher. The opinions expressed in *THE NEW SOCIAL WORKER* are those of the authors and are not necessarily shared by the publisher.

Photo/art credits: Image from BigStockPhoto.com © Rido81 (page 6), DNF-Style (page 12), Aquasnap (page 14), Anatols (page 16), Joe Seer (page 18), Marmion (page 22), Photojohn830 (page 32).

**Editorial Advisory Board**
Vivian Bergel, Ph.D., ACSW, LSW
Joseph Davenport, Ph.D.
Judith Davenport, Ph.D., LCSW
Brad Forenza, MSSW
Sam Hickman, MSW, ACSW, LCSW

Send all editorial, advertising, subscription, and other correspondence to:

**THE NEW SOCIAL WORKER**
**White Hat Communications**
**P.O. Box 5390**
**Harrisburg, PA 17110-0390**
**(717) 238-3787 Phone**
**(717) 238-2090 Fax**

lindagrobman@socialworker.com
http://www.socialworker.com
http://www.facebook.com/newsocialworker
http://www.twitter.com/newsocialworker

**Print Edition:**
http://newsocialworker.magcloud.com

## Write for The New Social Worker

We are looking for articles from social work practitioners, students, and educators.

Some areas of particular interest are: social work ethics; student field placement; practice specialties; social work careers/job search; technology; "what every new social worker needs to know;" and news of unusual, creative, or nontraditional social work.

Feature articles run 1,500-2,000 words in length. News articles are typically 100-150 words. Our style is conversational, practical, and educational. Write as if you are having a conversation with a student or colleague. What do you want him or her to know about the topic? What would you want to know? Use examples.

The best articles have a specific focus. If you are writing an ethics article, focus on a particular aspect of ethics. For example, analyze a specific portion of the NASW *Code of Ethics* (including examples), or talk about ethical issues unique to a particular practice setting. When possible, include one or two resources at the end of your article—books, additional reading materials, and/or websites.

We also want photos of social workers and social work students "in action" for our cover, and photos to accompany your news articles!

Send submissions to lindagrobman@socialworker.com.

# Susan Vanino

## *by Barbara Trainin Blank*

Susan Vanino isn't the type to let challenges daunt her. Diagnosed with macular degeneration since childhood, her vision has deteriorated throughout her life, leaving her almost entirely blind.

Many years after earning an associate degree in early childhood education and raising two children with her husband of 37 years, she returned to school as a non-traditional student for a Bachelor of Social Work (BSW) at Ramapo College of New Jersey. Some say she is following in her child's footsteps, as her daughter also earned a BSW from Ramapo 12 years earlier. Now, Susan is pursuing her MSW at New York University's Silver School of Social Work, in the advanced standing program.

"I chose NYU because of its outstanding academic reputation and its strong focus on clinical work," says Susan, who graduates in May.

Before returning to college, Susan worked for five years as the Adjustment to Vision Loss (AVL) Program Coordinator in Hackensack, NJ. AVL is an extensive network of peer support groups located throughout New Jersey. These groups provide individuals experiencing vision loss with relevant information, emotional support, and a special kind of understanding that might not be found elsewhere.

Susan continued full-time work with AVL during her undergraduate studies at Ramapo College, while also attending classes full-time. Currently, her social work internship is with Comprehensive Behavioral Healthcare, Inc., where she facilitates individual and group psychotherapy sessions with adults diagnosed with paranoid schizophrenia, as well as major depressive and bipolar disorders.

For her achievements, Susan is receiving a National Scholastic Achievement Award from Learning Ally, a nonprofit founded in 1948 as Recording for the Blind. It now serves individuals with print disabilities, as well as dyslexia and learning disabilities.

Learning Ally has the world's largest library of audiobooks, which Susan uses in her schoolwork, along with computer technology. A screen reader that works with MS Office allows her to do what seeing people can.

Susan and other awardees were awarded a scholarship and will be honored at a dinner in Washington, DC, on April 26.

"Susan was chosen because she demonstrates leadership in the community and is a role model to so many others," says Doug Sprei, national media director at Learning Ally. "She is always reinventing herself and moving forward, constantly trying to reach her potential. She has a lot of inner vision and is resilient."

Susan is an inspiration in a world in which the blind are often "woefully unemployed," he adds. "She wants to give back."

Kim Lorber, associate professor of social work and convener of the gerontology minor at Ramapo College, agrees. Having taught Susan in two classes, social work research methods and human behavior in the social environment, she calls her a "stunning student."

"She's brilliant, but also very easygoing," says Lorber. "Other students adore her. One can debate who learned more from whom, but I learned a lot."

"She cuts herself no slack," using technology and her own intelligence to achieve a near-perfect GPA, adds Lorber.

Susan has won a number of awards and scholarships. She is a mentor for the

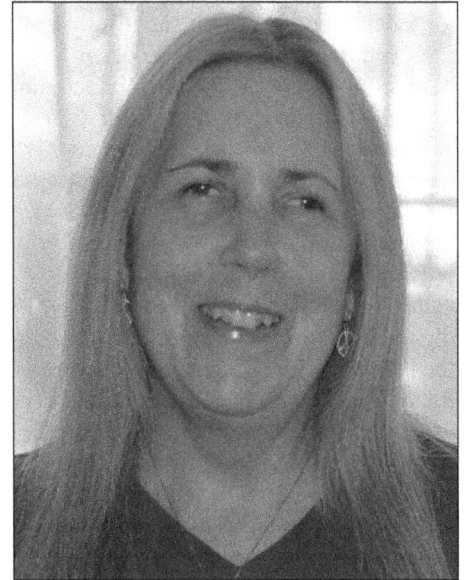

*Susan Vanino*

Bell-Ringer Program of the Joseph Kohn Training Center, and sits on the board of the Garden State Guide Dog Users and the Glen Rock Handicapped Persons Advisory Board.

Last July, Susan was honored at Arm & Hammer Park, in Trenton, New Jersey, by the members of the Trenton Thunder Baseball Team, the New Jersey State Library Talking Book and Braille Center, and the New Jersey Commission for the Blind and Visually Impaired. The 2013 Trenton Thunder Scholarship for Leadership and Community Service was awarded on the ball field at a pre-game ceremony to Susan, who was accompanied by her guide dog "Q."

Outside of work and school, Susan likes "any kind of concerts, but mostly rock and '60s-'80s bands," such as the Eagles and Journey. She also enjoys spending time with her husband and two adult children, as well as her two golden retrievers and black Labrador guide dog.

Through working with individuals with mental illness and physical disabilities, "I realized how a lot of people are not as fortunate as I am," Susan says. "As a social worker, I can touch a lot of lives."

*Freelance writer Barbara Trainin Blank, formerly of Harrisburg, PA, now lives in the greater Washington, DC, area.*

# Ethics Alive!

# Do Involuntary Clients Have a Right to Self-Determination?

## by Allan Barsky, JD, MSW, Ph.D.

Social workers often suggest that self-determination is a cornerstone of the profession. In fact, the first two standards in the NASW *Code of Ethics* (2008) say that our primary obligation is to our client and that we should honor a client's right to self-determination

Self-determination is built on the values of autonomy and respect for the dignity and worth of all people. So, given the primacy of self-determination, how is it that social workers can ethically justify working with clients who are mandated to social work services? By definition, if a client is mandated to services, isn't the social worker breaching the client's right to self-determination? Do involuntary clients have a right to self-determination, and if so, what does self-determination mean in such a context?

Let's start by considering what the NASW *Code* says about self-determination:

*Standard 1.02: Social workers respect and promote the right of clients to self-determination and assist clients in their efforts to identify and clarify their goals. Social workers may limit clients' right to self-determination when, in the social workers' professional judgment, clients' actions or potential actions pose a serious, foreseeable, and imminent risk to themselves or others.*

Note that this standard does not specifically speak to the issue of involuntary clients. Its one exception to self-determination arises when a client poses "a serious, foreseeable, and imminent risk to themselves or others." This exception typically applies to situations of suicidal or homicidal ideation–thus, if a client is about to commit suicide or homicide, the worker is ethically justified in taking steps that run counter to client self-determination to protect the client or potential victim.

Ethically speaking, the *Code* is giving priority to the principle of protecting life over the principle of respecting self-determination. This could include initiating processes that may result in involuntary admission to a psychiatric facility. Note, however, that committing a client involuntarily should be considered a course of last resort.

Standard 1.02 does not say social workers may ignore self-determination. It says they may *limit* self-determination. Implicit in this language is the notion of the "least intrusive" course of action. As much as possible, social workers should honor self-determination. Given that involuntary commitment is highly intrusive, social workers should first consider less intrusive approaches. This includes

> As professional social workers, however, we realize that respect for the dignity and worth of people includes ALL PEOPLE, including those who have harmed others or pose risks of serious harm.

approaches that respect and expand self-determination as much as possible, without undue risk to the life of the client or other person. Consider the following alternatives:

- Using crisis intervention strategies to de-escalate the client's suicidal or homicidal thoughts and plans.
- Developing a voluntary safety plan with the client that may include protective care or monitoring by family members, friends, or other informal support systems.
- Requesting the client's permission to inform the intended target of the crime.
- Offering the client alternatives, such as a referral to another mental health professional for a second opinion, or to a physician who can prescribe appropriate medication.

Working with suicidal or homicidal clients is not the only situation in which social workers serve involuntary clients.

Clients may also be mandated into services when:

- They are involved in the criminal justice system (e.g., convicted of a crime, placed on probation, or given parole with a requirement to participate in counseling or other social work services).
- They are involved in the child protection system because of allegations or findings of child abuse or neglect.

In these situations, our legal system is basically saying that the safety of others (the public, children, and so forth) is more important than self-determination.

The NASW *Code* has just one standard that specifically refers to involuntary clients:

*Standard 1.03(d): In instances when clients are receiving services involuntarily, social workers should provide information about the nature and extent of services and about the extent of clients' right to refuse service.*

This standard recognizes that, even though involuntary clients are being pressured into services, they still have certain rights. First, social workers need to inform clients about the services being offered. For instance, what are the purpose and goals of the services, what model of intervention will be used, what does research say about the benefits and risks of the services, and what are the expectations of the client as a participant in the services? Although providing such information does not constitute informed consent, it does provide informed notice.

Further, even when clients are mandated into services, social workers do not physically force clients into the services. As the above standard explains, workers should inform clients about the extent of their right to refuse services. In particular, workers should clarify what the client is mandated to do, and what the client may refuse to do. The worker should also help clarify the consequences if the client does not fulfill what has been mandated (e.g., will the client go back to court or to incarceration, will the client be denied access to his/her children?). If the client needs legal advice, the worker should ensure that client has access to such advice.

Social workers should also go beyond what Standard 1.03(d) states and strive to honor self-determination as much as possible. Self-determination is not simply an either/or situation. Although social workers should recognize that self-determination may be imperfect for involuntary clients, workers are able to enhance self-determination through various strategies:

- Social workers may engage clients by empathizing with clients, acknowledging pressures on the client, building trust, and validating client concerns, so the client is more willing to participate in services.
- Social workers may empower clients by helping them set goals and objectives that they genuinely want to pursue—even if they did not initially choose to participate in services.
- Social workers may offer clients a range of choices, including which methods and models of intervention will be used (e.g., individual vs. fam-ily counseling, cognitive vs. narrative therapy).

- In appropriate cases, social workers may advocate with authorities to honor client wishes and revise court orders or other mandates.

It may be easy for people to say, "This person committed a heinous crime. He doesn't deserve self-determination," or "These parents abused an innocent child. Of course, we have to take away their rights." As professional social workers, however, we realize that respect for the dignity and worth of people includes ALL PEOPLE, including those who have harmed others or pose risks of serious harm. Honoring self-determination as much as possible may be more difficult with some clients than with others. For the profession of social work, this is a challenge that we accept with conviction and pride.

*Dr. Allan Barsky is Professor of Social Work at Florida Atlantic University and Chair of the National Ethics Committee of the National Association of Social Workers. He is the author of Ethics and Values in Social Work (Oxford University Press), Conflict Resolution for the Helping Professions (Brooks/Cole), and Clinicians in Court (Guilford Press). The views expressed in this article do not necessarily reflect the view of any of the organizations with which Dr. Barsky is affiliated.*

# Field Placement

## Starting Where the Student Is: Reflections of a First-Year Social Work Graduate Student

### by Katherine Freeman

We sit down. "My name is Katherine Freeman, and I'm the social work intern at the clinic." She can hear my voice shaking. *Is her eyebrow raised in suspicion, or am I just imagining that?* "What can I help you with today?" *Just dive in. There's no other way,* I think to myself. I lean forward onto the desk, smile, and am sure that I sit with an open posture to the client, giving her my undivided attention as we were taught in our Social Work Practice Lab.

I'm not sure if my experience as a first-year social work graduate student exactly mirrors that of others. Actually, I believe it unfair to assume that there is one "standard" experience of a student in this field, as the beauty of this profession is that it attracts people with such a rich and diverse array of experience that it is impossible to identify a "typical" student.

The one thing that binds us all together is the opportunity we were offered to recreate ourselves as professional social workers–delicately, and at times clumsily, weaving together our experiences, worldview, compassion, and sense of self into the work we do. With the best of intentions, we learn to apply the principles of social work, while at the same time we are still diligently taking notes late at night on exactly what those principles are.

As I finish my first year of graduate school, I would like to reflect and share the experiences I have had with those entering the field. The challenges that I have faced have been internal as well as external, as at times I have found myself in the position of examining where I come from and how I view the world, to learning the seemingly endless implications of providing physical and emotional care to those in need. I would like to give a voice to first-year graduate students, and shed light and calm anxieties about what this experience might be like for incoming students, as well as serve as a validation for students in their first few months of field work that it's okay to not have all the answers.

## Anxieties of the Unknown

Prior to starting my field work in the fall, I had no idea what to expect. I knew my placement was at a community health center in West Harlem, New York City, and that I would be working with two social workers to provide case management and therapeutic support to the clinic's patients. When classes started and I began to meet my fellow students, the second question out of everyone's mouth after "What's your name?" was "Where's your field placement?" It felt reassuring to know I wasn't the only one with anxieties. However, the constant assurances from faculty members to relax and learn to "sit with your discomfort" seemed to simply mock my sweaty palms and beating heart.

My first few weeks at the clinic, I was guided through the roles and responsibilities that the social workers carry out and what was expected of me. I spent a great deal of time sitting in on assessments that my supervisors would carry out, and observing the kinds of questions they would ask, and the way they would respond to patients' differing attitudes, questions, and presenting problems. I was grateful that I was given this time to observe, process, and ask questions.

In this time, I learned that the clinic serves members of the surrounding community, which predominantly consists of first- or second-generation Latino immigrants. I began to learn just how pivotal the role of a social worker is in securing benefits for our patients, and also just how much the patients depend on our assistance in navigating the system to receive them.

The myriad of needs that our patients presented with was overwhelming to me at first. I feverishly took notes after observing every session, and I did my best to remember the exact dialogue that was carried out between my supervisors and the patients to report in my process recordings. My supervisors and I would discuss the details of the session afterwards, and I felt a rise in my confidence in how I would eventually carry out such a session on my own.

## Working Through the Discomfort

When I began to carry out my first assessments independently, I experienced countless emotions. I felt excited and eager to delve into the work, but also nervous and questioning about how much I would really be able to do on my own. My supervisors were close by if I had a question, and I utilized their guidance often.

Reflecting upon my first few months at the clinic, I recognize that I felt very unsure of myself and conflicted over the way I felt I was perceived, and how I would be able to relate to patients. I felt it possible that there were judgments being passed on me in regard to my appearance and what that seemed to symbolize to the population I was working with. Given that I was a young, white American female seemingly in this position of power, I felt that many of the patients were wary of me and had guarded responses to my questions.

At times, I began to feel a sense of inadequacy to help, given that the presenting problems of many of our patients are ones that I personally have not experienced. Being in a position in which you are expected to be of help, but have absolutely no idea really how to do so, can be quite disconcerting.

Furthermore, I also realized that the position I held often allowed me to provide patients what they needed, despite the fact that I often felt unworthy of being privy to the very personal aspects of the patients' lives that they discussed with me. Given that I personally did not view myself as being in a position of power, as I was a student who felt as though she was stumbling along the helping process herself, it was a very uncomfortable situation to be in.

On top of this, at times there seemed to be cultural and linguistic barriers. Although I can speak Spanish fluently and lived abroad for years, all the cultural competency and ability to connect through shared experiences that I thought I had prior to starting this work seemed inadequate. The concept that in certain situations I could be perceived as being part of the dominant majority group, instead of someone who can connect and understand based on shared cultural experiences, was unsettling to me.

It was through the process of working through this discomfort and acknowledging the systemic context of identity and culture that I was able to come to terms with my position. As stated by Mo (2003), especially when the clinician belongs to the dominant majority group and the client to a minority group, it is important for the clinicians to explicitly address and acknowledge the dynamics of power as an integral part of the therapeutic process. After all, it is of paramount significance for social workers to engage in mindful practice meaningfully with people of different and multiple identities, while also examining one's own social location in the "web of these power relations" (Wong, 2004).

I began to understand that my anxiety about how I was perceived and in what ways I could help our patients was a necessary part of the learning process that propelled me toward understanding myself as an aspiring professional as well as the needs of those I was serving. As stated by Shulman (2005), students must experience "adaptive anxiety" as a neces-

sary feature of their learning experience, as "uncertainty, visibility, and accountability inevitably raise the emotional stakes of the pedagogical encounters" (p. 57). Students must be emotionally invested in their work and experience some anxiety, as it serves as a motivating factor that stimulates students to work harder (Shulman, 2005).

I also found that if I ally myself with the patient, who in essence is the expert on his or her own life situation, and work toward finding a solution together by combing both our knowledge on the subject, we are able to make progress. As stated by Ann Hartman (2000), "knowledge and power are one, and when clients and subjects are collaborators in the discovery process, if their expertise is valued and affirmed, they are empowered" (p. 22).

## The Year Draws to a Close

Since beginning my work at the health center, I have learned how to find the balance between empowering the patients we work with and making them active participants in the problem solving process. Simultaneously, I also learned that meeting agency demands, as well as the expectations of professional and practice etiquette as a social worker, is a difficult and ongoing process. It has taken hours of supervision with my mentors, as well as a great deal of self reflection, to understand that it is an ongoing process and one that is inherent in the professional life of a social worker.

Although there are still times when I find myself rolling my eyes when I hear my professors saying to sit with our discomfort, I begrudgingly have to admit that the concept holds weight. This experience is challenging, overwhelming, exciting, and fulfilling, all at once.

What I can assure students entering this field is that you will be uncomfortable, and you will be forced to examine where you came from and what that signifies for the population with whom you are working. Not only will your supervisors, professors, and classmates be an integral source of support and understanding throughout this process, but I also believe the clients you work with will be, as well.

I have learned that when I ally myself with clients, it is as if the environment in the room has changed. I have found that if I crack a smile, allow a

chuckle, or feel comfortable in asking patients to elaborate on exactly what they mean, we are able to establish a working alliance that eventually will allow them to get what they need.

I am a student, and I continue to be inexperienced in comparison to the multitudes of amazing and inspiring social workers I have met so far in my budding career. However, I still have the capacity to help, and I believe that keeping that truth alive inside of me, despite all of the inner and external conflicts that one faces in this situation, is the key to a successful and ongoing learning process.

## References

Hartman, A. (2000). In search of subjugated knowledge, *Journal of Feminist Family Therapy, (11)* 4, 19-23.

Mo, Y. L. (2003). A solution-focused approach to cross-cultural clinical social work practice: Utilizing cultural strengths. *Families in Society, 84* (3), 385-395.

Shulman, L. S. (2005). Signature pedagogies in the professions. *Daedalus, 134* (3), 52–59.

Wong, Y. R. (2004). Knowing through discomfort: A mindfulness based critical social work pedagogy. *Critical Social Work, 5* (1).

*Katherine Freeman is a second-year graduate student at the Silberman School of Social Work at Hunter College, City University of New York. Katherine has a bachelor's degree in international relations and Spanish from the State University of New York, College at Geneseo and has experience working with at-risk youth in the United States and Chile. Katherine's current field placement is at an agency that provides trauma-focused therapy to children in the Bronx. She wrote this piece at the end of her first-year field placement.*

# GO FAR! A Useful Framework for Developing Career Success in Social Work
## by D.J. Williams, Ph.D., MSW

New social workers often feel overwhelmed trying to remember and apply what seems to be mountains of information to become effective and successful practitioners. There is always more knowledge to learn and master. And most of us commonly feel somewhat inadequate as we begin working with clients.

I remember more than a dozen years ago, when I first began my social work education, wondering if I could ever gain the knowledge and many skills needed to help clients with serious issues. After completing my MSW, I began my social work career in the correctional system. As in all areas of social work, many of my cases were difficult, and I found myself utilizing knowledge from all aspects of my liberal education. Fortunately, I had excellent training and supervision, and I gradually became more comfortable in the development of my unique professional self. Still, the learning curve from student to professional appears to be very steep.

Today, as the director of social work at Idaho State University, I see many of our students struggle with this same transition into the world of practice. At the same time, our social work standards and competency expectations have increased since my days as a social work student. In brainstorming how to distill so much valuable information into a user-friendly framework to facilitate the professional growth of our students, I came up with the GO FAR! framework.

I wanted to find an acronym that reflects both the science and art of social work, is easy to remember, and is a useful summary for students and new professionals but can also be applied by established social workers. GO FAR! is the result of this brainstorming, and our students, faculty, and community partners really like it. We now invite you to GO FAR! in the field of social work with us. GO FAR! stands for genuine, optimism, fun, accountability, and rigor.

## G is for Genuine

Effective social workers are genuine and authentic people. We are honest and "real" with ourselves, clients, colleagues, and people with whom we associate. When we are real with other people, then they also tend to be real with us. Many social workers are drawn to the profession because they genuinely want to help people. This, of course, is a strength that is often associated with compassion, and both are key ingredients for a positive therapeutic alliance.

Although most of us genuinely want to help, we sometimes tend to idolize teachers and professionals we perceive as being perfect at what they do. I remember being in awe of some of my teachers and clinical supervisors and wondering if I might ever be as adept as they were at navigating thorny clinical issues. Often, we copy the style of a mentor or two before later developing our own unique styles.

Encouraging genuineness, however, also means helping students recognize that each of us, including the very best teachers and clinicians, has strengths, limitations, problems, and personal issues, which is perfectly fine. Successful social workers accept themselves as they are, yet continually work on their own personal growth as human beings. Some of my mentors shared a few of their early mistakes and how they had learned and corrected these. Hearing these veteran social workers, who I greatly admired, share such stories was very helpful. As Harry Stack Sullivan used to say, "We are all more human than otherwise," so allow yourself to be human, too, and appreciate the journey.

## O Stands for Optimism

Years ago in my MSW program, one of my social work professors stated that an important thing we could always do to help clients is to give them hope. Although any situation possibly could get worse, most situations can improve by recognizing and utilizing strengths. Thus, strengths-based practice fits under the optimism dimension of GO FAR! Don't forget to identify and utilize your own personal and professional strengths to become a more effective social worker. For some of us, it is easier to notice the strengths of others than our own useful strengths.

Optimism is also critical to increasing motivation. So, consistent with a strengths-based approach and a wealth of scholarship on human motivation, try to give lots of positive feedback to people with whom you work, including your clients and your colleagues. In our program at Idaho State University, we strive for approximately a 4:1 ratio of positive statements for every negative. Although punitive approaches tend to increase motivation for a short time, positivity is far more conducive to building lasting, intrinsic motivation and thus desired improvement. Frequent positive feedback keeps clients engaged and motivated, and it makes for a fun learning and work environment.

## F Means To Have Fun!

Many of the people we work with struggle with serious issues, including debt, health issues, and legal problems. Clients sometimes can feel consumed by these problems and the constant grind of trying to get even their basic needs met. Social workers often manage high numbers of such cases, which amplifies our common need for adequate self-care. Choose modes of self-care that are personally fun and enjoyable. You will feel refreshed, and you'll be more effective at your job.

You will GO FAR if you instill lots of fun wherever you can in your world, including your professional practice. Fun and professionalism are not mutually exclusive! There are numerous health benefits associated with fun and regular laughter, but unfortunately, as we move from childhood to adulthood, we are often socialized away from having as much fun. I think this is a big mistake. Add lots of fun into your world at any age! You're likely to be happier and more satisfied, overall, with your life.

Years ago as a forensic social worker, I managed an aftercare clinic for parolees who were reintegrating back into the community. As part of their reintegration, they would attend group therapy once each week. Given their particular stage (community reintegration) in the correctional process, I believed it was important for them to report something they had done with family or friends during the previous week that was particularly fun or enjoyable. Group members seemed to really enjoy this.

At the beginning of one particular group experience after they had reported their fun experiences for the previous week, one of the members looked out the window and noticed that it was raining very hard outside. "We should all go outside and dance in the rain!" he suggested. After a short discussion and realizing that all members seemed excited about the possibility of playing in the downpour, I decided that this may be an unusual therapeutic and memorable moment for all of us. All these years later, I have forgotten nearly all of the other group sessions, but I will never forget that one! The entire group of men, myself included, went in the courtyard and danced, sang, and laughed in the pouring rain! We were all soaked through and through, but we came in with huge smiles on our faces. Everybody had a blast! That spontaneous experience modeled our ongoing emphasis on the need to laugh and have fun, and it certainly broke the monotony of a typical group experience. Several group members later mentioned that for them, that day when we all went and played in the rain had a more beneficial effect than any other single group experience of their aftercare programming.

Be ethical, of course, but look to have fun whenever you can! Have fun with your continuing education. Have fun with your clients and coworkers. Have fun with your self-care. Look to be creative! There may be an occasion or two when we cry with our clients, which is part of being genuine and compassionate, but every now and then we should laugh together, too.

## A is for Accountability

If you are going to be successful at virtually anything, including social work, you must be accountable and responsible. Know your role in the organization and your responsibilities. Take accountability for your own personal and professional growth. Keep up on knowledge in your area of practice. Don't be twenty (or more) years behind current knowledge in your field. Make sure that you know how to do your job, and look for ways to do it better and more efficiently.

Sometimes it is difficult for new social workers to let their clients be accountable. In other words, there is the temptation to overstep our boundaries and to do too much for clients. One of my wise forensics mentors once said, "You shouldn't be working harder at your clients' therapy than they are. Explore with them and give them opportunities, but they have to do their own work."

Sometimes when discussing with my students the importance of maintaining boundaries while working with clients, I joke that "I have enough difficulty just trying to manage my own complicated life!" Thus, I don't want to overstep boundaries and take on others' responsibilities.

## R is for Rigor

Rigor is the "meat and potatoes" of what we do. In GO FAR!, rigor refers specifically to the substance of professional practice—ethics, research, theory, and critical thinking. Each is important. Whatever you do as a practicing social worker, your work should be strongly shaped by social work ethics, research, theory, and critical thinking. Always be prepared

to explain and defend why you do what you do in your practice.

I remember my first time called into court to testify in a forensic social work case. One of my clients had been released from prison and was in a community transitional program, but he had not made therapeutic progress in several weeks since his release. My colleagues and I tried everything we could think of to help him engage in programming, yet he remained resistant. Our recommendation was that he be terminated from the program because of lack of progress. He was going to be sent back to prison, but had disputed this decision that eventually went before a judge.

I was very nervous when I was called to the stand. The judge asked what I had done to help this client and why I believed that he had not made progress. I calmly and briefly explained the planned change process in social work, along with empirically-tested behavioral change theories, including the transtheoretical model (behavioral change generally) and the risk-need-responsivity model (specific to offender rehabilitation). I explained what, theoretically, we would expect to see behaviorally from this client if he was, indeed, making progress. I also noted that while I have ethical obligations to this particular client, my job as a forensic social worker includes the ethical responsibility to help protect the public. My assessment and best clinical judgment of our entire treatment team was that this client was a very high risk to reoffend. He was likely to commit another crime. The judge nodded and agreed, and that was it. Our entire team had applied rigor to that case, and our thorough practice and evaluation was very evident in the courtroom.

## Conclusion

The GO FAR! framework provides a fun, focused, highly usable, mnemonic device for facilitating professional growth in social work. It may be especially helpful for new social workers who often feel overwhelmed with trying to remember and apply seemingly endless knowledge to social work practice, yet it can also be handy for students, established practitioners, administrators, and faculty members. The simple GO FAR! reminders to be genuine, liberally express optimism, have fun personally and professionally, be accountable, and practice with rigor function together to

help structure professional knowledge and gently move it into the realm of practice. Try it out and have fun with it, and see how far you can go in your social work career.

*Dr. D. J. Williams is the Director of Social Work at Idaho State University in Pocatello and the Director of Research for the Center for Positive Sexuality in Los Angeles. He holds an MS and an MSW degree from the University of Utah*

*and a Ph.D. from the University of Alberta. For several years, Dr. Williams worked as a licensed clinical social worker in corrections. His expertise focuses on issues involving forensic social work, sexual diversity, and social justice.*

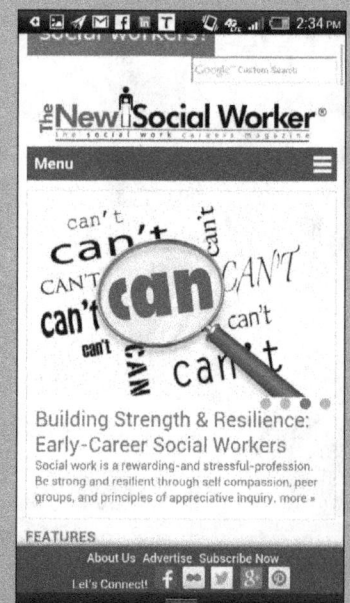

# Finding Families for Children—Not Children for Families: Social Workers and Adoption

*by Shelley Steenrod, Ph.D., LICSW*

Through the use of strengths and empowerment perspectives, social workers are in a unique position to support all members of the adoption triad (see Figure 1), including birth parents, child, and adoptive parents. Consider the following three scenarios.

*Stacy, a Caucasian 15-year-old high school student, is five months pregnant. She has decided to place her child for adoption. A social worker in a private adoption agency is working with Stacy to interview and select a family for her baby. Together, they will discuss and plan for the type of relationship Stacy wants with the family going forward. The social worker will support Stacy with her feelings following the adoption.*

*Jasmine and Jayden, a multi-racial couple both in their late 40s, have had numerous failed attempts at infertility treatment. They have decided to adopt a child from Africa and are working with a private adoption agency with programs in Ethiopia, the Democratic Republic of the Congo, and Uganda. After meeting with a social worker several times, they have decided that they would like to adopt an older child, many of whom are harder to place than babies. Jasmine and Jayden's social worker will not only help to match them with a child, but will assist with the emotional transitions of the parents and child following the adoption.*

*Rose (18 months), Alana (3), and Rowan (5) are a sibling set in need of a permanent home. They are currently in separate foster homes and in legal custody of the public child protection agency in their state. The social worker in charge of their case is searching diligently for a family that is able to adopt all three children together, knowing that it is in their best interest to be together. The children's social worker will either provide for or link to post-adoption services for the entire family.*

These case studies illustrate the three primary types of adoption—domestic infant adoption, international adoption, and adoption from foster care. Domestic infant adoption occurs when a pregnant woman seeks help from an adoption agency to select a "forever" family for her child and when a couple who wants to adopt seeks help in finding a baby. International or inter-country adoption is facilitated by agencies with programs in host countries. In international adoption, children have generally been relinquished by their families of origin as a result of death, disease, or extreme poverty. Foster to adopt programs can be delivered by public child protection agencies, which often have children in their care as a result of neglect or abuse.

Whether public or private, domestic or international, adoption agencies hire social workers to conduct home studies, provide pre-adoption education, match children with families, and offer post-adoption support. A brief description of each service is described below.

*Home study:* This is the process by which a social worker decides the suitability of an individual or couple to adopt. A home study is a comprehensive evaluation of each potential adoptive parent's emotional and physical health, experience or ability to parent, finances, home environment, and general ability to provide a safe, consistent, and nurturing family for a child. A home study generally involves meeting with and interviewing the individual or couple over several sessions.

The social worker asks specific questions and invites discussion pertinent to parenting and adoption. Some of these questions include: *Why adopt? What is your parenting philosophy? How do you resolve conflicts? What are your expectations about the process? What is your worst fear about adoption? How do you intend to balance work and family? What specific medical, emotional, behavioral, and cognitive issues are you prepared to handle? What are you prepared to do to help your child in the attachment process?*

In addition, the social worker visits the family home to ensure that there is appropriate, safe, and adequate space. Ultimately, the social worker writes a formal home study document that is submitted to domestic and international courts and governments as appropriate.

*Pre-Adoption education:* Pre-adoptive parents often have romantic notions of what parenting is like. First time parents may expect an adorable, sleepy baby who likes to cuddle. Instead, they may be faced with an inconsolable, teething child who won't sleep unless he or she is held. Parents adopting from other countries may expect a child who is grateful to have a full plate of food, and instead be met by a child who wants to return to his or her native country despite extreme poverty and despair.

Social workers provide pre-adoptive education to prepare families for both the realities of first-time parenting and the challenges of parenting children

## Figure 1
## The Adoption Triad

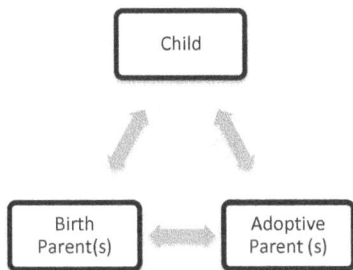

```
                  ┌─────────┐
                  │  Child  │
                  └─────────┘
                   ↗       ↖
        ┌──────────┐     ┌──────────┐
        │  Birth   │ ←→  │ Adoptive │
        │Parent(s) │     │Parent(s) │
        └──────────┘     └──────────┘
```

from hard beginnings. Some examples of workshops and trainings that social workers facilitate in this domain include topics such as: grief and loss, attachment, the effects of institutionalization, cross cultural issues, transracial parenting, and open adoption. Most, if not all, agencies require prospective adoptive parents to participate in a set amount of pre-adoptive education and show proof of completion.

*Matching Children with Families:* Social workers are tasked with finding the best family for children, not the best child for families. As such, they rarely make child placement decisions in a vacuum. Most agencies have committees that meet regularly to consider the mutual needs of children and families and to make matching decisions together. In these profound decisions, social workers can utilize their hard-earned knowledge from BSW or MSW courses on child development, human behavior, child and family welfare, research, cultural diversity, and values and ethics.

*Post-Adoption Support:* After adoption, social workers are an important part of a child's and parents' "village." Individuals and couples who adopt are not only faced with the same challenges of first time parents; they may also be faced with special issues—especially when adopting internationally or from foster care. Children from hard beginnings may bring with them a host of medical, neurological, emotional, and behavioral problems and require extra support and specialized parenting and educational strategies. An extreme example of the need for professional post-adoption support is the case of adoptive mother Torry Hansen, who in 2010 bought a one-way ticket to Moscow to return her 7-year-old son, whom she had adopted from Russia.

Some social workers have private practices that provide specialized counseling services to each member of the adoption triad. For example, adoptive children may bring issues of loss, guilt, shame, anger, and cultural dissonance to therapy. Birth parents may bring issues of loss, guilt, and shame, from their own unique perspective. Adoptive parents may have residual issues around infertility or question their true legitimacy as parents. All members of the triad may experience anxiety about searches or reunions between birth children and parents. Social workers in private practice apply various theoretical perspectives, especially family systems theory, ecological theory, and person-in-environment theory.

Are you interested in adoption? BSW and MSW students can test their interest by requesting field placements at public or private adoption agencies. New graduates should consider employment in adoption agencies. Finding families for children is truly life-changing work, and clients like Stacy, Jasmine, Jayden, Rose, Alana, and Rowan will all benefit from the knowledge, skills, and values that you bring to work each day.

*Dr. Shelley Steenrod is an associate professor of social work at Salem State University in Salem, Massachusetts. She received her Master of Social Work from Boston University and her Ph.D. from the Heller School at Brandeis University. Dr. Steenrod, a mother of four, has become interested in the role of social workers in the field of adoption since adopting siblings from Ethiopia in 2010.*

---

# Congressional Research Institute for Social Work and Social Policy (CRISP)

As deputy chief of staff for the office of Congressman Edolphus Towns, Dr. Charles E. Lewis, Jr. recognized the importance of creating an organization that would complement the mission of the Congressional Social Work Caucus (CSWC). Through hard work and perseverance, the Congressional Research Institute for Social Work and Policy (CRISP) was founded on October 22, 2012, by Congressman Towns, Dr. Lewis, Jr. and Dr. Angela S. Henderson. CRISP functions as a non-partisan organization committed to expanding the participation of social workers in federal legislative and policy processes.

According to CRISP's Executive Director, Dr. Henderson, "the organization acts as a bridge between social work researchers and the federal government to ensure their research is known to federal policy makers. CRISP is additionally committed to expanding opportunities for students to find field placements in federal government offices, both on Capitol Hill and in offices near their schools."

SOCIAL JUSTICE SOLUTIONS

CRISP will provide social workers with an opportunity to have critical roles in planning, developing, and implementing legislation and policies that affect the individuals, children and families, and communities that we serve on an everyday basis. For the upcoming year, CRISP will focus on producing and disseminating policy reports, holding congressional briefings and student networking events, and increasing the involvement of social workers in public policy media discussions (i.e. radio, Internet, and television). "It is in the nation's best interest to include social workers in public policy. After all, social workers employ problem-solving strategies daily to meet the needs of various populations," states Dr. Henderson.

For more information about CRISP, or to find out how to get involved, see: *http://www.crispinc.org*

*This article is is provided by CRISP as part of a collaboration between The New Social Worker and Social Justice Solutions. You can find Social Justice Solutions online at http://www.socialjusticesolutions.org.*

# What Every Social Worker Needs To Know About...
## The Universal Accreditation Act of 2012
### *by Grace R. Kennedy*

The Hague Adoption Convention on the Protection of Children and Co-operation in Respect of Inter-Country Adoption (Hague Adoption Convention) is an international agreement to safeguard intercountry adoptions. Concluded on May 29, 1993, in The Hague, Netherlands, the Convention establishes international standards of practices for intercountry adoptions.

With the passage and enactment of the Hague Adoption Convention, adoptions from countries that are signatory to the Hague Convention have become highly regulated. Pursuant to the Hague Adoption Convention, adoption service providers are required to become accredited to provide adoption services to adoptive parents. This means that the adoption professionals they employ receive training and that their adoption practices and procedures are subject to review by a government-appointed body.

The Hague Adoption Convention has been enacted by almost 90 countries around the world. Signatories include just about every "first world country" there is, most of Latin America, and a chunk of Asia. But the countries with bigger problems than child trafficking shied away from signing on to a convention that they were either too poor or too distracted to enforce.

The United States can't do much about what another country does with its most vulnerable citizens, but we recognized that we could do a better job safeguarding our part in the international adoption process. In an attempt to bolster our efforts to protect intercountry adoptees, the United States recently passed The Universal Accreditation Act of 2012 (UAA).

The UAA extends the safeguards provided by Hague accreditation to orphans born in countries that are not signatories to the Hague Adoption Convention, their adoptive parents, and birth parents. This is accomplished by ensuring that adoption service providers are all held to the same federal standards. Safeguards under the UAA are universal, because the UAA applies Hague Adoption Convention-compatible standards to both Hague Adoption Convention and orphan cases.

Before the Intercountry Adoption Act of 2000 (IAA), adoption service providers in intercountry adoption were exclusively regulated by state law. State licensing authorities in the 50 states have different standards; some had few specific standards governing intercountry adoptions, especially relating to agencies' conduct abroad. Many state licensing authorities were unable to hold service providers accountable for illicit practices in intercountry adoption cases. State laws often did not apply to the activities of licensed agencies outside the United States, and states often lacked the resources to investigate and take action against agencies involved in such cases.

The UAA provides for uniform standards and accountability for service provider conduct, regardless of whether the case falls under the Hague Adoption Convention or the orphan process. The IAA and the regulations implementing the Hague Adoption Convention protect against illicit activities and practices of the past that threatened the best interests of children.

Accreditation of adoption service providers ensures ongoing monitoring and oversight of adoption service providers to verify their compliance with federal accreditation standards. This holds accredited providers accountable for failure to be in substantial compliance with the standards.

Key protections include:

- Children may not be obtained for adoption through sale, exploitation, abduction, and/or trafficking.
- Parents receive training in advance of the adoption to understand what to expect when raising an adopted child and prepare them for some of the challenges.
- The agency or person must ensure that intercountry adoptions take place in the best interests of children.
- Fees must be transparent for services performed both in the United States and abroad and may not result in improper gain for the service provider.
- U.S. Department of State-appointed accrediting entities monitor and assess accredited agency compliance with federal standards.
- Accrediting entities ensure accountability when accredited agencies do not comply with the standards by taking appropriate adverse actions against them and may suspend or cancel their accreditation.
- Accrediting entities ensure that accredited agency personnel are qualified and appropriately trained and provide adoption services in an ethical manner.
- Accredited agencies must respond to complaints about their services and activities and may not retaliate against clients who complain.

Here is the text of the Act with all of the "legalese" deleted to make for easier reading:

*The Intercountry Adoption Act of 2000 shall apply to any person offering or providing adoption services. Accrediting entities shall have duties, responsibilities, and authorities with respect to a person offering or providing such adoption services, irrespective of whether such services are offered or provided in connection with a Convention adoption. The provisions of this section shall take effect 18 months after the date of the enactment of this Act.*

What does this mean? In a nutshell, anybody providing any adoption services relating to an intercountry adoption from a non-convention country on or after July 14, 2014, will have to be accredited.

The six adoption services are:

- Identifying a child for adoption and arranging an adoption;
- Securing the necessary consent to termination of parental rights and to adoption;
- Performing a background study on a child or a home study on a prospective adoptive parent(s), and reporting on such a study;
- Making non-judicial determinations of the best interests of a child and the appropriateness of an adoptive placement for the child;
- Monitoring a case after a child has been placed with prospective adoptive parent(s) until final adoption;
- When necessary because of a disruption before final adoption, assuming custody and providing (including facilitating the provision of) child care or any other social service pending an alternative placement.

But what about cases that have been partially completed before the 2014 deadline? Here's what you need to know:

- If the United States Citizenship and Immigration Service (USCIS) made a decision on either Form I-600A or Form I-600 before July 14, 2014, then no accreditation is required for adoption services that are provided before July 14, 2014.
- Accreditation is also not required when the prospective adoptive parents have filed either Form I-600A or Form I-600 before July 13, 2013, even though USCIS does not make a decision until after July 14, 2014.
- If the adoptive parent has made an "appropriate application" to a foreign adoption authority before July 13, 2013, then accreditation is not required.
- If form I-600A or Form I-600 was filed after July 13, 2013, then accreditation is not required for adoption services rendered before July 14, 2014, but will be required for adoption services rendered after July 14, 2014.
- If the prospective adoptive parent files Form I-600A or Form I-600 on or after July 14, 2014, then accreditation is required for all adoption services rendered in connection with this adoption.

What about private or independent adoptions? The State Department gives the following guidance in response to the question, "Can I complete an intercountry adoption doing an independent adoption in which I do the adoption work myself without the help of an accredited or approved provider?"

Answer: "No. An accredited primary provider is required in every intercountry adoption case, unless a public domestic authority is providing all of the adoption services." However, it goes on to state in a somewhat labyrinthine manner that if the adoptive parent is acting alone, then the adoptive parent is exempt from obtaining accreditation. So essentially, according to the State Department website, you cannot complete an independent adoption on your own because an accredited provider is needed in all intercountry adoptions, unless you are completing the adoption independently, in which case, it's fine. You do not need accreditation. Huh?!

I think that what they meant to say is that any adoption services must be provided by an accredited provider (after the July 2014 cutoff date) and that pre-placement training and post placement supervision may be required for visa issuance.

I called the State Department directly to get more clarification on this issue and was told that any adoption services rendered in connection with an independent adoption would need to be provided by an accredited provider. So, the home study will need to be done by an accredited provider or someone working under the supervision of an accredited provider. But will a child be eligible to have a visa issued if that child was not placed by an adoption service provider? It looks as if the child will still be eligible for a visa, but be prepared for the home study provider to have extra added responsibility to ensure that the placement is properly documented, that the local law has been complied with, and that post placement work is completed. As an aside, I also asked the State Department how a social worker in the U.S. could ensure that local laws had been complied with in a Pakistani slum or a remote Afghan province and was told, "We don't know that yet."

Do I think that the UAA signifies the end of private adoptions? No, I don't. The Immigration and Nationality Act and corresponding regulations specifically envisage and provide for situations in which children are orphaned but no agency or entity ever has custody of them. Children who are deserted (the biological parents refuse to parent them) or whose parents have disappeared are considered orphans; so too are the children of sole and surviving parents.

Congress intended that United States citizens should be able to adopt orphans from overseas and emigrate them as immediate relatives. If USCIS suddenly requires that an accredited child placing entity be involved in every independent or private adoption, then we are excluding from our definition of visa-eligible orphans an entire class of children that Congress explicitly and purposely intended to include in this class of children. Furthermore, existing regulations specifically prohibit children being placed in the custody of a child placing entity in anticipation of a particular adoption. It would seem counterintuitive to now require an accredited adoption service provider to make a placement in all orphan adoption cases.

The UAA will provide a sorely needed set of checks and balances in intercountry adoption cases from non-Hague countries. Adoption professionals across the board will welcome the additional safeguards it provides to both the adoptees and prospective adoptive parents. Not only will adoptive parents be required to receive appropriate training to ensure that they will be prepared for their adoption journey, but they will also be protected from unscrupulous providers here and overseas. Adoption services will be provided in a clear and transparent manner and will be monitored by a central government authority. Perhaps most importantly, the UAA will protect against illicit activities and practices that threatened the best interests of children. All of this moves us closer to our goal of providing appropriate families for children from around the world.

*Grace R. Kennedy holds a Bachelor of Laws degree from the National University of Ireland, Dublin and a Master of Laws degree from Emory University School of Law. She has extensive experience in immigration-related adoption issues. Ms. Kennedy is one of a few attorneys in the United States who routinely handles complex adoption issues involving orphans from predominantly Muslim countries, including Pakistan and Afghanistan. She has researched issues present in intercountry adoption cases and is extremely knowledgeable on all facets of the intercountry adoption process.*

# Groups

## Rescuing the Creative Self: An Art Expression Group
### by Lou Storey, LCSW, LCADC

I can't even draw a straight line!"
"I have zero talent!"
"I'm no artist!"
"I'm so bad at art it's embarrassing!"

As a clinical social worker and artist, I have run art expression groups in an assortment of mental health care settings. Variations of these statements can be expected when people find themselves confronted by the task of making art.

The group is advertised as an opportunity for self-discovery through visual art, regardless of experience or proficiency in the arts. Despite this disclaimer, most of my group members begin the group with a degree of discomfort, reluctance, and sometimes even dread of making art. They express feeling unworthy of the activity, citing the fact that they are not artists. This attitude begs the question: is the experience of making art a privilege reserved only to the artist? And then, likewise, is making music meant exclusively for musicians, dancing for dancers only, poetry and prose for the writer alone?

Not all that long ago in our culture, creative pursuits were more commonplace. People kept personal journals, painted watercolor studies of their gardens, sketched while on vacation, and repurposed objects like spools and used bottles into toys or functional items. Social gatherings could include playing musical instruments or singing around a piano with friends and family. These self-generated arts, often born of necessity and limited access to more formal or professional products, was part of our cultural fabric.

Today, what was formerly self-generated is now experienced as highly accessible commodities—consumer goods, packaged and highly processed for our passive consumption, but not our active participation. As we begin to compare our efforts to these polished products, we may feel that we come up short. But is this evaluation fair, or is it one-dimensional, focusing on the final product alone while ignoring the value of all that the journey of creativity can offer?

## Creating a Net of Safety

Social workers are responsible for "being where the client is"—an adage that reminds us to take into account what the client is thinking and feeling, and to make that the foundation from which clinical activity begins. But if clients are in a place where they may believe they have no mastery and are feeling vulnerable to failure or even ridicule, we need to implement some action toward movement in more positive and secure directions. A therapist friend of mine who runs groups once said that she works to "cast a net of safety" over her clients, creating an atmosphere conducive to free expression and creativity.

After many years of responding individually to the insecurities involved in art making, I began to see a repeating pattern to these behaviors and some consistent themes emerging, as well, in my response. Examining this pattern revealed a set of underlying principles from which I drew up a simple list of statements that addressed those areas of uncertainty and self-doubt. I call that list the "Creativity Pledge."

At the introductory group session, I will ask the new members, "What are your feelings about making art?" This immediately elicits an enthusiastic response of negative self-deprecating statements. These declarations are so predictable that I have with me a pre-prepared set of file cards, and as each statement is made, I hold up the corresponding card, the text of which is a perfect match to what was just said. The group responds with delight, as if I am a magician doing a fancy card trick. There is no magic to my act, but rather, recognition of the degree to which the general population has been disenfranchised from their own artistic creativity. I then distribute a one-page handout of the Creativity Pledge.

## Creativity Pledge

*I acknowledge and affirm my right to creative pursuits, such as singing, dancing, making music, art, poetry and performance, and will value my curiosity as a motivator, rather than stymie myself through a judgmental notion of "talent."*

*I understand that each of us is unique in what we create, and I will respect that uniqueness, especially my own, by not comparing my artwork in a negative way to anyone else's artwork.*

*I will recognize my creative pursuits as a journey and will pay attention to and value my thoughts, feelings, ideas, choices, changes in direction and discoveries that occur throughout my creative process, knowing that the end result is just the tip of the iceberg.*

As we begin to read the Creativity Pledge, I raise my hand, as is done when making a pledge, and ask the members to do so as well. This elicits some chuckles. Anything that lightens the mood is welcome in the group. The pledge offers each group member license to abandon the self-defeating, apologetic, and judgmental dialogue-tapes and instead focus on simply enjoying the opportunity to exercise some creative energy, play with color and materials, and explore possibilities.

## Themes Blending Art and Life

The goal of the art expression group is not to make art, but rather to explore the many facets of how we experience life. Art making, art history, group discussions, and contribution are the tools that we use for this exploration. Each week introduces a new theme referencing a recognizable element of art and linking it to aspects of life. The first group begins with the creation of a personal mandala. The Sanskrit word "mandala" translates to "circle" and represents wholeness and connectedness in life, ranging from the micro-sized spinning of atoms and cells to the macro-sized ringing rotations of planets and galaxies. As a group, we examine how our lives navigate within circles of friends, family, and community. A personal mandala can reflect upon and give insight into the many meaningful ways we are connected to our world and offers a compelling first art expression group experience.

Other weekly thematic units of the art expression group, linking art to experience, include:

*Personal World–Personal Boundaries* explores landscape painting, examining how artists through the centuries have been creating landscapes that speak to their own personal vision of "a place." Examples from art history include the swirling and ephemeral seascapes of J. M. W. Turner, or the fanciful and spirited worlds created by the German artist Paul Klee. Group members are invited to imagine their own personal place, and to consider how we each are the creators of our own world.

*Support Systems–The Elements of Art* recognizes the ways in which our lives are in need of support from a variety of sources, both internally and externally, just as art is supported by visual and tactile elements such as line, tone, color, space, shape, pattern, and texture. To begin a drawing, we make choices of material, style, and approach. In life, we may do the same, recognizing, sustaining, and utilizing our support system for positive outcomes.

*Chronicle Art–Witnessing History* invites the group to observe the recounting of history through art. Some examples include Norman Rockwell's *The Problem We All Live With,* illustrating a moment from the 1960s American school integration, or Pablo Picasso's *Guernica,* depicting the loss and horror of the bombing of Guernica in Northern Spain. Members are invited to consider their own histories, their journey through public events as well as personal milestones and life passages, and to choose those they wish to capture elements of on the page.

*Portraits–The Roles We Play* investigates the art of portraiture through examination of the many roles we play in life. What can we learn from the ancient portrait of a young man painted on a Roman urn, from da Vinci's enigmatic *Mona Lisa,* or from Vincent Van Gogh's penetrating self-portrait? In portraiture, the artist makes the decision of what roles and characteristics will be expressed. Group members create lists of the various roles they play in life (parent, child, friend, taxpayer, gardener, chocolate lover), and working from that list find ways to illustrate their feelings and thoughts surrounding those roles.

*Word Art* is prevalent in our culture, from printed advertisements to product packaging. A classic example of Word Art is the iconic "LOVE" painting created by contemporary artist Robert Indiana where the letters L-O-V-E are used as a device to create a compelling and dynamic design. Constructing a compilation of words that have personal meaning and significance, group members play with conveying value through selections in color, shape, and form, as well as expressing meaning inherent to the word itself.

*Logic and Emotion–Geometric Design and Balance* gives attention to both feeling and logical thought to maintain effective functioning in the world. Dialectical Behavioral Therapy (DBT) posits that we have an emotional mind and a logical mind. What would each of those minds look like if illustrated? When emotion and reason work successfully together, a third entity, the wise mind, is created. Keeping this concept as a paradigm, group members recall and then illustrate, through geometric structured patterns and contrasting asymmetrical free flowing markings, personal moments when emotion and logic were at odds but found eventual balance.

Other weekly thematic units connecting life experience to art using a variety of perspectives include: discovering the personal voice in poetry, appreciation of humor and whimsy, reviewing the seasons in relation to lifespan, framing and reframing life stories, and others.

Members may create as many pieces as they desire, and if they find themselves inspired to move in directions that differ from the initial theme, all creative efforts are appreciated. Members are also encouraged to suggest themes and new avenues of art expression to investigate. The weekly artistic accomplishments are stored in individual portfolios made from oversized poster boards that are simply folded horizontally in half.

## Art Expression Group Portfolio Review

The last session of the art expression group involves reflection and assessment of time together as a group by reviewing the contents of the art expression group portfolios. The group begins with each member spending some time looking through his or her artworks and reflecting on which pieces hold strong personal meaning, with the goal of choosing a selection to share with the group. Members present their art and share their thoughts and feelings. The other members are asked to be conscious of their own feelings in regard to what is being said.

As each member finishes his or her narration, other members write out their reactions to what was presented and the notes are collected in an envelope. Each art expression group member will leave the group with not only his or her artworks, but with an envelope of heartfelt responses from fellow members that speak to his or her importance as part of the group.

As the group facilitator, my hope is that the group members will continue their journey of exploring the world through art expression, build confidence in their relationship to art, and continue to feel free to play and create through any and all forms of art.

The groups are not without their challenging moments. Once, in the first session of an art expression group, during the part of the creativity pledge that affirms the "right to creative pursuits such as singing, dancing, making music, art, poetry and performance," I was confronted by a group member who exclaimed, "You're an artist. This is easy for you to say. What if I told you it's okay to sing out loud, would you be able to do that right now?" The challenge was intuitively a good one, as I immediately experienced fear of failure and embarrassment that no doubt paralleled their own apprehension of art-making.

"Well," I said, taking a deep breath as the group leaned forward, eager to see how this situation might play out, "I would consider doing so, with the support of the group." I was remembering back to the last time I'd really enjoyed singing, a journey that took me far back into childhood. With some trepidation, but willing to give it a try, I began, "Row, row, row your boat, gently down the stream." At this point, I gestured to the table, inviting others to join in–and they did. Soon, we had several spirited rounds going. The net was cast. Creativity was now safe to join us.

*Lou Storey, LCSW, LCADC, is in private practice at Meaningful Therapy Center, LLC, in Red Bank, New Jersey. He is an adjunct professor in the graduate social work school at Monmouth University. He is also an exhibiting artist.*

# Social Work Goes to the Movies

## The Oscars and Thanking Those Who Helped Along the Way

### by Addison Cooper, LCSW

*Matthew McConaughey, Cate Blanchett, Lupita Nyong'o, and Jared Leto at the 86th Academy Awards in Los Angeles.*

The 2014 Academy Awards were celebrated recently. It was the 86th ceremony, but only the second one I've watched. (I started writing Adoption at the Movies in 2012, and it seemed like I should probably find out who won the Oscars.) This year, I was particularly excited to watch, because I've reviewed several of the nominated films, including two Best Picture nominees (the grippingly emotional stranded-in-space survival story *Gravity* and the thought-provoking story of the pain caused by closed adoptions, *Philomena.*) I also was happy to see three of the films I reviewed up for Best Animated Feature—*Frozen, The Croods,* and *Despicable Me 2.* They are all fun, and they present good opportunities for family discussions.

Surprisingly, the highlight of the night for me wasn't finding out who won what; it was Lupita Nyong'o's enthusiastically grateful acceptance speech for Best Supporting Actress. If you missed her speech, you can find it pretty easily with a Google search. In the film adaptation of Solomon Northup's 1841 memoir, *Twelve Years a Slave,* Nyong'o played Patsey, a female slave who was abused by her master. Nyong'o thanked the spirits of Patsey and Solomon, acknowledging that her role in the film was a reflection of "so much pain in someone else's" life.

She thanked her director, the other actors, her family, her drama school, her friends, her brother, and her "chosen family," and encouraged every child that, "no matter where you're from, your dreams are valid." It was powerful and uplifting, and perhaps the most joy-filled three minutes I've heard on television.

N'Yongo's speech reminds me of the value of gratitude. She acknowledged who made her successes possible, and in genuinely thanking them, her joy increased.

As I think of her speech, I remember one other. In 1997, Fred Rogers won a Daytime Emmy Lifetime Achievement Award for his decades of work on *Mr. Rogers' Neighborhood.* After being introduced as "the best neighbor any of us has ever had," Rogers quietly took the stage to a standing ovation. He chatted briefly with the presenter. After the presenter profusely honored Rogers for telling children "over and over again that they have worth," Rogers accepted the award. Then he said, "So many people have helped me to come to this night. Some of you are here. Some of you are far away. Some are even in Heaven. All of us have special ones who have loved us into being." He then asked the celebrities in attendance, "Would you just take, along with me, ten seconds to think of the people who have helped you become who you are. Those who have cared about you, and wanted what was best for you in life." Then he said, "I'll watch the time." And then he did. After the time elapsed, Rogers commented, "Whomever you've been thinking about, how pleased they must be to know the difference you feel they've made." Then he proceeded to thank those who have helped him.

It's not only celebrities that have people who have cared about them and influenced their lives. It's also our clients. The phrase that sticks with me is: "Those who have cared about you, and wanted what was best for you in life." As social workers, perhaps we are some of the people that our clients will think of when they reflect on people who have cared for them and wanted the best for them. I hope that's the impression our clients take from our work with them. Whether that is the case is probably influenced both by the work we do, and the spirit we do it in.

It's not just our clients, though. We, too, have been helped and brought to where we are by others who have cared about us and wanted the best for us. It might have been friends, colleagues, supervisors, parents, professors, or mentors, but none of us make it into social work without support. Someone helped guide you to higher education. Somebody influenced your life—knowingly or not—to make you consider social work as a field of study or a field of work. And now, here you are.

Would you just take, along with me, ten seconds to think of the people who have helped you become who you are? Those who have cared about you, and wanted what was best for you in life? I'll watch the time.

*Addison Cooper is a Licensed Clinical Social Worker in California and Missouri. He reviews films and writes movie discussion guides for foster and adoptive families at Adoption at the Movies (www. adoptionlcsw.com), and is a supervisor at a foster care and adoption agency in Southern California. Find him on Twitter @AddisonCooper.*

# The New Social Worker Student Role Models Through the Years

*Throughout the years, The New Social Worker has recognized the accomplishments of social work students by featuring a student each quarter in our Student Role Model column, written by Barbara Trainin Blank since 1996. Many of them have gone on to get more advanced degrees and become leaders in the profession. Here is a listing of all our student role models.*

Spring 1994, Nicole Jesser, MSW student, University of Tennessee-Nashville

Fall 1994, Cory Frese, graduate student, University of Nebraska (BSW from Briar Cliff)

Spring 1995, Toni Pipkin, BSW student, Pembroke State University

Fall 1995, Bill Gray, MSW student, University of Maryland at Baltimore

Spring 1996, Andrea Bazan Manson, MSW/MPH graduate, University of North Carolina-Chapel Hill

Fall 1996, Myrlene Augustin, MSW student, Barry University

Winter 1997, Laura Wernick, MSW student, Columbia University

Spring 1997, Altaf Ali, graduate student, Florida International University

Summer 1997, Leslie Schwartz, MSW student, Bradley University

Fall 1997, Marijo Upshaw, BSW student, Central Missouri State University

Winter 1998, Becky Terhark, MSW graduate, University of Iowa at Des Moines

Spring 1998, John Potash, graduate of the Columbia University School of Social Work

Summer 1998, Jennifer Geller, MSW student, University of Connecticut

Fall 1998, Misty Sanders, BSW student, Frostburg State University

Winter 1999, Winnifred Whitaker, MSW graduate, University of Central Florida

Spring 1999, Laura Langner, MSW applicant, BSW graduate from University of North Carolina-Pembroke

Summer 1999, Carlita Owens, BSW student, Shippensburg University

Fall 1999, Jennifer Gracin, MSW student, University of Southern Mississippi

Winter 2000, Rich Bott, BSW student, University of New Mexico in Las Cruces

Spring 2000, Kristi Disney, BSW student, University of Tennessee-Knoxville

Summer 2000, Deborah Goldfarb, MSW student, University of Michigan

Fall 2000, Jenny Freer, MSW student, University of Arkansas at Little Rock

Winter 2001 Monisha Butler, BSW graduate, Southern University

Spring 2001, Melissa Bailey, BSW student, Michigan State University

Summer 2001, Patrick Hanlin, BSW graduate, Central Michigan University

Fall 2001, Kang Pha, BSW student, California State University Chico

Winter 2002, Aimee Perron, MSW student, Virginia Commonwealth University

Spring 2002, Todd Drazien, MSW student, Temple University-Harrisburg

Summer 2002, Kristen Hoye, MSW student, Hunter College School of Social Work of the City University Of New York

Fall 2002, Norma Viola Cantu, MSW student, Eastern Michigan University

Winter 2003, Delene Porter, MSW student, University of Georgia

Spring 2003, Paz Caisip, BSW student, Austin Peay State University

Summer 2003, Mary Mattson, BSW graduate, University of Wisconsin-Superior

Fall 2003, Anne Hills, MSW student, Marywood College

Winter 2004, Nathan Wood, MSW student, Radford University

Spring 2004, Azure Robnett, MSW student, University of Missouri-Columbia

Summer 2004, Oscar Rivera, MSW student, University of Central Florida

Fall 2004, Leina Yamamoto, MSW student, San Francisco State University

Winter 2005, Sheree Stutzman, BSW student, Stephen F. Austin State University

Spring 2005, Missy Jenkins, BSW graduate, Murray State University, and MSW student

Summer 2005, Teresita Hurtado, MSW graduate, University of Pennsylvania

Fall 2005, Chika Okonkwo, BSW student, University of North Carolina-Pembroke

Winter 2006, Zip Zimmerman, BSW student, Central Michigan University

Spring 2006, Alisha Ellis, MSW student, Smith College

Summer 2006, Libby Berry, MSW student, Monmouth University

Fall 2006, Darnell Morris-Compton, MSW student, University of Maryland at Baltimore

Winter 2007, Amal Elanouari, MSW student, University of California-Berkeley

Spring 2007, Greta Martin, MSW student, West Virginia University

Summer 2007, Susannah Bourbeau, BSW student, Marymount

Fall 2007, Kevin Douglas, BSW student, Eastern Connecticut State University

Winter 2008, Christina Michels, BSW student, Central Michigan University

Spring 2008, Joseph Marrazzo, MSW student, University of Wyoming

Summer 2008, Patricia Ann White, recent BSW graduate, Coker College

Fall 2008, Katie Schmidt, BSW student, Missouri State University

Winter 2009, Jason Luey, recent MSW, University of British Columbia

Spring 2009, Ashley Bunnell, BSW student, University of North Carolina Pembroke

Summer 2009, Kelly Lee, BSW student, Tarleton State University-Central Texas

Fall 2009, Joan Edwards, recent MSW graduate, Touro College

Winter 2010, Justine Naylon, MSW student, University of South Florida

Spring 2010, Mark Williams, recent MSW, Ohio State University

Summer 2010, Nanci Woodson, MSW student, Delaware State University

Fall 2010, Jael Cornelio and Laura Tellez, MSW students, Stephen F. Austin State University

Winter 2011, Carrie Amber Rheingans, MSW student, University of Michigan

Spring 2011, Shammrie Brown, BSW student, Aurora University

Summer 2011, Cristen Cravath, MSW and MPH student, University of Maryland

Fall 2011, Keyon Mitchell, MSW student, University of Southern California

Winter 2012, Carmelina Gilberto, BSW student, Catholic University of America

Spring 2012, Stephanie Maldonado, BSW student, University of IL at Urbana-Champaign

Summer 2012, Tayloe Compton, recent BSW, University of North Carolina Pembroke

Fall 2012, Christine Webb, BSW student, University of Indiana at Bloomington

Winter 2013, Sean Hudson, recent BSW, University of Alabama

Spring 2013, Brooke Schipporeit, BSW student, Nebraska Wesleyan University

Summer 2013, Cheryl Hershey, BSW student, Shippensburg University

Fall 2013, Ashley Stroud, MSW student, University of Georgia

Winter 2014, Erick Fugett, recent BSW, Morehead State University

Spring 2014, Susan Vanino, MSW student, New York University

# Understanding the Involuntary Commitment Process: Helping Patients Maintain Their Right to Self-Determination

*by Lauren Dennelly, MSW, LCSW*

Through my work as a social worker on a voluntary inpatient psychiatric unit, I have seen how complicated the mental health system can become when a state entity must get involved with psychiatric care. Despite the paperwork that patients sign stating that they are "voluntary" for treatment, when they begin treatment on the unit, their attitudes often change quickly and dramatically from when they were seen in screening. Suddenly, I have tearful patients in my office, stating, "I don't belong here. I want to sign out."

Now, in situations like this, our basic social work instincts kick in and

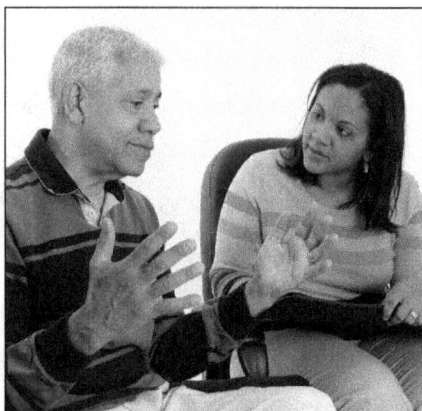

we "start where the client is," right? I console patients, let them know we are all here as a team to help them, and encourage them to take medications and go to group therapy.

This usually works well, and patients are able to calm down and discuss feelings of fear and shame about being hospitalized and in need of psychiatric care. We can begin work on how to focus on what one can and can't control, and with the assistance of intensive 24-hour support from the inpatient team, patients are able to see that they are experiencing a temporary scenario.

However, there are some instances in which patients are simply not convinced (despite having signed paperwork to indicate otherwise) that any of the treatment on the unit will be helpful. They vehemently deny that they tried to commit suicide and/or will try to commit suicide (again, despite screening reports that indicate otherwise), and

launch into the "this was all just a big mistake" speech.

Again, we start where the client is. Working on a voluntary psychiatric unit does not mean that, as the practitioner, I am free from seeing patient denial. In an acute inpatient facility, however, there is not much time to work through the denial process with the patient as I might in an outpatient setting. I have a week, tops, and that's if the insurance company will give me that much. If the patient continues to insist on signing out, I then respond with, "There's a document called a 48-hour notice...."

This is when the process becomes complicated. In researching the New Jersey laws on my own, I came across a document entitled *The Involuntary Civil Commitments Resource Binder,* published by the New Jersey Court system to help make sense of the basics of the process. Involuntary commitment procedures vary by state. In New Jersey, the patient can sign a document called a "48-hour notice," in which patients have 48 hours to be rescreened by the original screening entity that found them to be appropriate candidates for the inpatient setting.

Many patients incorrectly interpret this as having to spend only 48 hours on our unit and state that they have been told by the screening entity that after 48 hours, they are free to go. Whether or not patients are actually told this or this is their interpretation is something I may never know. However, I do know I see the aftermath of this incorrect assumption on a weekly basis, sometimes multiple times in one week.

I provide education to patients, informing them that it is their right to sign the notice if they so choose, but that in doing so, if the screening entity continues to feel they are a danger to themselves or others if released, the screening entity may then involuntarily commit them, and they will be transferred to another facility that has an involuntary bed. Often, exasperated patients will ask me, "How is this place really voluntary if you either go voluntarily or they [screeners] commit you?"

It is at this point in the conversation that the idea of self-determination

comes to my mind. How can I assist patients in maintaining their right to self-determination while underlining the importance of making a decision that is going to be in their best interest? The NASW *Code of Ethics* states:

*Social workers respect and promote the right of clients to self determination and assist clients in their efforts to identify and clarify their goals. Social workers may limit clients' right to self determination when, in the social workers' professional judgment, clients' actions or potential actions pose a serious, foreseeable, and imminent risk to themselves or others. (1.02 Self Determination)*

In assisting clients to "identify and clarify their goals," I can take the approach of asking them to discuss what their goal is—getting better or getting out. Getting better may mean further treatment—specifically the treatment that professionals are currently recommending. Being discharged before treatment is provided may be in direct conflict with patients' goals of getting better, as it doesn't allow the treatment process to begin. "But I DO want to get better," I've heard in response. "I just don't think being here is going to help me do that. This is making me feel worse."

Refocusing patients on their goals and respecting their right to disagree with the treatment they are receiving while firmly informing them of their rights as patients relates to respecting patients' dignity and worth:

*Social workers treat each person in a caring and respectful fashion, mindful of individual differences and cultural and ethnic diversity. Social workers promote clients' socially responsible self determination. Social workers seek to enhance clients' capacity and opportunity to change and to address their own needs. Social workers are cognizant of their dual responsibility to clients and to the broader society. They seek to resolve conflicts between clients' interests and the broader society's interests in a socially responsible manner consistent with the values, ethical principles, and ethical standards of the profession. (NASW Code of Ethics, Ethical Principles)*

Encouraging patients to be advocates for themselves while at the same time teaching them to take responsibility for their behavior is something I view as an important part of helping them resolve the conflict between what they want and what society at times dictates is appropriate. Many times, I come across patients who are willing to lay the blame on the mental health system or even society as a whole, but fail to recognize their own self-efficacy. It is often difficult for me professionally to see a client's full potential and have to watch patiently as he or she spends precious treatment time fighting the very system that is trying to help him or her, rather than engaging in treatment.

A colleague once said to me, "Maybe this *is* the treatment." More specifically, maybe helping to support patients while they go through their process of fighting the system is exactly the kind of support they need in that moment, even though it may not be the practitioner's idea of productive treatment.

For myself, staying grounded and understanding that I'm not the solution to a client's problems but rather a support along his or her journey, however bumpy that journey may be, has been a vital realization in my work.

## References

New Jersey Courts. (2008). *Involuntary civil commitments resource binder*. Retrieved from http://www.judiciary.state.nj.us/civil/ICC_ResourceBinder.pdf

## Additional Reading

Kaplan, L. E., & Bryan, V. (2009). A conceptual framework for considering informed consent. *Journal of Social Work Values and Ethics, 6* (3). Retrieved from http://www.jswvearchives.com/content/view/130/69.

Cameron, L. (2009). The day self determination died. *The New Social Worker, 16* (2). Retrieved from http://www.socialworker.com/feature-articles/ethics-articles/Ethics%3A_The_Day_Self-Determination_Died/

*Lauren Dennelly, MSW, LCSW, works as a licensed clinical social worker in Pennsylvania. She has also worked in New York and New Jersey in a variety of settings.*

## Greetings From the Phi Alpha Honor Society for Social Work

The deadline for the below Phi Alpha programs is May 31, 2014. The electronic application can be found on the Phi Alpha website at: *http://www.PhiAlpha.org*

- 4 Chapter Service Awards
- 3 Patty Gibbs-Wahlberg Scholarships
- 1 Advisor of the Year Award
- 3 Student Leadership Awards

Upon approval of the October 2014 International Council meeting in Tampa, Florida, future Phi Alpha programs will include two Chapter Grant Programs, and Phi Alpha will provide Student Support Memberships at each local chapter for those who are financially unable to join Phi Alpha.

Kind regards,
Tammy Hamilton
Executive Secretary
*PhiAlphaInfo@etsu.edu*

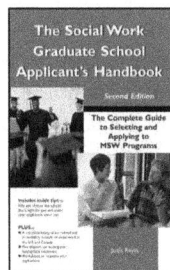

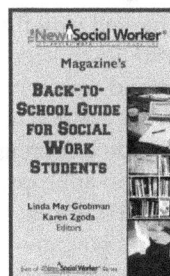

# Making the Tough Call: Social Workers as Mandated Reporters

## Part VII: I Made the Report—Now What?

### by Kathryn S. Krase, Ph.D., J.D., MSW

*Editor's Note: This article is part of an ongoing series.*

Congratulations! You used your education, experience, expertise, and critical thinking skills to make a tough call. Now you're wondering what's next...

## Working with CPS After Making a Report

For most reporters of suspected child maltreatment, their responsibilities end after the call is accepted by Child Protective Services (CPS). For social workers who make a report to CPS, this may not always be the case. In cases in which the social worker as mandated reporter cannot or does not make the report anonymously, CPS may reach out to the worker after the report to ask for clarification of concerns. (For information on when you can/cannot make an anonymous report, see *Making the Tough Call Part III: How do I make a report?* in the Summer 2013 issue of *The New Social Worker*). You, as the mandated reporter, also have the right to contact CPS yourself.

When you communicate with CPS after you make a report, it is important to remember that you are still responsible to protect your client's confidential communications. Even though the law allows you to breach client confidentiality to make a report of suspected child maltreatment to CPS, you are required to minimize the breach. (See *Making the Tough Call Part IV: Conflicted Over Confidentiality,* in the Fall 2013 issue of *The New Social Worker*).

The NASW *Code of Ethics* highlights the social worker's responsibility to minimize harm to a client from the kind of disclosure made in a report to CPS. Social workers are expected to provide the least amount of confidential client information necessary. When you make a report to CPS about a client, you only need provide the information necessary for fulfilling your legal obligation to report, as well as your ethical obligation to the larger society, while protecting as much of your client's privacy as you can.

Depending on the length and depth of your relationship with your client prior to making the report, you may know much about your client that he/she has never shared with anyone else. When you work with CPS, it is important to remember that not all client information is appropriate to share. Generally, you should limit the information you share with CPS to that which informed your decision to make the report, and information you have received since making the report that is relevant to the concerns you expressed in your report (Lau, Krase, & Morse, 2009).

CPS can (and will often) ask for more information, including client records. Client records are protected by client confidentiality, and the decision to share them with CPS should be made with care. In states like New York, the law says that when requested by CPS, mandated reporters must provide records "that are essential for a full investigation" (New York State Social Services Law, Section 415). New York law specifies that these records could relate to "diagnosis, prognosis or treatment, and clinical records." What the law does not specify is WHO gets to determine if the requested records are "essential for a full investigation" (emphasis added).

As a professional, charged with the ethical and legal responsibility to keep your client's information and communications confidential, you are entitled to exercise your discretion in determining what information YOU deem appropriate to share with CPS. If CPS wants more information than what you are providing, then they can ask for more. The legal way CPS can ask for more is by serving a subpoena. A subpoena is a legal tool that seeks to force a person (or business) to provide information (written or oral) for the purposes of furthering a legal action. CPS has the authority to issue a subpoena or ask the court to issue a subpoena. You have the right to challenge the breadth of the subpoena issued by CPS. You can ask a judge to conduct an "in camera" review of your records or your testimony. This means that you tell/show the judge what evidence you have, and it is up to the judge to determine what it "essential" for CPS to know and what is not. This may sound scary, but remember, you're responsible for protecting your client's confidentiality!

## Working with your Client After Making a Report

Negotiating your relationship with CPS after making a report may seem easy compared to figuring out how to work with your client. Should you tell the client you made the report, or not? That decision is up to you. The law does NOT require you to inform your client when you make a report about her/him or his/her family.

When making the decision whether or not to tell your client that you made a report to CPS, safety should be your biggest consideration. Consider any concerns you have regarding your safety, and that of your client and other people. If you feel that anyone's safety would be in question were you to share this information with your client, then, by all means, do not tell the client that you made a report.

If you determine that no one's safety is at risk, then you can tell your client, but you still are not required to. Consider the impact that such a disclosure would have on your relationship with your client, and your client's participation in whatever service he or she is receiving from you. A client may decide that he/she no longer wants to receive services from a social worker who made a report to CPS. Although this decision may seem unfortunate, you also need to remember that the client has the right to self-determination (see NASW *Code,* Section 1.02). In the case in which a client refuses to continue services with a social worker because he/she made a report to CPS, the social worker should provide the client the opportunity to work with someone else within the agency, or provide a referral to a social worker in another setting.

If you decide NOT to inform your client that you made a report to CPS, consider the impact that this omission might have on your relationship with your client. Consider a client who knows a report was made to CPS, but does not know who made the report. The client may process her or his feelings with the social worker, without knowing that it was that social worker who made the report.

Whatever you tell the client or not, use your education, experience, expertise, and critical thinking skills to make this decision, too. They've worked well for you so far, and the more you exercise them, the better they will serve you in the rest of your professional career!

## References

Lau, K., Krase, K., & Morse, R. H. (2009). *Mandated reporting of child abuse and neglect: A practical guide for social workers.* New York: Springer.

National Association of Social Workers (2008). *Code of ethics.* Retrieved from: http://www.socialworkers.org/pubs/code/code.asp

*New York State Social Services Law, Section 415.* Retrieved from: http://codes.lp.findlaw.com/nycode/SOS/6/6/415

*Kathryn S. Krase, Ph.D., J.D., MSW, is an assistant professor of social work at Long Island University in Brooklyn, NY. She earned her Ph.D. in social work, her Juris Doctor, and her Master of Social Work from Fordham University. She has written and presented extensively on mandated reporting of suspected child abuse and neglect. She previously served as Associate Director of Fordham University's Interdisciplinary Center for Family and Child, as well as Clinical Social Work Supervisor for the Family Defense Clinic at New York University Law School.*

# The Staggering Talents of Bayard Rustin: Lessons From Backstage

## *by Melinda Pilkinton, Ph.D., LCSW*

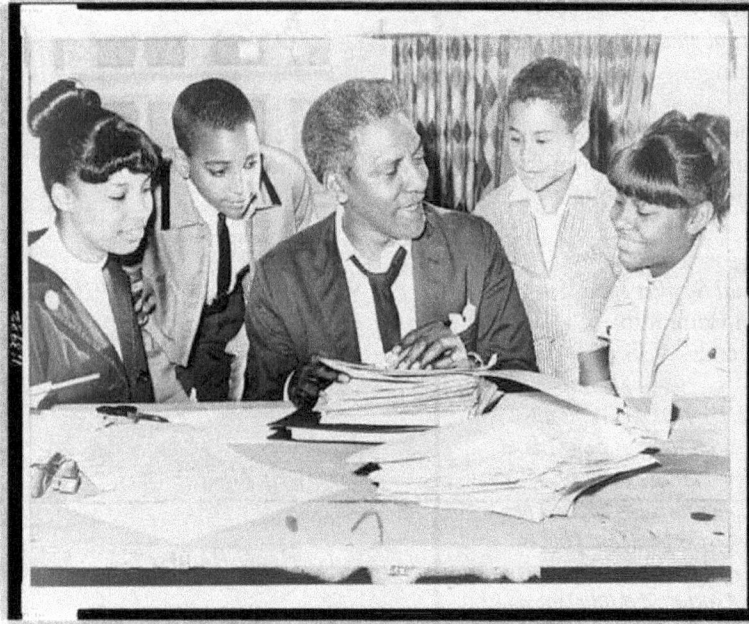

*Bayard Rustin (center) speaking with (left to right) Carolyn Carter, Cecil Carter, Kurt Levister, and Kathy Ross, before demonstration.*

*For decades, this great leader, often at Dr. King's side, was denied his rightful place in history because he was openly gay. No medal can change that, but today, we honor Bayard Rustin's memory by taking our place in his march towards true equality, no matter who we are or who we love.*

>    President Barack Obama, November 20,
>    2013, Presidential Medal of Freedom
>    Ceremony (Wall Street Journal, 2013)

Bayard Rustin (1912-1987) is not a well-known figure in the history of the American Civil Rights Movement. His skills as an organizer, planner, and leader were highly valued by prominent leaders in the Civil Rights Movement; yet, Rustin was relegated to the background during the Movement. He was a gay man, which he guarded from public scrutiny. He and other leaders feared that his sexual orientation would diminish the progression of the movement and reflect badly on the image of Civil Rights leaders.

Rustin was brought up with well-respected grandparents who exposed him to social justice from an early age. Julia Rustin, his grandmother, was one of the first members of the NAACP after it was founded (D'Emilio, 2003). From a young age, Bayard was exposed to the influences of his grandparents as they helped others, including using their home as a way station for the "Great Migration" of African Americans who left the south to escape Jim Crow laws (D'Emilio, 2003). Rustin was a gifted athlete and scholar, which later made him indispensable as an organizer and writer. He was a talented vocalist and a well-known poet within his high school. Known to be a personable young man, he had many friends, both Black and White (D'Emilio, 2003). He was able to attend college when he received a scholarship to Wilberforce University in Ohio. However, Rustin did not graduate. His departure from Wilberforce was possibly due to his sexuality, although no clear evidence exists (D'Emilio, 2003, p. 29).

Rustin discussed his sexuality (in an oblique fashion) with his grandmother, although he never admitted openly to her that he was gay (Miletta, 2006). After Rustin left Wilberforce, Julia warned Rustin that he should associate only with those "who [had] good reputations," further stating, "people who do not have as much to lose as you have can be very careless" (D'Emilio, 2003, p. 29). What he could not know at that time was the impact that his sexuality would have on his life's work.

As a young person who had been exposed to Quaker meetings, anti-war sentiment, stories of the Underground Railroad, and Civil Rights leaders, Rustin was concerned about inequities within society (D'Emilio, 2003; Perlstein, 2007). His values concerning human rights and concepts of nonviolence were rooted in the Quaker belief system. These beliefs led to his studies of non-violence in India with Mahatma Gandhi's son in 1948 (Carbado & Weise, 2004). In the following years, his knowledge and ability to teach others about these beliefs were critical to the Movement.

Rustin's knowledge of and commitment to passive resistance (as Gandhi termed it) and non-violence was tested throughout the Civil Rights Era. When he challenged segregation by refusing to give up a bus seat, he was beaten savagely. He endured verbal abuse for his passive protests. He was arrested and sentenced to a chain gang for violating Jim Crow laws (Carbado & Weise, 2004; Haughton, 1999). Rustin was true to his values of non-violence throughout his life, at whatever the cost.

Rustin experienced embarrassing moments. He was arrested for violating a morals law in Pasadena, California in 1953. Rustin, age 41, had spoken to the American Association of University Women (Carbado & Weise, 2004). Afterwards, he wandered the streets until about 3:00 a.m. when he was approached by some White men in a car. According to the testimony, Rustin offered to perform oral sex on the three men in the car, which they accepted. When police approached the parked car, they arrested all three men for public lewdness (Carbado & Weise, 2004; Cassuto, 2006; D'Emilio, 2003). All of the men were arrested, convicted, and sentenced to 60 days in jail (Cassuto, 2006; D'Emilio, 2003). Rustin was "broken" to be in jail for something other than his beliefs about civil rights (Carbado & Weise, 2004). That particular arrest was followed by other arrests for public solicitation (Allman, 2008; D'Emilio, 2003). During the time period (mid-20th century), every state had criminal laws against homosexuality (D'Emilio, 2003). Rustin's arrests in California on a morals charge and in New York on public solicitation were typical for gay men of the time; if they were observed engaged sexually in public, then trouble came their way. Rustin was arrested many times for his sexuality, effectively eliminating any possibility of public recognition for the work that he did for the

Civil Rights movement (D'Emilio, 2003; Lewis, 2009), and excluding him from his rightful place at the center stage of the movement. In spite of his enormous strengths, he was not able to escape the shadow placed on him by those in the movement who disapproved of his sexuality.

Rustin was aware that the attention brought by his arrests would negatively affect the movement; indeed, he was threatened to have these incidents revealed. For example, Adam Clayton Powell, Jr., threatened to link Martin Luther King and Bayard Rustin as romantic partners (D'Emilio, 2003; Greene, 2006). Rustin was reported to be Dr. King's "closest friend and confidante" (Marable, 2008) and his "key adviser" (Cassuto, 2006), but there is no evidence that a sexual relationship existed between them. Prior to the March on Washington, innuendo and rumors were perpetuated by agents of the Federal Bureau of Investigation (Glenn, 2004) and among Dr. King's advisors (Cassuto, 2006). Nevertheless, Rustin persevered from the sidelines. His influence was massive and his "signature" is evident, but little recognition was given for Rustin's work in the Movement.

Roy Finch referred to him as a "four-way outsider," which was explained as "Black, an artist, a homosexual," and a "pacifist-Quaker" (Kurtz, 2005). Rustin was an outlier compared to other Movement leaders and could not survive public scrutiny of his personal life.

Rustin's role in the organization of the 1963 March on Washington is legendary. He was the coordinator of travel, finances, and details for A. Philip Randolph, Chair of the March. Colleagues described Rustin's organization as phenomenally efficient (Lee & Diaz, 2007). Rustin sent four succinct organizational memos. The first announced the March, the second presented information about non-violence, the third discussed transportation, and the fourth outlined methods for a safe return trip home for the protestors (Lee & Diaz, 2007). That this feat was accomplished at all is amazing, but it is difficult to visualize without the benefit of modern technology and while under surveillance by the federal government (Branch, 1988).

Rustin's organization of the March on Washington included an army of volunteers. Riverside Church in New York prepared 80,000 cheese sandwich lunches to provide the crowd with food

(Branch, 1988). Four thousand volunteer marshals provided security and crowd control (Branch, 1988). Rustin also planned for first-aid stations, water stations, and 200 toilet facilities (Branch, 1988).

As the protesters arrived in Washington for the March, crowd management was challenging. Rustin advanced the program nearly one hour in order to accommodate the attendees (Branch, 1988). As problems with speakers unfolded, Rustin mediated conflicts. He inserted Reverend Fred Shuttlesworth (who was not scheduled to speak) into the events and assisted in mediating a dispute about the content of John Lewis' speech (Branch, 1988) with the Student Nonviolent Coordinating Committee (SNCC) leaders, who felt that other leaders (NAACP, for example) were not forceful enough in demanding civil rights (Branch, 1988).

There was criticism of Rustin's planning. Some leaders thought he relegated Dr. King to speak last at the March because of a rift in their relationship (Carbado & Weise, 2004). Rustin had been approached by other speakers for the event asking Rustin not to put them on the program following Dr. King; they

were intimidated by Dr. King's oratory skills and suspected that the speeches would be over as far as the crowd was concerned once Dr. King spoke (Carbado & Weise, 2004). This is an example of the criticism directed toward Rustin; others assumed conflict where there was none. Dr. King and Rustin had been estranged for about three years at the time of the March, primarily because of Adam Clayton Powell's threat to blackmail Dr. King (Branch, 1988). However, Rustin was not influenced by this breach of their association; he was organizing something much bigger than two men and their personal conflicts.

In the years following the 1963 March on Washington, Rustin distanced himself from civil rights organizations (Perlstein, 2007). He linked with the labor movement and used his well-honed organizational skills for other causes, although this decision separated him further from Black activists (Carbado & Weise, 2004; Perlstein, 2007). The March on Washington was the peak of Rustin's career as a peaceful activist. Arguably, he orchestrated the most influential and widely known demonstration of the American Civil Rights Movement in the shadows of other greats: A. Phillip Randolph, Martin Luther King, Jr., Roy Wilkins, and others. In recent years, credit has been given to Rustin's extraordinary skills. He has been called the "most accomplished organizer of the civil rights movement" (Kurtz, 2005). Upon Rustin's death, Ronald Reagan, a conservative Republican president, praised the socialist activist:

*We mourn the loss of Bayard Rustin, a great leader in the struggle for civil rights in the United States and for human rights throughout the world.... Though a pacifist, he was a fighter to the finish. That is why over the course of his life he won the undying love of all who cherish freedom.* (Reagan, 1987)

## References

Allman, J. (2008). Nuclear imperialism and the Pan-African struggle for peace and freedom: Ghana, 1959-1962, *Souls: A Critical Journal of Black Politics, Culture & Society, 10* (2), 83-102.

Branch, T. (1988). *Parting the waters: America in the King years 1954-63*. New York: Simon & Schuster.

Carbado, D. W. & Weise, D. (2004). The civil rights identity of Bayard Rustin, *Texas Law Review, 82* (5), 1133-1195.

Cassuto, L. (2006). The silhouette and the secret self: Theorizing biography in our times, *American Quarterly, 58* (4), 1249-1261.

D'Emilio, J. (2003). *Lost prophet: The life and times of Bayard Rustin*. Chicago: University of Chicago Press.

Glenn, D. (2004). From protest to.... Dissent, 126 -131.

Greene, C. (2006). What's sex got to do with it: Gender and the New Black Freedom Movement Scholarship, *Feminist Studies, 32* (1), 163-183.

Haughton, B. (1999). Bayard Rustin Civil Rights Leader. *Quaker Studies*. Retrieved 28 October 2013 from http://www.quakerinfo.com/quak_br.shtml

Kurtz, J. B. (2005). Bearing witness still: Recovering the language and the lives that made the Civil Rights Movement move, *Rhetoric & Public Affairs, 8* (2), 327-354.

Lee, S. S. & Diaz, A. (2007) "I was the one percenter": Manny Diaz and the beginnings of a Black-Puerto Rican coalition. *Journal of American Ethnic History, 26* (3), 52-80.

Lewis, A. B. (2009). *The shadows of youth: The remarkable journey of the civil rights generation*. New York: Hill and Wang Publishers.

Marable, M. (2008). The crisis of Black leadership: Introduction to an international symposium, *Souls: A Critical Journal of Black Politics, Culture and Society, 10* (1), 1-4.

Miletta, A. (2006). Brother Outsider: The life of Bayard Rustin, 19 (2), 63-64.

Perlstein, D. (2007). The dead end of despair: Bayard Rustin, the 1968 New York school crisis and the struggle for racial justice, *Afro-Americans in New York Life and History, 31* (2), 89-121.

Reagan, R. (1987, August 25). *Statement on the Death of Bayard Rustin*. The Public Papers of President Ronald W. Reagan. Ronald Reagan Presidential Library. www.presidency.ucsb.edu/ws/?pid=34735#axzz2j3ATc9F1 (accessed 28 Oct 2013).

The Wall Street Journal (2013, November 22). *Transcript of Obama's remarks at the Medal of Freedom ceremony*. Retrieved from: http://blogs.wsj.com/washwire/2013/11/20/transcript-of-obamas-remarks-at-the-medal-of-freedom-ceremony/

## Additional Resources

*Bayard Rustin: Biography*. (n.d.) Retrieved May 22, 2010 from http://www.spartacus.schoolnet.co.uk/USArustin.htm.

Carbado, D. W. & Weise, D. (2003). *Time on Two Crosses: The Collected Writings of Bayard Rustin*. San Francisco: Cleis Press.

Kates, N. (Producer) & Singer, B. (Director). (2003). *Brother Outsider* [Motion picture]. USA: Public Broadcasting System.

Naegle, W. (n.d.). *About Bayard Rustin*. http://www.rustin.org

*Melinda Pilkinton, Ph.D., LCSW, is Associate Professor and Program Director of the Social Work Program at Mississippi State University.*

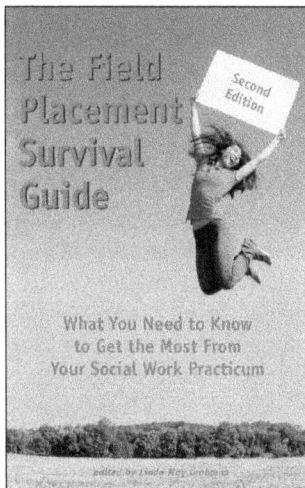

# THE FIELD PLACEMENT SURVIVAL GUIDE
## What You Need To Know To Get the Most From Your Social Work Practicum
## 2nd Edition

Field placement is one of the most exciting and exhilarating parts of a formal social work education. It is also one of the most challenging. This collection addresses the multitude of issues that social work students in field placement encounter, including choosing a placement, getting prepared, using supervision effectively, working with clients, coping with challenges, and moving on to a successful social work career.

This collection is a goldmine of practical information that will help social work students take advantage of all the field placement experience has to offer. Each chapter (many written by seasoned experts in field educa-tion; others by students) presents a different aspect of the practicum and offers students insight into the importance of both the challenges and the joys of this unique learning experience.

This book brings together in one volume the best field placement articles from THE NEW SOCIAL WORKER. Packed with practical, essential information for every student in field placement!

*"As an older (52), non-traditional student working my internship for my B.A. in social work, I ordered your book. It was so reassuring that others had survived and gone on to successful careers!"*

*Linda Chamberlain*

Edited by Linda May Grobman, ACSW, LSW
Founder, publisher, and editor of **THE NEW SOCIAL WORKER**.

*ISBN: 978-1-929109-26-5  2011  Price: $22.95  284 pages*  *Shipping/Handling: add $8.50/first book, $1.50/each additional book in U.S.*
*Canadian orders: add $14.00 first book, $4 each add'l book. Other orders: contact us. If ordering from Pennsylvania, add 6% sales tax.*
*Order from White Hat Communications, PO Box 5390, Harrisburg, PA 17110-0390*
*http://shop.whitehatcommunications.com  717-238-3787 (phone)  717-238-2090 (fax)*

# IS IT ETHICAL? 101 Scenarios In Everyday Social Work Practice
## A Discussion Workbook
### by Thomas Horn, MSW, RSW

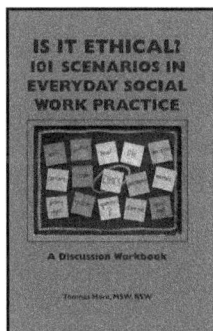

What would you do if you were asked to be your hairdresser's social worker? How about if you developed a crush on a client? Or if you unexpectedly received a $100 check in the mail from an agency to whom you had referred a client?

Social work is filled with these kinds of questions. They come up every day in professional life. Will your students be prepared to make the ethical decision?

Very few social workers go to work looking for ways to exploit, manipulate, or mislead the people with whom they work—clients, colleagues, managers, the government, or the general public. Yet, it is possible to cross into unethical behavior unintentionally, often as a result of poor decisions that are misguided. The line between ethical and unethical can become blurred.

This workbook provides students with 101 different everyday scenarios and challenges them to think about what the ethical and unethical choices might be in each situation. Through examining these scenarios on their own and in discussion with classmates and others, they will become more familiar with how to apply the ethical guidelines and standards that they will be required to follow as professional social workers.

Space is provided after each scenario for readers to write their own responses as they prepare to discuss the scenario with classmates, supervisors, and others. There is space for students to write their own scenarios, as well.

Resources are listed, including Code of Ethics Web addresses for nine different social work associations, as well as ethics journals.

*"...if you need a resource to begin a discussion of ethics in a classroom or agency in-service, this workbook qualifies for Social Work Ethics 101."* Paul Dovyak, ACSW, LISW-S, University of Rio Grande, Journal of Social Work Values and Ethics

### ABOUT THE AUTHOR

Thomas Horn, MSW, RSW, is a Registered Social Worker (RSW) with both the Ontario College of Social Workers and Social Service Workers (OCSWSSW) in Ontario, Canada, and the General Social Care Council (GSCC) in England. Tom is also a graduate member of the British Psychological Society. He has worked in the social services field for more than 20 years in a variety of settings, including residential developmental care, residential and outpatient child and adolescent mental health, residential drug/alcohol treatment, and inpatient psychiatry. Currently, Tom works with an inpatient forensic mental health team at a large psychiatric hospital in Ontario. He routinely provides field supervision to social work students at the undergraduate and graduate levels.

2011 • ISBN: 978-1-929109-29-6 • 118 pages, 5½ by 8½ • $14.95 plus shipping

White Hat Communications, P.O. Box 5390, Harrisburg, PA 17110-0390 Phone: 717-238-3787 Fax: 717-238-2090 shop.whitehatcommunications.com

# Turn Up the Tech in Social Work

## Microaggressions and the Internet
### by Ellen Belluomini, LCSW

This winter, I attended the Evolution of Psychology conference in Anaheim, California. Dr. Derald Wing Sue presented a session on microaggressions and their impact on minorities. Microaggressions are "brief and commonplace daily verbal, behavioral, or environmental indignities, whether intentional or unintentional, that communicate hostile, derogatory, or negative racial slights and insults toward people of color" (Sue, et al., 2007, p. 271). Oppressed categories affected by these comments can include people of color, as well as those of minority gender, sexual orientation, and ability status. This discussion prompted my thoughts on how microaggressions occur online, their influence on the client populations we serve, and a reflection on my own online behavior.

The online environment is rampant with prejudicial statements against many different populations not in the majority. Microaggressions are about power imbalance and privilege afforded the dominant culture. These subtle forms of prejudice can create a hostile environment for minorities. The subtleness and frequency of these acts create a sense of "losing one's mind" because "it must be me," support an underlying lack of confidence, and/or generate impotence in action (Sue, et al., 2007). The reactions and frequency of these microaggressions in social media can prolong the impact of the statement or behavior. Vulnerable and marginalized populations are especially susceptible to these comments. There are three categories of microaggressions that flourish on the Internet—microinvalidation, microinsults, and microassaults (Sue, et al., 2007).

*Microinvalidation* is a verbal or nonverbal portrait refuting the experience of a population of a minority culture. This invalidating statement can be couched in a compliment. A Tweet from the Republican National Committee (@GOP) on December 1, 2013, stated "Today we remember Rosa Parks' bold stand and her role in ending racism." Later, the RNC changed the quote to "Today we remember Rosa Parks' bold stand and her role in fighting to end racism." The original Tweet is an example of microinvalidation, minimizing the experience of every person who experiences racism in America. Tweeting is a brief form of communication and does not lend itself to weighty topics. The statement in this Tweet may be an example of how the white majority is unconscious of the racism existing in society, or it may be an example of someone's incompetence in using Twitter. Either way, the ramifications intensified over the wording of this Tweet.

*Microinsults* are tactless or thoughtless statements conveying a subtle offense to minorities. The *Duck Dynasty* star, Phil Robertson, used microaggressions about African Americans he would work next to while picking cotton in the pre-Civil War Era south, stating, "They're singing and happy. I never heard one of them, one black person, say, 'I tell you what. These doggone white people'—not a word!" Initially stated to a reporter for *GQ Magazine,* this example exhibits his unconsciousness about the effects of racism. Microinsults on social media can range from "you write so well for a black person" to "this Pinterest is too Mexican for me." Whether these comments are from famous people or a stranger, the microinsult can be internalized.

*Microassaults* are purposeful messages of discrimination toward a minority group. Following the Boston Marathon bombing, multiple articles addressed the thought of Muslim involvement. Before the bombers were identified, police issued warnings for a "darker skinned or black male with a possible foreign accent in connection with the attack." This description initiated many microassaults through Tweets, memes, comments on social media, and news reports against persons who were Muslim or Middle Eastern. President Obama is consistently referred to online as a Muslim. Sadly, this is a microassault, not a positive adjective referencing our president.

I focused on social media here, but there are examples to be read on blogs, websites, Tumblr, Pinterest, through online course curricula, YouTube videos, or other forms of communication and play on the Internet.

When you see different forms of microaggressions, do you choose to ignore it or confront it? What are the best ways to communicate when microaggressions occur? How do we help people understand the issues with a comment or content in a way that will not put them on the defensive? Who do you trust to give you feedback on your microaggressions? How do you let down your defenses in listening to feedback? These are conversations needing to happen in all of our online circles.

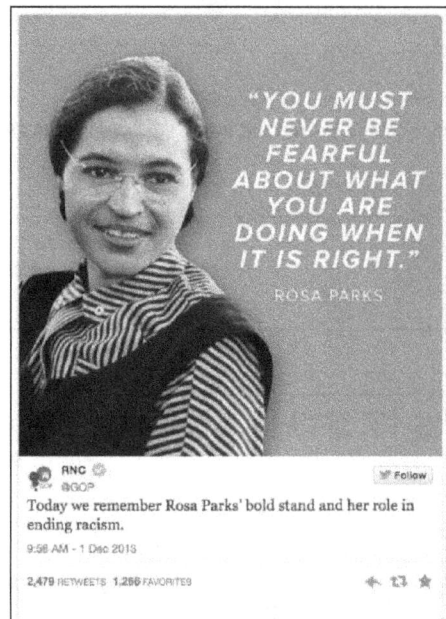

I do not know if microaggressions are more acceptable through an online format, or if people's prejudices are easier to identify because they are shouted to the world. Both seem to be the answer. When a congressperson's speech includes microinvalidations or an actor tweets a microinsult, the communication is spread globally in an instant. There are usually two sides, either supporting or denouncing the comment. This debate occurs throughout social media. Facebook friends argue back and forth linking articles or statistics to prove their point. Memes are created to support a person's viewpoint. Tweets shout their message to the Tweetosphere. Minority groups are inundated with microaggressions. How do these statements add to internalized oppression? The effect this form of racism (and other isms) has is yet to be determined, but the first step to change is awareness.

My final evaluation is with myself. Although microaggression is not a new term for me, as a person who is white, I need to re-remember this concept more frequently. Coming home from this conference, I re-evaluated my blog writing with a new lens. I did not find any offensive or negating verbiage in my content. This does not mean there is not any to be found. It means I am unconscious to some of the microaggressions I exhibit. Unconsciousness is an easy state to fall back on when I am in the majority. I am not confronted daily on negative characteristics my "whiteness" brings to the world. As I continue to write on my blog, create curricula online, or post comments on social media, there is a pressing responsibility. Vigilance of my microaggressions is as important to me as my confrontation of other's microaggressions. This is an instance of "be the change you want to see in the world."

Examples of microaggressions can be read at The Microaggressions Project (microaggressions.com) or you can view Microaggressions in Every Day Life at: https://www.youtube.com/watch?v=BJL2PQJsAS4

# Reference

Sue, D.W., Capodilupo, C., Torino, G., Bucceri, A., Holder, A., Nadal, K., & Esquilin, M. (2007). Racial microaggressions in everyday life. *American Psychologist, 62* (4), 271-286.

*Ellen M. Belluomini, LCSW, received her MSW from the University of Illinois, Jane Addams School of Social Work and is currently a doctoral student at Walden University. She is an educator at National Louis University and Harper College. She has developed online and blended curricula with an emphasis on integrating technology into human services practice. She writes a blog "Bridging the Digital Divide in Social Work Practice" to increase awareness about technology's uses. She presents and consults on various issues related to social services. Her clinical work has been in private practice, management of nonprofit agencies, and programming for vulnerable populations.*

# Accessing Apps: Encouraging Multiculturalism
*by Ellen Belluomini, LCSW*

Multiculturalism is making its way onto the digital learning highway by developing apps for adults and children. These apps offer an opportunity to understand and experience other cultures. This is a small step toward the appreciation of differences in our world. Place app name in browser to find (App name, android or App name, Apple).

## General App
SmallTalk Intensive Care
What I would have given for an app like this when I worked in a hospital. This picture-based app helps patients express their medical needs. Instead of trying to gesture what the client wants, they have universal pictures of "I have chest pain, I need suction, or I need a doctor." The only thing that would make it better is using different languages with the pictures.
Cost: Free

## Multicultural Apps for Children
**Drum Kids, ABC Music**
Music and its rhythms have a way of connecting every culture. These apps help children explore global cultures through sound, both listening and creating.
Cost: $2.99

**Round is a Mooncake or other eBooks**
There are many books about different cultures to explore with children. Some of these books include games. Others are picture eBooks. Premio Publishing (http://gozobooks.com/it-aint-flat.php) offers eBooks showing many different cultures as the characters.
Cost: $2.99

**The Amazing Train**
This is an interactive book about children visiting India, helping the reader experience India's culture. The interactive features allow kids to interact with the culture.
Cost: 2.99 Apple

**The Big Myth**
Potentially one of my favorites for kids, this app helps children understand the myths from each culture about how the world began and how the first humans came into being. It will encourage critical thinking about differences.
Cost: Apple $3.99

## Multicultural Apps for Adults
**Kick it Out**
This app surprised even me. Have you ever been at one of your adolescent's sports games and heard the parent next to you yelling racial slurs toward the other team? Centering on negative interactions in the bleachers during football (soccer) games, this app addresses discrimination in the crowd. The information goes to the designated administrator. Every report is confidential. I am sure it could be adapted for use by little leagues in the United States.
Cost: Free

**S-Translator, iTranslator, Languages, Universal Translator**
Have you ever wanted to communicate with someone who did not speak your language? These apps are not just your Google search anymore. They provide a way to connect with a person speaking any language. Just write or speak your sentence, and it will translate it to a verbal example.
Cost: Free to $2.99

**Melteampot**
This multicultural group's app connects people from different countries in groups. The app features icons for various languages spoken. These icons can be viewed on everyone's profile. People can meet up in their cities or when they travel on vacation. Go to *Melteampot.com* to see a tutorial.
Cost: Free

**No Racism in Islam**
This instructional app informs users about the Islam religion. The app dispels myths by providing examples in the text about racism, equality, and manners.
Cost: Android Free

# Compassionate Competence:
# A New Model for Social Work Practice
*by Marian L. Swindell, Ph.D.*

As a social work practitioner and educator, I have always felt something lacking in my practice philosophy. I encourage my undergraduate students to develop a practice "philosophy" or "mantra" that they will try to live up to every single day. Upon graduation from my MSW program, I embraced my practice "mantra" or philosophy as stemming from the Wesleyan Doctrines of Goodness. As I was raised within the church setting, I became very familiar with this doctrine, which encour-

ages people to "do all the good you can, by all the means you can, in all the ways you can, in all the places you can, at all the times you can, to all the people you can, as long as ever you can."

As I graduated with MSW in hand, I was prepared to go out and "do good." I was blessed with an amazing graduate program that encouraged MSWs to go out into the world and make a huge, positive difference. Thinking back upon that educational program, I realize that they were, in fact, giving me permission to go out, be brave and courageous, and really seriously change the world.

During my education, one fundamental skill I was taught and worked to develop was the skill of cultural competence. A great definition of cultural competence is:

*the process by which individuals and systems respond respectfully and effectively to people of all cultures, languages, classes, races, ethnic backgrounds, religions, and other diversity factors in a manner that recognizes, affirms, and values the worth of individuals, families, and communities and protects and preserves the dignity of each.... Cultural competence is a set of congruent behaviors, attitudes, and policies that come together in a system or agency or among professionals and enable the system, agency, or professionals to work effectively in cross-cultural situations.... Operationally defined, cultural competence is the integration and transformation of knowledge about individuals and groups of people into specific standards, policies, practices, and attitudes used in appropriate cultural settings to increase the quality of services, thereby producing better outcomes* (http://www.naswdc.org/practice/standards/naswcultural-standards.pdf).

The fundamental interpretation of culturally competent social work is different for each social worker. This difference in interpretation can make social work one of the most enriching, colorful, tactile, soul inspiring careers of all time. As a student, I fundamentally "got" exactly what cultural competence was.

Being culturally competent meant that upon graduation, I would know how to ethically and effectively work with different types of people, from different towns, cities, regions, countries, with different dialects, speech patterns, belief systems, family systems, values, abilities, gifts, income, and educational backgrounds. Basically, I should be able to embrace the differences and similarities that each client would bring into my office and to remain open-minded and willing to learn new things about human beings when working with my clients. So, fundamentally, I was competent at being a culturally competent social worker.

After years of talking with clients, students, and colleagues, I knew my practice philosophy was changing–evolving–shifting. I was going deeper into doing what I was doing as a social worker. I was looking at a bigger picture, basically how I was changing the world, one person at a time. I was seeing that I was having universal impact, and that was terrifying.

I understood and fully comprehended that my actions with my clients had gone past being competent and had become compassionate. I understood cultural differences, and also that compassion included all cultures, all peoples, all walks of life. I understood that compassion was much bigger than culture. This understanding and the ultimate transformation took place solely because I yearned for a deeper connection to my profession.

I struggled with not feeling like "I had been called." So many people say that social work is a "calling." My problem, however, was that I never felt or heard this "calling." I sometimes felt that I was a fake social worker or that I was "faking it" because I didn't get "called," and I thought I was surrounded by all these great, and magical, mystical people who had gotten this miraculous call.

As the years passed and I began to authentically talk with my clients, my students, and colleagues, I understood that, yes, I needed to understand cultural competence, and I needed to be good at it. But that was just the beginning for me.

I began to understand that cultural competence was a foundation upon which to enrich my career–a building block of sorts. Yes, yes. I knew I was competent. I was very technically efficient. But that wasn't enough for me. In addition to being *competent* (the black/white side of social work), I also wanted to be *compassionate* (the colorful side of social work).

A great definition of compassion, defined by the Merriam-Wesbster dictionary, is:

> *a feeling of wanting to help someone who is sick, hungry, in trouble, etc.: a sympathetic consciousness of others' distress together with a desire to alleviate it. (http://www.merriam-webster.com/ dictionary/compassion)*

I posit that we, as social workers, embrace a new philosophy about our profession. I no longer want to be merely culturally competent. I do not want to be seen as a technically efficient integrator and transformer of knowledge, skills, and policies to produce a better outcome. Yes, that technical, efficient, productive philosophy is about "answering a call." That philosophy is very black or white.

Let's consider a blending of these two ideas into one revolutionary practice goal–one that will change how social workers view our profession and how others view us, as well. Social workers should desire a career philosophy filled with black and white, and all the bright and beaming colors in between. We should embrace both competence and compassion. Thomas Merton states that "the whole idea of compassion is based on a keen awareness of the interdependence of all these living beings, which are all part of one another, and all involved in one another" *(http://www. fiercelight.org/resources).* As social workers, we understand and embrace systems theory and ecological theory. Compassion embraces these theories as well.

The competent aspect of social work is crucial; we are worthless if we are incompetent. The compassionate aspect of social work is crucial, as well; without compassion, we are just automaton/robots going through the motions of our day. We need both competence and compassion, black/white and color. Based on the definitions explained above, I encourage social workers to embrace a new term with a new definition: *Compassionate Competence.* Building on the two

previous definitions, I would loosely define "compassionate competence" as:

> *an ethically, successful integration and transformation of knowledge, skills, attitudes, behaviors, and policies to sympathetically and consciously alleviate suffering* (Swindell, 2013).

The first section of the definition, "an ethically, successful integration and transformation of knowledge, skills, attitudes, behaviors, and policies" focuses on the technical and competent aspect of our social work–successfully completing a task and doing so correctly. The second section of the definition "sympathetically and consciously alleviating suffering" focuses on the humanitarian, unselfish aspect of our profession–helping those who are suffering–AND includes all people, all cultures, all religions, all socioeconomic classes, all human beings. The definition is written clearly, simply, and succinctly and reads "alleviate suffering." This means all suffering, not just certain types of suffering. Suffering is suffering, regardless of how it is presented. All cultures suffer. People within all cultures experience suffering. The original language in the definition of compassion reads "alleviate suffering." It does not matter what culture, gender, age, disability, poverty level, religious affiliation...all that matters is suffering and the alleviation of that suffering.

It is important to note that culture is indeed a significant aspect of a person's life and that this article is in no way diminishing the importance of culture. The article is only suggesting that we focus more on compassion (which includes cultural awareness and knowledge) than just on culture itself.

In conclusion, I feel that I must explain that this article comes from my own personal and spiritual journey within myself from a social worker's perspective. Many readers may completely agree or disagree with the notion of a new practice goal. Some may say that they have been practicing this way their entire career and that this notion of "compassion" in social work is nothing new. I agree. There are approximately 995 articles with the terms "social work" and "compassion," according to a search of *Academic Search Complete.* The majority of these articles focus on self-compassion, compassion fatigue syndrome, and compassion satisfaction. So this relation-

ship between compassion and social work is not new. The purpose of this article, however, is to formally introduce the term "compassionate competence" as a practice goal within our profession. Whether one chooses to embrace this practice goal and include it within the practice repertoire is purely personal.

The culturally competent social worker is a technically proficient, efficient, effective, successful worker. Once social workers become successful at this, they can complete tasks with their eyes closed. The difference is that compassionately competent social workers become successful ONLY AFTER they open their eyes.

Joel A. Barker affirms that "Vision without action is merely a dream. Action without vision just passes the time. Vision with action can change the world." *(http://www.brainyquote.com/quotes/quotes/j/ joelabark158200.html)*

The vision of compassion plus competent action can indeed change the world. The time is now for social work to shift into a higher calling, based on a higher vision, far reaching just culture, but embracing all of humanity.

## References

BrainyQuote. (2013). Joel A. Barker quotes. Retrieved from *http://www. brainyquote.com/quotes/quotes/j/joela-bark158200.html.*

Fiercelight. (2012). Fiercelight: Where spirit goes deeper. Retrieved from *http:// www.fiercelight.org/resources.*

*Compassionate.* (n.d.). In Merriam-Webster's online dictionary (11th ed.). Retrieved from *http://www.merriam-webster. com/dictionary/compassion.*

National Association of Social Workers. (2001). *NASW standards of cultural competence.* Retrieved from *http://www. naswdc.org/practice/standards/NAswcultural-standards.pdf.*

Swindell, M. (2013). *Compassionate competence: A letter to MSU-Meridian social work students.* Student Orientation, Fall, 2013.

*Marian L. Swindell, Ph.D., is an associate professor of social work at Mississippi State University.*

# Reviews

*Research Methods for Social Workers (2nd ed.), by Samuel S. Faulkner & Cynthia A. Faulkner, Lyceum Books, Chicago, 2014, 256 pages, $54.95.*

As a doctoral student in social work, I'm privileged to both instruct and enroll in social science research courses. During this process of training to become an academic, I'm also engaged in a variety of research projects. These experiences have stoked my interest in the generation of knowledge, offering fascinating opportunities to design and implement studies, analyze data, and consider various venues to support dialogue and dissemination of findings.

The second edition of this text by the Drs. Faulkner, published in 2014, marks a seminal advancement in training related to social work research. Updating content from the premier edition, CSWE Core Competencies, self-assessments, and suggestions for the cultivation of practice-informed empiricism are integrated throughout the 13 chapters. Whereas many of the profession's research training publications primarily read like textbooks, the style, tone, and content of this resource are differently engaging and informative. In fact, students and practitioners alike may discover that this new release resembles a practice manual, an attribute that is likely to reduce the hesitation often accompanying studies of research. Carefully crafted and concise treatments of literature reviews, inferential and descriptive statistics, and research proposals further enhance applicability.

Despite its many achievements, a third revision of the text may address some of the limitations. Absent from the book are more critical considerations of key elements in the research process. For instance, the ways in which social science theories can inform the design of studies and analyses of data need to be considered. Qualitative and quantitative processes are occasionally framed to imply a mutual exclusivity, with an implicit privileging of the latter paradigm; unfortunately, this duality prevents a more dynamic discussion of mixed methods research. Mostly absent from the text, also, are reviews of timely topics of great importance to data analyses, including the centrality of mediation and moderation and strategies for exploring alternate approaches like structural equation modeling. Although these shortcomings are unlikely to impede the orientation of new trainees in social work research, those committed to more advanced learning may need to acquire supplemental materials to accompany their studies.

Well written and with tremendous readability, this latest text by Drs. Faulkner and Faulkner makes an invaluable contribution to the development of new knowledge related to practice-informed research and evidence-based practice. Students, practitioners, and scholars in social work and allied social sciences are certain to be challenged by and appreciate the rich ideas discoverable within these pages.

*Reviewed by Jeff T. Steen, LCSW, Ph.D. candidate, New York University, Silver School of Social Work.*

---

*Transcending Dementia Through the TTAP Method: A New Psychology of Art, Brain and Cognition, by Linda Levine Madori, Ph.D., CRTS, ATR-BC, Health Professions Press, Baltimore, Maryland, 2013. 243 pages, $42.95 paperback.*

*Transcending Dementia* is an amazing resource and a must read for anyone working with older adults. Dr. Madori presents her cutting edge, evidence-based technique, the Therapeutic Thematic Arts Programming Method (TTAP Method) and systematically explains how it can be used in working with clients with Alzheimer's disease. The book is well organized and, just as the title suggests, discusses how the TTAP Method can genuinely transcend dementia through presenting practical, very feasible activities for practitioners to do with their clients, both individually and in groups.

The strengths-based nature of the TTAP method and the diversity of creative expression Madori presents in how to use the method are both exciting and empowering for social work practitioners. For example, from photographs, painting, sculpting, and drawing, to music and movement, the TTAP method can be used to make significant, measurable positive impacts in the lives of clients.

Although the text was not written specifically for social workers, every aspect of the book parallels social work values, theories, and evidence based practice, as well as our commitment to building on client strengths. The text is very relevant for the social work practitioner, as its inter-disciplinary nature is very apparent, and it will likely ignite exciting collaboration among helping professionals working with clients with dementia.

One of the strongest elements of the book is Madori's presentation of the research on the efficacy of the TTAP method. The data are presented in a way that is exciting to read, and are also very practical, thorough, and relevant to the social work practitioner. In fact, tools and resources are presented in the back of the book for practitioners to implement the technique and track its effectiveness. In reading the book, I felt an invitation to participate in collecting research and be a part of using this method to enhance client well-being.

Another stand-out feature of the book is an extremely well written and comprehensive chapter titled *Aging and Human Development Theories: Understanding and Meeting the Needs of Older Adults, Including Those with Dementia*. Madori presents several theories in a very succinct way, highlighting the "meat" of the theory, and uses visuals that enhance the reader's understanding. The theories are not just presented, but tied to application of the TTAP method.

In summary, this book is not just a great read, but a teaching tool for practitioners in gerontology. It teaches you, step by step, about the current research on Alzheimer's, the TTAP method and how to use it, and how to track its effectiveness with clients.

I recommend this text as a handbook for gerontology social workers and educators. Madori's work is a great example of innovation, creativity, and research that stemmed from practice experience working with older adults. For me, this book was extremely empowering. Working with clients with a degenerative disease can sometimes feel disempowering, and this book counteracts that and sets the stage for practitioners to be creative in building on client strengths through applying the TTAP method.

*Reviewed by Satara M. Crandall, Ph.D., MSW, Associate Professor, Social Work Department of Behavioral and Social Sciences, College of Adult and Professional Studies, Indiana Wesleyan University.*

---

*The Children's Bureau: Shaping a Century of Child Welfare Practices, Programs, and Policies, edited by Katherine Briar-Lawson, Mary McCarthy and Nancy Dickinson, NASW*

Press, Washington DC, 2013, 342 pages, $55.99.

The title of this text would seem to indicate that the book is about the history of the influence of the Children's Bureau, but what is most beneficial to educators and practitioners alike is the relationship to current trends in child welfare practices. The editors chose experts across the nation to present viewpoints about the varying issues relative to child welfare practice and included a wealth of research information on the subject.

Chapters discussing trauma-informed care practice, working with clients with co-occurring disorders, and family-centered practice all contribute to the understanding of child welfare practice today. The chapters on workforce and leadership development, as well as organizational imperatives, will help social workers new to child welfare or those who influence program development to understand some of the challenges and dynamics facing the field today. The text provides specific attention to working with tribal entities and nicely articulates the roles for partnership and collaboration across systems of education, training, and service.

Practitioners will appreciate the chapter on engagement. The authors used stakeholder reflections to highlight areas in which social workers can adjust their practice to improve engagement and utilize the skill set that is helpful to promote professional relationships. The authors did not stop there, however, also including factors at both the peer and systems levels that can facilitate engagement.

Each chapter outlines the history of Children's Bureau efforts, research evidence within the topic area when possible, the role of social work, and implications for both educators and practice. As in any edited text, the authors approach the focus of the chapter differently within the given framework. If I were to indicate a limitation of the text, it would be that there appeared to be some repetition regarding the Children's Bureau history across several chapters. The information was connected to the specific chapter focus, but was repetitive. The framework did not always fit well for the topic of the chapter, resulting in cursory coverage of some of the topic areas, which is not unexpected in what is essentially a reference book. I would like to have seen more discussion of systems issues in the chapter on trauma informed practice

and information on racial disparities, compassion fatigue, and self-care, for example.

This book is a wonderful resource for individuals interested in child welfare systems and would be a great addition to agency and academic reference collections. In the classroom, I could see the text as a supplement within courses directed to child welfare or even to provide a more specific child welfare focus in policy courses at all levels. The topic-specific chapters can bridge understanding between other areas of practice and child welfare. In more advanced level course work with an emphasis on child welfare practices, the text could be used for further discussion, critique, and investigation of those societal factors that influence the treatment of children and families. The authors are to be commended for pulling together child welfare history across so many dimensions.

*Reviewed by Joan Groessl, MSW, Ph.D., LCSW, Lecturer and BSW Field Coordinator, University of Wisconsin-Green Bay.*

---

*Multiple Minority Identities: Applications for Practice, Research and Training, edited by Reginald Nettles and Rochelle Balter, Springer Publishing Company, New York, 2012, 280 pages, including 2 appendices and index, $70.*

*Multiple Minority Identities* explores how professionals interact with clients who identify with more than one minority status. The volume focuses specifically on therapists' interactions with clients who identify as LGBTQ, as persons with a disability, and/or as an ethnic minority (to utilize the language of the authors).

The book is divided into three sections. The first section focuses on research conducted about the impact of multiple minority identity. Beginning with a chapter about the development of theories of stigma, additional chapters highlight discussions of mental health issues for those who identify with more than one minority group and the clinical implications for this group. The book includes a chapter detailing issues to consider if a client is both deaf and has one of the other minority statuses described above.

The second section focuses on practice interventions. Chapters provide historical information and clinical applications for therapists working in group psychotherapy, as well as those utilizing cognitive-behavioral, psychodynamic, and positive psychology frameworks in prac-

tice. Case studies illustrate the concepts advanced within each chapter.

The third section focuses on training those who will serve clients with multiple minority identities. Chapters outline techniques for therapists utilizing psychodynamic or group relations perspectives. In addition, a chapter emphasizes the need for in-depth and thoughtful diversity training. The final chapter outlines "next steps" for professionals.

All chapters encourage helping professionals to explore all aspects of a client's identity, being careful to listen for the client's self understanding of each identity without assuming that one identity takes precedence over another. Several writers emphasize the need for therapists to explore how each identity provides resilience or creates pain for the client: for example, exploring the intersectionality of issues for a gay Hispanic man with a European partner.

Each chapter begins with a set of learning objectives for the chapter and concludes with a set of review questions. In that respect, the volume appears to be student focused rather than professionally focused. In addition, all the authors are psychologists, so case examples often are provided from within the clinical boundaries of psychology rather from the perspective of clinical social workers.

The profession of social work celebrates diversity and trains students at both the BSW and MSW levels toward cultural intelligence. The need for workers to be willing to engage clients as whole persons rather than focusing only on particular aspects or parts of who they are is a critical skill for social workers. This book provides a brief overview of research regarding the specific therapeutic modalities mentioned above and up-to-date information as to how these specific modalities can be used by psychologists in therapy. In addition, it emphasizes the need for clinicians to be competent to assist those who have multiple minority identities.

For master's level students, or those social workers new to the field, the book can be useful to both strengthen understanding and to utilize sound practice when working with those who identify as multiple minorities.

*Reviewed by Jane Hoyt-Oliver, ACSW, LISW-Supv., Ph.D., Chair, Social Work Program, Malone University, Canton, OH.*

## Network With *The New Social Worker!*

As of April 1, 2014, we have reached 57,129 fans (or "likers") of our page on Facebook at *http://www.facebook.com/ newsocialworker.*

Besides providing information about *The New Social Worker* magazine, the page has features of a typical Facebook timeline. We list upcoming events and send updates to our "likers" when there is something interesting happening!

Are you on Facebook? Do you love *The New Social Worker?* Show us how much you care! Be one of our Facebook "likers" and help us reach 75,000 (and beyond)!

We also have a Facebook page for our SocialWorkJobBank. com site! Go to *http://www. facebook.com/socialworkjobbank* to "like" this page. New job postings at *http://www.socialworkjobbank.com*

are now automatically posted to the Facebook page, as well.

Finally, stay up-to-date on our latest books at *http://www.facebook. com/whitehatcommunications.*

In addition, we'd like to know how *you* are using Facebook. Have you found it a useful tool for networking with social work colleagues, searching for a job, or fundraising for your agency? Write to lindagrobman@socialworker.com and let us know.

Facebook address: *http://www.facebook.com/newsocialworker*
*Also check out our other pages:*
http://www.facebook.com/socialworkjobbank
http://www.facebook.com/newsocialworkerbookclub
http://www.facebook.com/whitehatcommunications

AND...look for The New Social Worker's group on LinkedIn.com:
http://www.linkedin.com/groups?gid=3041069

Twitter: http://www.twitter.com/newsocialworker

Google+: https://plus.google.com/+Socialworkermag/posts

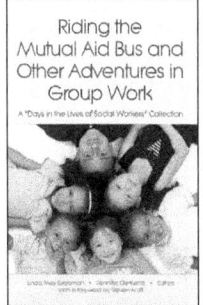

# Beginnings, Middles, & Ends
## Sideways Stories on the Art & Soul of Social Work
Ogden W. Rogers, Ph.D., LCSW, ACSW

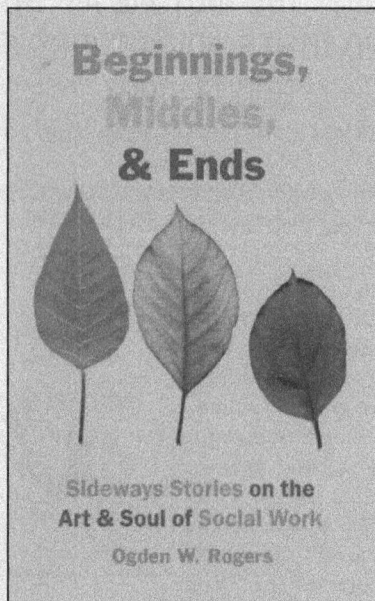

A sideways story is some moment in life when you thought you were doing one thing, but you ended up learning another. A sideways story can also be a poem, or prose, that, because of the way it is written, may not be all that direct in its meaning. What's nice about both clouds, and art, is that you can look at them and just resonate. That can be good for both the heart and the mind.

Many of the moments of this book have grown from experiences the author has had or stories he used in his lectures with students or told in his office with clients. Some of them have grown from essays written for others, for personal or professional reasons. They are moments on a path through the discovery of social work, a journey of beginnings, middles, and ends.

With just the right blend of humor and candor, each of these stories contains nuggets of wisdom that you will not find in a traditional textbook. They capture the essence and the art and soul of social work. In a world rushed with the illusion of technique and rank empiricism, it is the author's hope that some of the things here might make some moment in your thinking or feeling grow as a social worker. If they provoke a smile, or a tear, or a critical question, it's worth it. Everyone makes a different journey in a life of social work. These stories are one social worker's travelogue along the way.

## PRAISE FOR THE BOOK

"As someone near the end of a long career in social work and social work education, I found the stories of Ogden Rogers in his collection, Beginnings. Middles, and Ends, to reflect so much of my own experience that I literally moved back and forth between tears of soulful recognition and laugh-out-loud moments of wonderful remembrances. There is something truthful and powerful about the artist who is willing to put a masterpiece together and leave the telltale signs of failed attempts. Too many who reflect on their past do so to minimize imperfection, setting standards unreachable by others. Ogden Rogers has charted a course of professionalism that encourages creativity, allowing for errors, and guided by honest reflection and dedication to those whom he would serve. This read is a gift to all, whether they are starting or ending their journey of service to others."
    Terry L. Singer, Ph.D., Dean, Kent School of Social Work, University of Louisville

"I found the stories humorous, sometimes painful, and incredibly honest and real. There is really nothing else out in our literature that is quite like this. It reminds me of when we teach the art and science of social work practice—this is the art."
    Jennifer Clements, Ph.D., LCSW, Associate Professor, Shippensburg University

"...a profound piece of creative literature that will reinstill idealism within senior social workers who are on the threshold of being cynical about their work."
    Stephen M. Marson, Ph.D., Professor, University of North Carolina Pembroke

"Recommended reading for new social workers, experienced social workers, friends and families of social workers, and future social workers because of the variety of anecdotal case presentations and personal perceptions. Truly open and honest portrayals of social work and the helping professions with touching, easy-to-read entries fit within the beginning, middle, and ending framework. This book is suggested for both public and academic libraries to support the career services and/or professional development collections."
    Rebecca S. Traub, M.L.S., Library Specialist, Temple University Harrisburg

For the complete
Table of Contents of
Ogden Rogers'
**Beginnings, Middles, & Ends**

and other information
about this book, see:

**beginningsmiddlesandends.com**

Available directly from the publisher now! Available in print and Kindle editions at Amazon.com.

## ABOUT THE AUTHOR

**Ogden W. Rogers, Ph.D., LCSW, ACSW,** is Professor and Chair of the Department of Social Work at The University of Wisconsin-River Falls. He has been a clinician, consultant, educator, and storyteller.

ISBN: 978-1-929109-35-7 • 2013 • 5.5 x 8.5 • 249 pages • $19.95 plus shipping  Order from White Hat Communications, PO Box 5390, Harrisburg, PA 17110-0390
http://shop.whitehatcommunications.com  717-238-3787 (phone)  717-238-2090 (fax)

# The New Social Worker ®

### the social work careers magazine

Summer 2014
Volume 21, Number 3

*Hawaii Pacific University (HPU) BSW 2014 graduates proudly celebrated their pinning ceremony on Wednesday, May 14, 2014, at the Hawaii Loa Campus, which overlooks the beautiful Ko'olau Mountains in Kaneohe, Hawaii. (L-R) Row 1: Queayla Camacho Sablan. Row 2: Gabrielle Schwing, Maricel Lorenzo, Francis Jessica Agtarap Galera, Carly Jean, and Samantha Lorenzo. Row 3: Ana Maria Snyder, Jimberly Valenzuela, Jessica Valdez, Jazmynn Kapua Oliveira, Breana-Malia Asuncion and Mia Arceo. Row 4: Nathan Alfaro, Tobias Tenorio, Samantha Leutu, and Jeremiah Tubon. Photo credit: Evalani Lorenzo.*

# FEATURES

## Turn Up the Tech in Social Work

## Social Work Goes to the Movies— Belle

## Reviews

# In This Issue

Student Role Model: Whitney Sewell

## ...and much more!

# DID YOU KNOW...

...Depending on your state of practice, you may be required to report or warn about a potentially harmful or dangerous client?

**NASW does.**

Our Risk Management Helpline exists to help you navigate important state-specific issues like the duty to warn.

State Licensing Board Inquiries | Conflicts of Interest | **Duty to Warn** | Supplemental Liability | Tail Coverage | Deposition Expense Coverage *

**NASW™**
Assurance Services
*Where Social Workers Come First™*

······················· DUTY TO WARN ···············

## How This Affects You

If you are working with a client who has admitted anger issues, you may discover that he or she has harmed someone in the past. Depending on your state of practice, you may be required to warn about your client's risk to do harm again — either to him/herself or to another person. For many social workers, this causes an ethical and legal dilemma: keep your client's information confidential or fulfill an obligation to warn your state about a potentially dangerous situation?

*5% Premium discount included when you sign up online!*

## What the NASW-Endorsed Policy Can Do to Protect You

The NASW-Endorsed Professional Liability Insurance Program offers an exclusive Risk Management Helpline to support insured policyholders with such questions. Staffed by personnel experienced in risk and claims management, the helpline provides assistance on how to handle such situations.

**Want to know more?**
Visit us online today!

**Don't have NASW-Endorsed Professional Liability Insurance? ENROLL NOW!**
Visit **www.naswassurance.org/pli** to sign up online. Or, call **855-385-2160** to enroll over the phone. You must be a member of NASW to participate in our exceptional program.

*  Learn about all the issues you face and what the NASW-Endorsed Policy can do to protect you. Visit **www.naswassurance.org/pli** today.

ILLUSTRATION: CAROLYN BELEFSKI

# CONTENTS

THE NEW SOCIAL WORKER®
Summer 2014
Volume 21, Number 3

## FEATURES

## DEPARTMENTS

# Publisher's Thoughts

Dear Reader,

I hope you are having a great summer so far! In this column, I want to take a moment to recognize THE NEW SOCIAL WORKER's Editorial Advisory Board. We welcome two new members to the board, Brad Forenza and Mozart Guerrier. Brad and Mozart are relatively new social workers who will bring a fresh new perspective to the group. Vivian Bergel, Joseph Davenport, Judith Davenport, and Sam Hickman are long-time members of the board. I appreciate the input, dedication, and support of all of our Editorial Advisory Board members!

*The publisher/editor*

This issue could be called the "tips" issue! I love articles that provide real ideas for readers to help them with a concern. In this issue, we have tips for students new to field placement, tips for writing a great résumé, and tips for new/young social work supervisors.

In addition, we look at how one school of social work is teaching cultural competence, a social worker's reflections on war, and a poetry therapy group for hostility reduction in a correctional facility. Other articles focus on what happens when a non-social worker becomes a social worker and realizes she has been an "impersonator," how strong foster kids are, and a new model for screening and treating people with substance disorders.

I want to call your attention to a new section of our website! In April, we launched the nonprofit management and nonprofit ethics pages. On these pages, you can read the FULL text of several nonprofit management books, including a brand new book on nonprofit ethics. These books and pages are not specifically for social workers, but for all nonprofit managers. Please take a look, and share these resources with colleagues. The ethics pages are at *http://www.socialworker. com/nonprofit/ethics,* and the management pages are at *http://www.socialworker.com/ nonprofit/management.*

To subscribe to THE NEW SOCIAL WORKER's Social Work E-News and notifications of new issues of the magazine, go to the "Subscribe" link on our website at *http://www.socialworker.com.* (It's free!)

Until next time—enjoy the rest of the summer, and happy reading!

*Linda M. Grobman*

## Write for The New Social Worker

We are looking for articles from social work practitioners, students, and educators.

Some areas of particular interest are: social work ethics; student field placement; practice specialties; social work careers/job search; technology; "what every new social worker needs to know;" and news of unusual, creative, or nontraditional social work.

Feature articles run 1,500-2,000 words in length. News articles are typically 100-150 words. Our style is conversational, practical, and educational. Write as if you are having a conversation with a student or colleague. What do you want him or her to know about the topic? What would you want to know? Use examples.

The best articles have a specific focus. If you are writing an ethics article, focus on a particular aspect of ethics. For example, analyze a specific portion of the NASW *Code of Ethics* (including examples), or talk about ethical issues unique to a particular practice setting. When possible, include one or two resources at the end of your article—books, additional reading materials, and/or websites.

We also want photos of social workers and social work students "in action" for our cover, and photos to accompany your news articles!

Send submissions to lindagrobman@socialworker.com.

# The New Social Worker

Summer 2014
Vol. 21, Number 3

*Publisher/Editor*
Linda May Grobman, MSW, ACSW, LSW

*Contributing Writers*
Barbara Trainin Blank
Allan Barsky, JD, MSW, Ph.D.
Addison Cooper, LCSW
Ellen Belluomini, LCSW
Kathryn A. Krase, Ph.D., J.D., MSW

THE NEW SOCIAL WORKER® (ISSN 1073-7871) is published four times a year by White Hat Communications, P.O. Box 5390, Harrisburg, PA 17110-0390. Phone: (717) 238-3787. Fax: (717) 238-2090. Send address corrections to: lindagrobman@socialworker.com

Advertising rates available on request.

Copyright © 2014 White Hat Communications. All rights reserved. No part of this publication may be reproduced in any form without the express written permission of the publisher. The opinions expressed in *THE NEW SOCIAL WORKER* are those of the authors and are not necessarily shared by the publisher.

Photo/art credits: Image from BigStockPhoto.com © Monkeybusinessimages (page 4), iqoncept (page 6), Ragsac (page 10), Mr. Smith (page 18), chrisroll (page 28). Photo from Pixabay: page 8 and page 14.

## Editorial Advisory Board
Vivian Bergel, Ph.D., ACSW, LSW
Joseph Davenport, Ph.D.
Judith Davenport, Ph.D., LCSW
Brad Forenza, MSSW
Mozart Guerrier, MSW
Sam Hickman, MSW, ACSW, LCSW

Send all editorial, advertising, subscription, and other correspondence to:

**THE NEW SOCIAL WORKER**
**White Hat Communications**
**P.O. Box 5390**
**Harrisburg, PA 17110-0390**
**(717) 238-3787 Phone**
**(717) 238-2090 Fax**

lindagrobman@socialworker.com
http://www.socialworker.com
http://www.facebook.com/newsocialworker
http://www.twitter.com/newsocialworker

**Print Edition:**
http://newsocialworker.magcloud.com

# Whitney Sewell

*by Barbara Trainin Blank*

Whitney Sewell's high energy level might stem partly from a "full childhood."

"My four brothers and I had a great imagination and were involved in intricate play, inside or outside," she says. "I loved playing."

Still, life had its challenges. Sewell's parents were divorced, although her father remained active in their lives. Her mother was on welfare for a time–the family lived in Section 8 housing.

Then, as part of a welfare-to-work program, her mother got a job as a library assistant. "She came home every day with a bagful of books, and we dived in," Sewell recalls. "I remember learning about the Montgomery Boycott and photosynthesis and seeing videos like 'West Side Story.'" Even with her vivid imagination, Sewell never dreamed she would complete an MSW degree from the University of North Carolina, Chapel Hill. She has just completed that program and will enter a doctoral program in the fall.

Social workers once occupied a negative place in her life. "The overall attitude was that they were 'baby snatchers,' who came in and said parents weren't fit. I was socialized to have those perceptions."

The perceptions didn't budge much, even when helpful social workers found her mother work and "challenged my initial assumptions in a good way," Sewell says.

Yet, she was interested in going into the helping professions. The eye-opener came when she took some time off from college to work at the Veterans hospital and realized social workers were doing intake and therapy.

"I thought that was so cool," Sewell says. "I started doing research into the different helping professions, and things started clicking."

The road to a B.A. was rocky. Sewell spent time at Tufts and at Ashford University without getting a degree, because of financial difficulties. Finally, at Penn State University, she completed the goal. "I love Penn State for encouraging me," she says. "I did everything in three semesters."

The 28-year-old will start doctoral studies at Washington University's George Warren Brown School of Social Work in the fall. She has been awarded the university's generous Chancellor's Fellowship for Doctoral Studies.

"I definitely want to work at a university as a professor–doing a lot of research, adding to the body of knowledge, and producing future social workers," says Sewell, who initially wanted to be a clinician. "My professors definitely had a profound influence on me."

When Professor Anne Jones, clinical associate professor, met Sewell in class for the first time, she considered her a "firecracker."

"I remember that Whitney stood out–in her goals, dreams, interests, and vision for the future," Jones recalls. "It wasn't that she was tremendously verbal, but she had energy; there were real fires burning. When she had something to say in class, it was something meaningful."

Jones became Sewell's "informal mentor" and field instructor this past year. Typically, she said, graduate students don't have much to do with undergrads. But Sewell became active with the LGBTQ Center as a safe zone coordinator–on top of a full academic load and an internship–and "did an amazing job." Sewell was also one of only two students

in the "self-directed program" at UNC, combining macro and direct practice.

Assistant Professor Sarah E. Bledsoe also taught Sewell, who was part of Bledsoe's research team. Under Bledsoe's guidance, Sewell presented at the Society for Social Work and Research conference and is working on an additional presentation. One topic that particularly interested the MSW student was the impact of being a minority student on one's engagement in school, including which academic courses are chosen.

"Whitney is not only an incredible critical thinker, but is very intelligent and hard-working," Bledsoe states. "She sought out professors who shared areas of interest and goes above and beyond–taking a qualitative research course generally for doctoral students. She's the kind of student you want to go the extra mile for, because she has so much to offer."

Sewell was a graduate research assistant on four different projects at UNC and contributed to several research papers in peer-reviewed edited publications and a book.

While at UNC, Sewell served as the graduate advisor for the undergraduate student group Diversity and Inclusiveness in Collegiate Environments, formed in response to the high attrition rates and recruitment of ethnic minority students. She was one of eight students awarded

*Whitney Sewell continued on page 25*

*Whitney Sewell continued on page 25*

Whitney Sewell

# Ethics

# Teaching Cultural Competence: A Closer Look at Racial and Ethnic Identity Formation
## by Ebony Hall, Ph.D., M.Div., LMSW, and Shelia Lindsey

*Editor's Note: Our ethics columnist, Allan Barsky, will return in the next issue.*

The new social worker of tomorrow is emerging with a new way of critical thinking and a new way of application. *The new social worker is different, not settling or conforming for reasons of financial stability and job security. The new social worker is on a path of self-discovery and has embraced acceptance, where he or she is from, and all that it entails. The new social worker speaks with confidence about race and ethnicity and knows about his or her culture. Are we ready?*

For several decades, the social work profession has effectively saturated academia with various models of practice for students to be knowledgeable about other cultures in order to be culturally competent and sensitive (Sue, 1991; Locke, 1992; Poston, 1990; Rodgers & Potocky, 1998). As a younger generation of social workers emerges, the emphasis on identity not only creates a "more comprehensive view of cultural competence" (Garran & Rozas, 2013, p. 99), but attributes to a larger notion of being a healthy professional. The competency of social workers is limited when they do not possess tools of acknowledgment that can affect them when working with diverse populations. Teaching students to be mindful of and sensitive to issues, from potential language barriers to recognizing various religious sects, plays a role in effective practice. However, if the massive "elephant in the room" continues to be overlooked, ethnicity and race will continue to have an influence on professional and personal relationships, leading to insufficient cultural competence resulting in poor services (Seipel & Way, 2006).

The social work profession is built upon culturally sensitive practices that advocate for social and economic justice for those who are disadvantaged, oppressed, and/or discriminated against. Standard 1.05(c) in the National Association of Social Workers' (NASW) *Code of Ethics* (NASW, 2000), reminds social workers of their duty to be culturally competent and to purposefully "obtain education about and seek to under-

stand the nature of social diversity and oppression." NASW's National Committee on Racial and Ethnic Diversity (NASW, 2001) highlights this necessity by identifying standards that make up culturally competent practices, including self-awareness, cross-cultural knowledge, skills, and leadership. Although "diversity is taking on a broader meaning to include the sociocultural experiences of people of different genders, social classes, religious and spiritual beliefs, sexual orientations, ages, and physical and mental abilities" (p. 8), the historical impact of race on American society continues to play an integral part in the development and effectiveness of culturally competent practice.

*Race* is a social construct (American Anthropological Association, 1998) with the sole intention of separation and power based on the color of one's skin. More accurate terms of *ethnicity* and *ethnic origin* have begun to emerge, not to displace the term of "race," but rather to highlight a significant component of ethnic and national origin. Because of the impact "race" has had on society, it continues to be a necessary concept to acknowledge as the profession takes the journey toward fully embracing racial and ethnic identity.

Many institutions of higher learning create such space for students to explore identity formation through its emphasis on self-awareness. Within that emphasis is the basic act of each student to acknowledge one's own racial and ethnic identity, especially White social work students, who are too often lumped together and struggle with identifying their ethnic roots and culture. Because White social workers make up more than half of the social workers in the United States

(Whitaker, Weismiller, & Clark, 2006), it becomes vital for White students to take a journey of racial and ethnic self-discovery, not on the backs of students of color, but alongside them.

Some continue to ask, "Why is racial and ethnic identity important to social workers in practice?" The answer is that knowing who you are influences how you interact. Casey Family Programs (2013) promotes identity formation through a three-part curriculum for social work professionals. It assists professionals in knowing how to explore race and ethnicity. The *Knowing Who You Are* curriculum prepares social workers to foster "healthy development of their constituent's racial and ethnic identity" (Casey Family Programs, 2013).

Carolyne Rodriguez, LCSW, retired Texas State Strategy Director of Casey Family Programs, emphasizes the need to promote and instill identity formation for future and current social workers. She states, "It is essential that social workers providing services to children, youth, and families have a solid understanding of their own cultural identities. If they are to effectively promote racial and ethnic pride with clients and are to demonstrate an understanding of the importance of culture, race, and ethnicity, this starts with knowing themselves. It is from this foundation that children, youth, and families will experience respect and appreciation for their cultural identities from social workers who are working with them and on their behalf."

Efforts that promote racial and ethnic identity formation are beneficial. However, it means students have to acknowledge and accept a history that is filled with acts of hatred based on power and privilege. Acknowledging institutional and individual acts of racism is uncomfortable for both White students and students of color, but all students need to learn about the history of racism and its role in American society. Racism continues to be "a silent code that systematically closes the doors of opportunity to many individuals" (NASW Delegate Assembly, 1998). As stated by Blank (2006), "Despite the decades that have passed since the beginning of the civil rights movement, racism is still a major issue in America." This fact urges students to acknowledge the role that race plays in society, but also to accept their responsibility to acknowledge their own racial and ethnic identity and the role it plays and will play in their personal and professional life. Without such awareness, "social workers contribute to [the] oppression when working with clients" (Seipel & Way, 2006), and any other persons with whom they may interact.

Having a healthy sense of racial and ethnic identity needs to be fostered in the classroom. Many social work programs offer a course that speaks to diversity and culture as part of the student's degree plan. These courses serve as great opportunities for students to begin or continue their self-awareness. Through its Center for Diversity and Social Economic Justice, the Council on Social Work Education (2013) promotes the integration of education that "fosters the achievement of diversity." Social work practitioners are charged with delivering culturally competent services to the participants served. They should be able to respond to "people of all cultures, languages, classes, races, ethnic backgrounds, religions, and other diversity factors" (Garran & Rozas, 2013, p. 98). This charge is accompanied by the expectation of social work programs to instill such competency through active learning strategies, allowing students to examine their racial and ethnic identity and how it contributes to who they are personally and professionally. These courses are pivotal in equipping culturally competent and culturally sensitive social work practitioners.

The social work program at Tarleton State University continues to emphasize the importance of all social work students to acknowledge, accept, and activate their racial and ethnic identity as one of the first steps toward becoming a healthy social work professional. Similar to other smaller social work programs, Tarleton's main campus is primarily comprised of traditional White social work students with limited exposure to diverse groups and different cultures. The inception of the "Diverse Populations" course has provided an avenue of self-discovery, which has proven to be valuable for all of the students.

"The importance of learning your own race and ethnic identity is being able to understand and acknowledge where you came from. The more you understand about yourself, the easier it will be to work with all types of individuals who are trying to find themselves," wrote Alexis, an undergraduate sophomore of German and Hungarian descent.

Social work students of color are also learning from the course in a manner that allows them not only to share their personal stories of institutional racism, but to hear stories from their White colleagues to develop a better understanding of White culture, ethnicity, and White privilege. "When they ask me questions about my hair or about the music I listen to, I try educating them. Then I will ask them to tell me about some of their physical characteristics and interests," said Brandi, a senior of African American and Indian descent.

During a project for the course titled "Individual Diversity," students are encouraged to explore their own diversity. Christina, a junior with various racial and ethnic backgrounds (German, Blackfoot Indian, Swedish, and African American), utilized Poston's (1990) Biracial Identity Development Model to assist her on her journey toward racial and ethnic identity formation. She said, "I remember as a child receiving a Black doll for my birthday. I cried. At that time, I thought the color of your palm determined what color you were. It was at that time my mother told me that I was Black. I didn't understand."

Like Christina, many students who have taken this course and others similar have continued to support such educational activities to allow them to increase their self-awareness to better inform and equip them as generalist practitioners.

Overall, such efforts by accredited social work programs across the country value the importance of facilitating the racial and ethnic identity of all students and supporting an atmosphere of professional health. The course has proven to be effective for students of other majors as well. "Both parents came from Mexico at a very young age. My parents did a good job integrating their culture in my upbringing and I never felt ashamed. As a result, I am also teaching my son about my culture, not the Mexican American one," said Crystal, a junior of Mexican descent majoring in nursing. The course has evolved to include students pursuing degrees in child and family studies, criminal justice, nursing, and psychology.

## References

American Anthropological Association. (1998). *Statement on race*. Retrieved from: http://www.aaanet.org/stmts/racepp.htm

Blank, B. (2006). Racism: The challenge for social workers. *The New Social Worker, 13* (4).

Casey Family Programs. (2013). *Knowing who you are*. Retrieved from: http://www.casey.org/resources/initiatives/KnowingWhoYouAre/

Council on Social Work Education. (2013). *Diversity Center mission*. Retrieved from: http://www.cswe.org/CentersInitiatives/Diversity/AboutDiversity/51129.aspx

Garran, A., & Rozas, L. (2013). Cultural competence revisited. *Journal of Ethnic and Cultural Diversity in Social Work, 22* (2), 1-10.

Locke, D. C. (1992). *Increasing multicultural understanding: A comprehensive model*. Newbury Park: Sage Publications.

National Association of Social Workers. (2001). *NASW standards for cultural competence in social work practice*. Washington, D. C.: NASW.

National Association of Social Workers. (2000). *NASW code of ethics*. Washington, DC: NASW.

National Association of Social Workers Delegate Assembly. (1998). *Racism*. Retrieved from: https://www.socialworkers.org/pressroom/2013/Racism.pdf

Poston, W. (1990). The biracial identity development model: A needed addition. *Journal of Counseling and Development, 69*, 152–155.

Rodgers, A., & Potocky, M. (1998). Preparing students to work with culturally diverse clients. *Social Work Education, 17* (1). 95-100.

Seipel, A., & Way, I. (2006). Culturally competent social work: Practice with Latino clients. *The New Social Worker, 13* (4).

Sue, D. W. (1991). A conceptual model for cultural diversity training. *Journal of Counseling & Development, 70*, 99-105.

Whitaker, T., Weismiller, T., & Clark, E. (2006). *Assuring the sufficiency of a frontline workforce: A national study of licensed social workers*. NASW Center for Workforce Studies.

*Ebony L. Hall, Ph.D., M.Div., LMSW, is an assistant professor and campus coordinator at Tarleton State University. Shelia Lindsey is a BSW student at Tarleton State University. Shelia will graduate with her BSW in the summer of 2014.*

FOLLOW ME ON TWITTER

**The New Social Worker is on Twitter! Follow us at:**
*http://www.twitter.com/newsocialworker*

# Field Placement

## 8 Tips for New Social Work Interns
### by Sharon Young, Ph.D, LCSW

*Editor's Note: Within the context of this article, the terms intern and internship refer to the social work field placement or practicum.*

A year ago last fall, I began my academic career as the field coordinator at a medium-sized BSW program in Connecticut. Looking back over my first year, it was not unlike what a new intern experiences when beginning the semester at a new placement. The early days were both exciting and terrifying. There was so much to learn and process as I adjusted to my new role. I relied on the expertise of my new colleagues to teach me the ropes and to support me when I struggled. I found a mentor who provided me with guidance and a sounding board when I needed one.

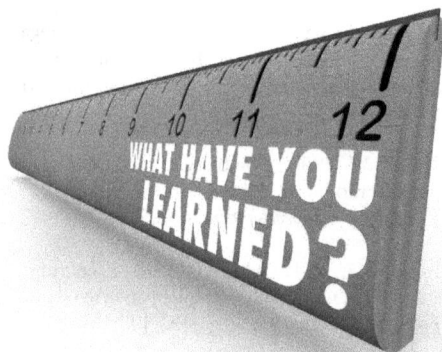

Like a social work intern, I learned on the job by applying the education and experience I brought with me. As you begin your fieldwork, you will learn how to apply your experiences to your new role as social work intern. This article will provide you with some tips and insider information that can make your transition to your internship smoother.

Social work is a demanding profession. As social workers, we understand and respond to a myriad of political, social, interpersonal, and intrapersonal forces that affect the people we serve. Social workers assume a broad range of roles and duties that span wider than those of other human service providers.

As a profession, we are the Jack (and Jill) of all trades. In just one position at a neighborhood agency, I have been a community organizer, a group worker, a clinician, a grant writer, and a program manager. Among my varied tasks, I have driven clients to the hospital, gone camping with a youth group, organized a task force of mental health care providers, and provided crisis support for grieving teens. I know my experience is not unique, in that all social workers will face a wide range of challenges, big and small. My job as a social work educator is to prepare students for the many roles they will play as professionals.

I am no expert on field education. Drawing from my experiences as a student, social worker, field instructor, field liaison, and now coordinator, I have been able to see all sides of the field education experience. I learned many valuable lessons, and I want to share them with you.

1.  *It's normal to be nervous and unsure in the beginning.* For some students, the first field placement is their initial step into a professional world. Even for seasoned students, each workplace brings a new set of challenges and expectations. There is a lot to learn in the beginning. Take your time and ask questions. No one expects you to know the job before you start.
2.  *Always begin with a learner's stance.* Learning involves watching, listening, asking questions, rehearsing, and practicing. You will find that there will be several people at your field placement who are happy to share their knowledge with you. You will likely learn as much from the clients or consumers as you do from the staff. Allow everyone the opportunity to share their expertise with you.
3.  *Practice, practice, practice.* Your internship not only provides you with exposure to the field of social work, but also allows you to try out your new skills. If you learned an engagement technique in your practice class, put it to use when meeting a new client. How about applying your knowledge about adolescent development when working with a parent group?
4.  *Beware of field placement envy.* When you are sitting in seminar listening to your classmate describe a fantastic field experience, don't despair about your own. Many placements start out bumpy, but they often improve as you become more skilled and empowered to take on more challenging work.
5.  *If you think your field instructor isn't providing you with challenging assignments, discuss it with him or her.* Field instructors sometimes like to start students out slowly, so they can be sure the intern is prepared for what is to come. It is helpful to go over your learning agreement with your field instructor throughout the semester, to make sure your agency assignments match your learning goals.
6.  *If you are having difficulty at your agency, tell someone.* Students sometimes have trouble discussing difficulties with new field instructors or faculty liaisons. Don't be afraid to ask for help. Your field instructor and professors are there to help you negotiate difficult situations and to aid you in reflecting on your practice decisions.
7.  *Develop your professional identity.* At your field placement, you will be learning what it means to be a social worker, especially if working in a multi-disciplinary environment. What roles do social workers play on treatment teams, in community meetings, in a residential setting? Remember to identify yourself as the *social work* intern, not just the *intern*.
8.  *Remember, you are making professional contacts along the way.* Make sure you leave a good impression in every professional setting. You may be meeting potential future employers at your next community meeting or task force. Make sure you introduce yourself to others when at larger agency meetings, trainings, or when visiting other agencies.

I remember the feelings of anxiety I felt as an MSW student entering a new field placement. The first weeks of field placement bring many new challenges–establishing yourself as a professional, learning the organizational culture and structure, and finding a work-life balance. It becomes especially challenging when you begin to face clients and community groups and start to connect what you learned in Practice I to the real world.

Fieldwork gives social work students an opportunity to apply academic training to a professional setting. Practicing social work skills in field practicum leads to greater learning outcomes and higher satisfaction for students (Lee & Fortune, 2013). Make the most of your internship by applying and practicing your newly learned skills and knowledge.

As an intern, you are establishing the foundation for your social work career. As a professional social worker, it is important for you to develop supportive and open relationships with colleagues and supervisors. These relationships will provide a source of both support and challenge for you throughout your career. Make sure you develop a sound relationship with your field instructor and other supportive social workers and benefit from their knowledge and experience.

Having a strong on-site supervisor has been associated with greater learning satisfaction in social work interns (Cleak & Smith, 2012). Practicing social work can be stressful and emotionally difficult work, even for veteran social workers. It is important that you keep the lines of communication open with your field liaison, faculty members, and field instructors when things get difficult.

Social work students often turn to friends, family members, or fellow students to discuss stressful or emotionally charged field situations (Litvack, Mishna, & Bogo, 2010). Discussing difficult client situations with friends and family could lead to a breach of confidentiality and could also compromise your professional career. Your faculty and field instructors are there to help you and to guide you through sticky situations. Use them.

You are in the process of not only learning how to be a social worker but also how to manage the emotional toll this work can bring. Over the years, you will find the support of supervisors and colleagues to be important in avoiding burnout, especially when you are a new practitioner (Hamama, 2012).

## References

Cleak, H., & Smith, D. (2012). Student satisfaction with models of field placement supervision. *Australian Social Work, 65* (2), 243-258. doi:10.1080/0312407X.2011.572981.

Hamama, L. (2012). Burnout in social workers treating children as related to demographic characteristics, work environment, and social support. *Social Work Research, 36* (2), 113-125. doi:10.1093/swr/svs003.

Lee, M. & Fortune, A. E. (2013). Do we need more "doing" activities or "thinking" activities in the field practicum? *Journal of Social Work Education, 49* (4), 646-660. doi:10.1080/10437797.2013.812851.

Litvack, A., Mishna, F., & Bogo, M. (2010). Emotional reactions of students in field education: An exploratory study. *Journal of Social Work Education, 46* (2), 227-243.

*Sharon L. Young, Ph.D., LCSW, is an assistant professor and field coordinator in the Department of Social Work at Western Connecticut State University. Prior to her academic career, she was a clinical social worker in the substance abuse prevention and treatment field.*

# Finding the Wisdom:
## 5 Tips for Young Supervisors
### *by Ashley Blake, BSW*

One of the most inclusive and refreshing aspects of the social work field is the diversity of its constituents. Studying and working alongside people at different points in time in their life–with different backgrounds, and different levels of experience–is not uncommon. As a result, human service providers, perhaps more than any other group of people, recognize that a passion for helping others to reach their full potential knows no color, gender, faith, or age.

Upon graduating from college with my BSW, I moved to a medium-sized city to accept a job with a medium-sized nonprofit. Not long after starting my entry-level position, it became clear that my organization was thriving and that there would be a boom in hiring, particularly within my department. Otherwise put, we were an increasingly diverse department, in an increasingly diverse nonprofit.

Four years later, I am now the manager of my department, supervising a group of passionate, committed staff, some of whom are more than a decade older than I. Although I was fully aware of this fact when I accepted the position, it didn't negate my inherent discomfort about supervising people who were older than me.

It wasn't long before the apprehension crept in. In every team meeting, every performance review I conducted, and almost every moment of supervision, I found myself fretting: *Am I being taken seriously? Is this person willing to take direction from someone with less work experience? What could I possibly teach this person that he or she doesn't already know?*

For weeks, I could feel myself shrinking under these fears. Then I realized...I had nothing to fear all along. In fact, once I shifted my perception, I realized I had a treasure trove of learning experiences right in front of me. I just had to be willing to look past my own self doubt. Doing so wasn't always easy, but I took steps to work past my hesitance and fulfill my managerial role with confidence and humility.

For those of you similarly rising through the ranks at a young age, here are my top five tips for kicking the cold feet and embracing your manager status.

## 1) Recognize your strengths.

A strengths-based approach may be our go-to when working with clients, but many of us find it difficult to extend the same encouragement and acceptance to ourselves. Nevertheless, taking the time to recognize what it is about yourself that you value and appreciate goes a long way toward helping you understand why you're destined for success.

Eventually, as self doubt began to sneak in about my ability to lead and manage my department, I was forced to remember why I would be great at the job (cue forced smile)! Besides, what choice did I have but to show up every day and do my best? It may not have been as easy as willing my confidence and watching it appear, but I began to put the "I can do this" pieces together. After all, what the position needed was someone who was familiar with the field, familiar with the history of the department, excited about the job, compassionate, organized, and motivated. And what do you know–I was all those things! Slowly but surely, acceptance of my strengths far surpassed the ways in which I thought I was unsuitable for the job.

Alas, I've learned that feelings of defeat are not uncommon in our field, whether it's the seemingly endless budget cuts that diminish much-needed resources for the people we're serving, or a challenging interaction with our clients or co-workers. In the end, exercising the ease with which we're able to find the productive and valuable in any situation serves not only us, but our clients, as well.

## 2) Be willing to embrace your weaknesses.

Let's face it. Just as we each have areas of expertise, so too do we have areas of our career and personal life that we find challenging and tedious. Luckily, recognizing and working through these weaknesses is a task that we (hopefully) learned to address during our social work studies. In fact, it may have been one of the biggest takeaways from my time as a student, as I find it continually serving me in so many ways–not the least of which was to apply my ability for personal reflection and insight to the anxiety I was having around my new manager status. Just as I had to acknowledge the strengths that helped me get to where I was, I had to know the barriers that would prevent me from succeeding. Once I knew the areas in which I might falter, I knew where to step back as needed, and when to push myself harder.

More importantly, I knew what strengths to look for and cultivate in my staff. For instance, I sometimes struggle to see the proverbial forest through the trees. If you need someone to get lost in the details with, to think through every step in every process with, I'm your woman. If what you need is to see the biggest picture possible–to envision the outcomes of a program five years down the line–I may not be your go-to person. Knowing this, I'll often turn to one of my staff who I know has a knack for thinking broader and larger in scope. Asking for her input and explaining why I need it (don't be afraid to admit that you can't do it all!) has helped me to successfully address the task at hand. At the end of the day, I've learned something new, my staff knows they are valued members of the department, and both my team and I are stronger.

## 3) Trust the belief that others have in you.

My mom asked me once, after I shared my anxiety about supervising staff with more years in the field, "Do you think your boss is a smart woman?" "Yes, of course," I replied, somewhat confounded by the question. I elaborated, "She's knowledgeable, well respected, and trusted in the industry." "Why then," my mom responded, "don't you believe that she knew what she was doing when she picked you to run this program?" She was right. This pointed out a ridiculous oversight on my part, I must admit, but common of people moving through the throes of incertitude.

Thankfully, as we sometimes struggle aimlessly to see how we're doing absolutely anything right, there are people around us who can see just how well we're able to handle the multitude of responsibilities that come our way, and it behooves us to listen. Listen and trust. Once we accept the belief and encouragement we receive from people in our lives as more than nice sounding compliments, we will learn to see them as truth.

## 4) Stay open to growth.

Many people feel that to progress in life, one must be open to growth. Allowing the opportunity for new experiences, ideas, and tools to find their way into our lives is one way of ensuring that we get smarter, savvier, and more gracious with every passing year. Interestingly, these paths toward growth may be paved with rough roads, and what may actually be a blessing can sometimes feel like a curse.

Around the same time I was promoted to my current position, so was one of my co-workers. We were both thankful for our promotions but anxious to prove our worth. Soon, we found ourselves getting to work early, skipping lunches, leaving later, and even dreaming about work! We were tired, stressed, and terrified of failing. As we were leaving one night, long after everyone else, we stood in the parking lot questioning whether we had made the right decisions in accepting our new positions. We wondered whether we would ever get a handle on our roles and responsibilities. Satisfied with our grumbling, and knowing another day was looming large, we got in our cars and drove home. That same conversation happened many more times over the next few months, and yet, we continued to show up and push ourselves to do good work. In the end, we were simply doing what most of us do when faced with a challenge: Put one foot in front of the other and keep moving.

Now, I look back on those early days with fondness. It was a rough road, but so worth the journey. There are still weeks when I feel tired, stressed, and terrified of failing, but I know that I'm growing into that smarter, savvier, and more gracious person.

## 5) Remember your shared purpose.

Each of the tips I mention here acted as one of many tools in my toolbox, as no one affirmation was able to fully snap me back to a place of confidence and contentment—except one. At the end of every day, I found myself—if even for a moment—reveling in the camaraderie and inspiration that stemmed from working alongside such kind, smart, and hard-working people who share my vision for a more equitable, inclusive, and compassionate world. In those moments, it doesn't matter who is a manager and who is not; or who is older and who is younger. Ultimately, what matters in those moments, and every moment, is that you find a job, or a city or a family where your efforts, your wisdom, and your heart align with those around you, to help make this world a little bit better than how you found it.

*Ashley Blake is a manager at a nonprofit organization providing affordable housing and resident services to seniors and families earning low incomes. She graduated Summa Cum Laude with a Bachelor of Social Work from Eastern Michigan University and is a past contributor to* The New Social Worker. *Ashley resides in Portland, Oregon.*

# 10 Essential Tips for Your Amazing Social Work Résumé
## by Valerie Arendt, MSW, MPP

Is your résumé ready to send out to employers? You have Googled example résumé templates, perfected your formatting, and added appropriate action words. Everything is in the correct tense, in reverse chronological order, and kept to two pages or less. What else should you think about for an amazing social work résumé? Whether you are a clinical or macro social worker, student, new professional, or have been in the field for 30 years, these essential tips will keep your résumé ready to send out to your future employer.

## 1. Objective or Professional Summary?

Let's start at the beginning. I am not a fan of the objective, and neither are many hiring managers. If they are reading your résumé, they already

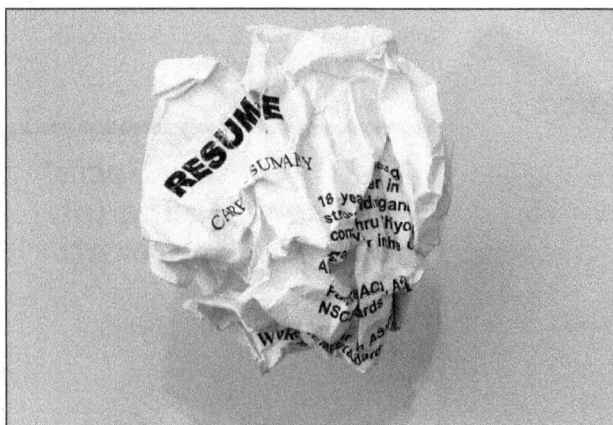

know you are seeking a position with them. Generally, an objective is used by someone who has recently graduated or has very little experience. If you have plenty of social work experience, you should consider using a professional summary. This is one to three sentences at the beginning of your résumé that help describe the value you bring as a social worker through your skills and experience. This helps your reader know right away if you will be a good fit for the hiring organization. It is much easier for a hiring manager to find that value in a short paragraph than trying to piece it together from a lengthy history of professional experience and education.

*DON'T: Objective: Seeking a social work position within a facility where I can utilize my experience to the benefit of my employer as well as gain knowledge and professional growth.*

*DO: Licensed Clinical Social Worker with 6+ years experience in medical and mental health settings, working with diverse populations in private practice, health care, outpatient, and inpatient treatment settings. Recently relocated to Georgia.*

## 2. Don't assume your reader already knows what you do.

This is one of the biggest mistakes I see when reviewing résumés. Write your résumé as if the person reading it has no idea what you do. Really? Yes! This will help you to be descriptive about your experience. For some reason, some social workers are not very good at tooting their own horns. Your résumé is exactly the place you need to brag about what an amazing professional you are. Don't assume that because your title was "Outpatient Therapist," the reader of your résumé will know exactly what you did. Be descriptive. Give a little information about the organization or program, the clients, and the type of therapy or work you performed. This can easily be done in three to five bullets if you craft thoughtful, complete sentences.

*DON'T: Provide psychotherapy to clients.*

*DO: Provide group and individual outpatient therapy to adult clients at a substance abuse treatment center utilizing Cognitive Behavioral Therapy (CBT), Dialectical Behavioral Therapy (DBT), psychoeducation, and motivational interviewing.*

## 3. List your accomplishments.

If you worked in a position for five years but don't list one relevant accomplishment, that is a red flag for a hiring manager. Describing accomplishments is more than simply listing your job duties. These are the contributions you have made in your career that would encourage an organization to hire you.

Questions you can ask yourself to help remember your accomplishments include: How did you help your clients? Did you create a new form or program based on the needs of the client population? Did your therapy skills reduce the relapse rate in your agency? Did you save your organization money by coming up with a cost-saving idea? Were you selected for special projects, committees, or task forces? Even if the only social work experience you have on your résumé is your field placement, you should be able to list an accomplishment that will entice the reader to want to know more.

*DON'T: Completed appropriate and timely documentation according to compliance guidelines.*

*DO: Recognized need for updated agency forms. Developed 10 clinical and administrative forms, including no-harm contract, behavior contract, and therapist's behavior inventory, which increased staff efficiency and productivity by 15%.*

## 4. Quantify your accomplishments.

Numbers aren't just for business professionals. Numbers also help with the bragging I mentioned that needs to happen on your résumé. The most convincing accomplishments are measurable and help your résumé stand out from the crowd. How many clients did you serve? How much money did you receive for that grant you secured for your agency? How many people do you supervise?

*DON'T: Wrote grants for counseling program in schools.*

*DO: Co-wrote School Group Experiences proposal, which received a $150,000 grant from State Foundation for Health, resulting in doubling the number of children served in group counseling from 120 children to 240 children, and increasing the percentage of minority children served from 20% to 50% of the total child population in group therapy.*

## 5. Tailor your résumé to the specific job.

You have heard this over and over, and it should make sense. Still, not many social workers do this correctly or at all.

Many big organizations, hospitals, and university systems use online applicant tracking systems to review résumés. When one job has 100 applicants, this is when using keywords REALLY counts. Look at the job description for keywords.

For example, what words do they use to describe the clients? Patients, clients, residents, victims, survivors, adults, children? If you have worked with the same client populations, used the same therapy techniques, or provided the supervision listed in the job description, make sure these SAME words are in your résumé. Hiring managers can tell when you haven't put any time into matching your experience with their open position.

DON'T: *Provide in-home therapy for families.*

DO: *(Similar language from job description) Perform individual and family, agency, and home-based therapy for medically fragile children and their families (parents and siblings) with goal of maintaining intact families and improving family functioning.*

## 6. Spell out all acronyms.

Social workers LOVE to use acronyms. Many social workers spend hours writing case notes, and to be efficient, they rely on acronyms to describe their work. For the same reasons you should use keywords, it is essential that you spell things out for the computer or human resources person who may not know what certain acronyms mean. I am a social worker with limited clinical knowledge, and I often have to Google acronyms when I review NASW members' résumés. The reader responsible for finding the right candidates to interview will consider this a waste of his or her time and might move on to the rest of the résumés in the pile if he or she has no idea what you are talking about.

DON'T: *Scored and analyzed clinical assessments to include SIB-R, CBCL, CTRF, or SCQ in packets for families scheduled for autism evaluations.*

DO: *Scored and analyzed clinical assessments for autism evaluations including Scales of Independent Behavior-Revised (SIB-R), Child Behavior Checklist (CBCL), Caregiver/ Teacher Report Form (CTRF), and Social Communication Questionnaire (SCQ).*

## 7. Bullets, bullets, bullets.

Most résumés I review are succinct and formatted very nicely by bulleting experience. But there are still some folks who use paragraphs to describe their experience. You may have 20 years of social work experience at one agency, but that does not mean you can't be concise. I guarantee you that hiring managers are not going to read a paragraph that is 15 lines long to look for the experience that will fit the position they are trying to fill.

---

## Cover Letters for Social Workers: Get Yourself the Interview
*by Valerie Arendt, MSW, MPP*

Should you submit a cover letter when one is not required? The answer is *yes.* Cover letters are essential to getting an interview. They are a concise way to communicate your value to an organization, and hiring managers do use them to winnow candidates. Your cover letter should tell the employer that you are the perfect match for the position. Do this by using the language from the job description and organizational mission. It is essential to tailor your cover letter to the specific job.

Here are some basics for writing an interview-winning cover letter:

• *Salutation:* Find out who will be reading your letter. This is essential. If it is easy to find out who will be reviewing applications and you don't take the time to do this, they probably won't take the time to read your letter.
• *Name of Organization and Position Title:* The organization may have multiple openings. Be sure to indicate which position you are applying for.
• *Referral Source:* If someone in or close to the organization suggested you apply for this job, mention that person in the cover letter. This will let the reader know you have a connection to the organization and will score big points.
• *Why do you want to work for them?* You need to describe to your reader how the organization's mission and goals are a good fit for you professionally. This shows them you know about the organization and have done your homework.
• *What can you do for their clients/organization?* Sell yourself. Let them know how your experience and education is a perfect match for the position and a good fit for the organization. This is where you use the keywords from the job description to really hit it home that you are a candidate worthy of an interview.

Below is a real job description with keywords highlighted. If you have the experience they are looking for, you should invariably use the same language in your cover letter.

**Title:** Social Worker
**Job Details:** Responsible for completion of *psychosocial assessment* of *patients* and *families* enrolled in *Hospice.* Will work as *part of a team* to address *end-of-life needs,* some *counseling* and emphasis on *case management.* Able to access *homes* in *Moore & Montgomery County* service areas. Must be able to take *call rotation.* Strong *organizational skills* needed.

After a strong introductory paragraph, the body of your cover letter should be concise and address the two to four most important details from the job description:

My experience and areas of expertise are an excellent match for the requirements stated in your announcement:

• **Hospice Assessments:** As a clinician with St. John's Hospital, I prepared extensive psychosocial assessments and treatment plans for patients.
• **End-of-Life Care:** I provided counseling and accurate case management to more than 1,000 patients and their families over 7 years as a member of the St. John's Hospital end-of-life team.
• **Home Visits:** I made regular home visits to hospice patients in Moore and Montgomery Counties and was responsible for two on-call shifts per month.

Close by stating that your experience and passion make you a perfect fit for the employer. Include the best way for them to contact you for an interview.

Write your résumé in such a way that it is easy to scan and find the keywords in 30 seconds or less. Use three to eight bullets to describe your experience and accomplishments.

## 8. Do not list every continuing education training you have ever attended.

Whether or not you are licensed in your state, you should seek out continuing education in social work. Don't forget, it is in the *NASW Code of Ethics: Section 4.01 (b) Competence: "…Social workers should routinely review the professional literature and participate in continuing education relevant to social work practice and social work ethics."*

It is great to show your reader that you are up to date on the latest clinical information on your client population, but the section on your résumé for Continuing Education or Professional Development should only list the courses that are relevant to the job you are applying for. It is a great idea to keep a list of all your continuing education, for your own reference and for your license renewal. You just don't need to list them all on your résumé.

## 9. Less is more.

I hope you are seeing a theme here. Recently, I have come across a few résumés that have all of the following sections:

- Professional Summary
- Education
- Relevant Social Work Experience
- Work Experience
- Additional Experience
- Summary of Skills
- Professional Affiliations
- Volunteer Experience
- Publications
- Relevant Coursework
- Activities
- Honors

Every résumé is personal and different. You don't need 10 categories on your résumé. Professional Experience and Education are musts. but after that, limit the places hiring managers need to search to find the information that will help them decide to interview you. Only put the information that is most relevant to the job to which you are applying.

## 10. Your references should always be available upon request and not on your résumé.

If the last line on your résumé is "References Available Upon Request," this one is for you. It is not necessary to tell your reader that you have references. If you get far enough in the interview process, they will ask you for your references. Have them listed in a separate document.

Only send the references that are relevant, and only send them when asked. It is imperative that you inform your references that they may be contacted, and always send them a copy of the job description and your recent résumé, so they can be prepared when contacted. Nothing is a bigger turnoff to me than getting a call to be a reference for someone I supervised five years ago and I can't remember exactly what their job duties were. It is great to get a heads-up and a reminder of what the person did under my supervision. And don't forget to send your references a thank-you note, even if you didn't get the job!

*DON'T: References Available Upon Request*

*DO: (Separate document with your contact information at the top) References:*

*Jessica Rogers, MSW, LICSW, Director of Family Programs, Affordable Housing Authority*
*Chicago, IL*
*Relationship: Former Supervisor*
*Phone: 543-321-1234*
*rogers@email.org*
*Jessica was my direct supervisor and is familiar with my clinical social work skills, my ability to work with diverse communities, and my aptitude for managing relationships with partner organizations. Jessica recognized my success in client outcomes and promoted me within 6 months of my hire date.*

Remember, your résumé is your tool to get an interview. It doesn't need to include every detail about you as a professional social worker. Use your cover letter to expand on details that are specific to the job you are seeking. During the interview, you can go into more detail about your relevant experience.

*Valerie Arendt, MSW, MPP, is the Associate Executive Director for the National Association of Social Workers, North Carolina Chapter (NASW-NC). She received her dual degree in social work and public policy from the University of Minnesota and currently provides membership support, including résumé review, to the members of NASW-NC.*

# Home From the War: Reflections on Memorial Day
## by Don McCasland, LMSW

This year, as in other Memorial Days past, I went to nearby Fort Campbell, KY, and paid my respects to friends and buddies no longer with us. I went to each of my former unit's areas where their memorials are located, as well as at the 101st Airborne Division Monument, and left an offering at each place. As I do so at each stop, I reflect on the memories and the loss we feel as fellow Soldiers on the battlefield, as well as the loss that family and friends in their hometowns felt and continue to feel every day for the rest of their lives.

Inevitably, as the day goes on, I'll think of my own journey, and the pain I carried for YEARS–and the pain my family endured because of the wound in my soul I brought home, and carried like so many jagged rocks in my "emotional rucksack." I did that for almost seven years before I got help and began the long, slow journey toward healing. No matter how well I'm doing, I'm still on that journey and always WILL be on it. That's why I'm on the path that I walk as a person, as a Warrior, and that I walk with others as a social worker. It's part of my healing to try to show Brothers and Sisters who continue to struggle that there's light at the end of that seemingly never-ending tunnel.

We lose people every day to bombs and bullets in war zones. And people come back to the "safety" of home and continue to fight life and death battles in their minds every day. We lose almost one veteran every hour to those battles–the battles for inner peace, for their souls, for the desperate need to feel whole again. These battles are fought because of combat trauma, as the result of sexual assault, and in some cases because of both while serving our country. They fight because, even after returning, they still haven't "come home." Some win and live to fight another day. However, for far too many, it's a battle they lose. It's one that we barely hear about, and too often we don't feel the effects of... even though our communities ARE the war zone and "combatants" are everywhere we go in our daily lives.

Until recently, there was a secret I've told very few family members about, and almost no friends–that I was one of those lucky few to live and fight another day. At my very lowest point, I thought

it would be better if I was dead, and I remember that exact moment like it was yesterday. It was during my mid-tour leave on my third trip to Iraq in 2008, and I was on the riding mower in the back yard. Suddenly, I thought, "If I was dead, this would all just stop." For many people in the place I was, it can be that simple, that quick, that matter-of-fact. A sudden realization that you feel as though you have no other choice, nowhere to go. All you can think of in that most painful of moments is you want the hurt to stop. I kept that secret for almost five years, even after I retired. After all, I was a Senior Non-Commissioned Officer, responsible for the lives of 45 people in combat. I couldn't allow anyone to

know I had these thoughts. How can someone like that be counted on to stay focused when they're barely keeping it together themselves?

As professional caregivers, I urge everyone to think about those fighting their own battles amongst us. Remember that just because many of us are physically "home from the war," it doesn't mean we are emotionally and spiritually "home." Too many of us are joining the ranks of our fallen buddies from the so-called "safety" of our communities and our stateside duty stations. We WANT to come home, but it's hard to know how sometimes. It can also be hard to know just how to facilitate that start toward a "new normal."

For social workers who interact with clients as individuals or through our respective agencies, it can be something as simple as bearing witness to our truth and allowing us to be heard. It's ugly, it hurts, and it's dirty, but try it. Even if you have no personal experience with the military community, one of the biggest things that can break down barriers and

allow you to help the veteran begin the journey down the path toward healing is to hear and listen. Often, veterans are asked questions such as, "What was it like?" but because of the subject matter, once a veteran begins to share the painful and unvarnished truth, often a person's reaction is to quickly change the subject, leaving the veteran feeling as though no one cares. This can sometimes be the case with well meaning social workers. That desire to get right to an assessment, goals setting, and a plan for treatment in the name of helping... and suddenly the listening and hearing takes a back seat. Many times, this can cause the veteran to shut down and possibly never come back.

Another challenge can be the veteran dealing with hyper-vigilance in crowds, among new persons, or with unfamiliar surroundings. In combat environments, or sometimes with veterans who are victims of sexual assault, the environment can be perceived as the threat. That sense or feeling that has been ingrained in our thought process: "What's in that room with the closed door?" "Why is that briefcase there, and what's in it?" "Where are the exits, and can I get to them in a hurry?" This can lead to increased tension, irritability, or anxiety–all emotions that can be major stumbling blocks to developing rapport and beginning the therapeutic relationship. A simple way to help avoid this is to lead the client into the room, rather than opening the door and letting them walk in first. In a high-threat situation, you can't control the actions of people who want to do you harm, but you CAN control your environment to an extent. Help clients feel "in control of the environment" by leading them into the office, reassuring them it's okay to relax. If possible, allow them to sit where they feel comfortable. Ask, "May I shut the door?" These are all things that can help the client feel more at ease and safe.

Another item to consider is the fact that they are in your office seeking help in the first place. Culturally, military and veterans are taught over and over again that to need or ask for help somehow shows weakness. Weakness equals unreliability, and to be seen as unreliable or a "weak link" means people can't count on you in life and death situations. This is a horrible label in a culture that values teamwork and watching each others' back. One way to reassure a veteran or active duty member is to show that needing help is okay and is not a reflection on their character. You can even frame it as a teamwork situation, and one that you look forward to, for example: "I'm sure this seems overwhelming/difficult to deal with, but WE can get through this with some teamwork, and I'm going to help you." This can help reframe the situation as the client being part of a team that will work toward reaching a goal or objective. They'll feel like a stakeholder in the outcome, and it can help them feel as if they are part of something, that they aren't weak and can contribute to something important.

As with any client, being culturally sensitive and aware of veterans' values is important on many levels. However, because of the ongoing and constantly-changing issues involving this particular demographic, the need to be flexible and to "think outside the box" is even more important, which makes social workers a huge asset in this ongoing fight. We have the ability to do things and connect with people and resources like no other profession. Use those skills and abilities and you can literally save a life.

*Don McCasland, LMSW, retired from the U.S. Army after 21+ years of service, including service in Desert Storm and three tours in Iraq with the 101st Airborne Division. He earned his BSW and MSW from Austin Peay State University in Clarksville, TN, and in June of 2010 he helped found The Lazarus Project, a nonprofit that provided free counseling services to active duty, veterans, and their families. In January 2012, they merged with SAFE (Soldiers and Families Embraced) in Clarksville, TN. Don is currently the Program Director at SAFE, which offers free counseling, as well as client advocacy and other "wrap-around" services. SAFE also facilitates professional mental health training specific to military psychology and workshops for civic organizations and the community at large.*

## Cross-Disciplinary Theater Production Focuses on Abusive Relationships

Abusive relationships and their origins were examined in a play staged in April 2014 by the University of Wisconsin-Milwaukee's Helen Bader School of Social Welfare (HBSSW). The Milwaukee premiere of *Surviving the Cycle* was performed by 17 college students and community members. It was written and directed by Milwaukeean Richard Gustin, a theater professor at UW-Fond du Lac.

*Surviving the Cycle* captures one abused wife's story, her husband's story, the couple's interactions, the children's repetition of the cycle, and a missed opportunity to perhaps break the cycle. "It has a profound effect on audience members," Gustin says. "They recognize elements of their own stories portrayed on stage, and when that happens, there can be a shift of awareness, the potential for change. Theater is meant to be a transformative experience. That's always the goal–the better society."

Roberta Hanus, clinical associate professor of social work, worked with Gustin to bring the play to UWM. Hanus teaches coursework dealing with issues of domestic abuse. "Many people are abused, humiliated, put down, bullied, or marginalized," she says. "In the play, characters' internal and external dialogs expose individual and cultural belief systems and how they play out in life choices, especially in regard to self worth and self esteem."

Hanus led talkbacks after each performance. During one talkback, audience member Cherie Griffin, executive director of the Women's Resource Center, Racine, pointed out how far we've come as a society in our discussions about domestic abuse

since the beginning of the movement in the 1970s. "Domestic violence in the '70s was a family problem that no one talked about. It was a family secret. Today the issue is being performed on a stage. That's progress that can make a difference for the next generation," she says.

As the lead female, Eileen Newsome, HBSSW social work master's student, had a difficult part. "It was uncomfortable for me to do it. But that is why this matters," she says. "I'm a survivor myself and walked on eggshells at my house." The experience, she adds, was irreplaceable. She gained a lot of empathy for people in abusive situations and gained insight into why it takes a person an average of seven times to leave such a situation.

*Surviving the Cycle* was first performed in Fond du Lac as part of St.

*Eileen Newsome (UWM social work student, actor), Maurice Pulley (community member, actor), and Richard Gustin (director, writer).*

Agnus Hospital's domestic violence awareness program.

At UWM, the cast was composed of UWM students from various areas of study (social work, criminal justice, acting, business, education, film, music, education, and communications), Marquette University's theater students, and community members.

Watch a video documentary about *Surviving the Cycle,* researched and produced by BSW student Maria Xiong, at: *https://www.youtube.com/watch?v=D_YUaMlnrqU&feature=youtu.be*

# What Every Social Worker Needs To Know About...
# Screening, Brief Intervention, and Referral to Treatment (SBIRT)
## by Shelley Steenrod, Ph.D., LICSW

*A social worker visits Mr. Henry, an older African American man who is attending a community-based day program for senior citizens. He is very insistent that the program social worker ask his doctor to refill a prescription for pain medication. The social worker is concerned that his medication-seeking behavior may indicate a substance abuse problem.*

*Yolanda, an 18-year-old Latina college freshman, is taken to a local hospital emergency room by ambulance. She is accompanied by her frightened roommate, who reports that Yolanda has passed out after consuming a "huge" amount of alcohol while playing a drinking game at a party.*

*Denise, a 33-year-old pregnant White woman meets with a social worker in an early intervention (EI) program to discuss her 3-year-old child who receives EI services. The Early Intervention Program social worker screens Denise for alcohol, tobacco, and drug use with the ASSIST. The screen reveals that Denise is abusing tobacco, alcohol, and methamphetamine.*

The cases above illustrate how social workers are often on the front line when it comes to interacting with individuals with substance use disorders. Unfortunately, social workers often feel under-prepared or untrained to intervene in cases in which substance abuse is present. The Office of National Drug Control Policy (ONDCP) and the Substance Abuse and Mental Health Services Administration (SAMHSA) have put forth a public health model to identify and provide treatment services to individuals with substance disorders. This approach, called *SBIRT,* is an acronym for Screening, Brief Intervention, and Referral to Treatment.

Why is the federal government interested in a screening program for substance disorders? Consider the following: One in every four deaths is the result of alcohol, illegal drugs, or tobacco use (National Institute of Drug Abuse, 2012). In addition, the economic cost of alcohol and illegal drug use in the United States is a whopping $426 billion per year (Substance Abuse and Mental Health

Services Administration, 2012; National Drug Intelligence Center, 2011). SBIRT is grounded in the belief that early identification of problematic alcohol or drug use can save lives and reduce costs related to health care and behavioral health care, crime and incarceration, and overall loss of productivity.

## What is SBIRT?

*Screening* is the first step in the SBIRT process. Screening is a universal process, meaning that an entire population group is screened for an illness or disease. For example, in the field of medicine, all female patients are instructed to begin regular mammography screening at the age of 40, all pregnant women are screened for gestational diabetes with a glucose tolerance test, and men and women alike are routinely screened for high cholesterol through laboratory tests.

It's important to note that screening is different from assessment. Screening is brief, time limited, and intended to simply identify clients with problem alcohol or drug use. In contrast, assessment is a deeper, more thorough process that may take several sessions. Assessment interviews are conducted by substance abuse specialists who consider multiple domains of a client's alcohol or drug use, including risk for withdrawal, medical complications, emotional/behavioral complications, stage of change, relapse potential, recovery environment, legal complications, family system, and employment history.

In the SBIRT framework, screening for substance use is conducted on every client who is seen in a particular program or agency. Settings may include emergency rooms, trauma centers, psychiatric crisis units, health centers, doctors' offices, child protection settings, and other medical or behavioral health environments.

A social worker or other clinician begins screening with the use of a standardized instrument. (See Table 1.) Some frequently used tools include the AUDIT (Alcohol Use Disorders Identification Test), the DAST (Drug Abuse Screening Test), the ASSIST (Alcohol, Smoking, Substance Involvement, Screening Test), the CAGE (Cut Down, Annoyed, Guilty, Eye-Opener), and the CRAFFT (Car, Relax, Alone, Forget, Friends, Trouble). The result of the screening dictates one of three clinical responses: no intervention, brief intervention, or referral to treatment (See Figure 1).

### Figure 1: Potential Outcomes of a Screening Interview

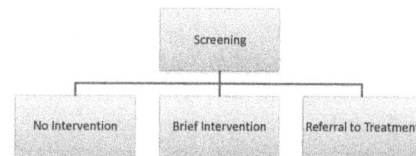

## Potential Outcomes of SBIRT

*No Intervention:* A screening interview with negative results requires no further action specific to substance abuse

### Table 1: Substance Abuse Screening Instruments

| Long Name | Acronym | # of questions | Website |
|---|---|---|---|
| Alcohol Use Disorder Identification Test | AUDIT | 10 | http://www.projectcork.org/clinical_tools/ |
| Alcohol, Smoking, and Substance Abuse Involvement Screening Test | ASSIST | 12 | http://www.who.int/substance_abuse/activities/assist_test/en/ |
| Cut Down, Angry, Guilty, Eye Opener Test | CAGE | 4 | http://www.projectcork.org/clinical_tools/ |
| Drug Abuse Screening Test | DAST | 28 | http://www.projectcork.org/clinical_tools/ |
| Car, Relax, Angry, Friends, Forget, Friends/Family, Trouble | CRAFFT | 6 | http://www.projectcork.org/clinical_tools/ |
| Michigan Alcohol Screening Test | MAST | 25 | http://www.projectcork.org/clinical_tools/ |

intervention or treatment. For example, after screening Mr. Henry for alcohol and drug use with an instrument targeted for older clients (MAST-G), the social worker is relieved to learn that he is not abusing his prescription medication as a way to manage his pain. However, she believes that Mr. Henry could benefit from a more holistic approach to pain management and makes a note to speak with Mr. Henry's physician about a referral to a pain management center that employs mind-body approaches to pain control.

*Brief Intervention:* A screening interview that indicates moderate risk requires a brief intervention, or "a discussion aimed at raising an individual's awareness of their risky behavior and motivating them to change their behavior" (Substance Abuse and Mental Health Services Administration, 2007). Brief interventions are conducted in the community sector, often at the same time and by the same clinician who conducted the screening interview.

There are several reasons why client behavior can change as the result of a brief intervention. A key component of brief interventions is to educate clients on safe drinking behavior, as well as the physical, social, and familial consequences of alcohol and drug abuse. Next, brief interventions require a treatment plan to be implemented to reduce or eliminate substance use. Third, scheduled follow-up appointments hold clients accountable for problem use and provide an opportunity for clinicians to recommend higher levels of treatment, if needed.

In Yolanda's case, once she is medically stable, Yolanda meets with a hospital social worker who interviews her using the CRAFFT, a screening tool for adolescents. The screen indicates that Yolanda rarely uses alcohol and never uses drugs. Her roommate corroborates these facts. However, because the consequences of this isolated incident are so serious, the social worker conducts a brief intervention to educate Yolanda on the consequences of alcohol misuse.

To this end, the social worker uses motivational interviewing practices to build rapport and set goals with Yolanda. Yolanda states that her goal is to continue to attend college parties, but not become so intoxicated that she embarrasses herself or gets sick. The social worker provides Yolanda with an overview of the dangers of binge drinking and some data on the number of deaths that are

attributed to excess alcohol use each year. She also offers Yolanda strategies to avoid consuming large amounts of alcohol in short periods of time. For example, she advises Yolanda to consistently snack at parties where alcohol is present and to alternate alcoholic drinks with non-alcoholic drinks. The social worker also educates Yolanda on what a standard drink is (1 ounce of liquor, 4 ounces of wine, and 8 ounces of beer), so she can quantify the amount of alcohol she ingests. Finally, the social worker helps Yolanda and her roommate establish a contract around when to exit campus parties. Yolanda leaves the emergency room armed with knowledge and strategies to avoid future binge drinking emergencies. The social worker follows up after two weeks and reports that Yolanda is utilizing the strategies that they discussed.

*Referral to Treatment:* A screening interview that indicates severe risk of dependence requires a referral to a specialized alcohol and drug treatment program for comprehensive assessment and treatment. In this instance, the referral process should be as "air tight" as possible. It is insufficient to simply give a client the name and number of an alcohol and drug treatment program. Instead, it is best for social workers to make an appointment with the client at hand and follow up to be sure the client follows through. Recommendations from a substance abuse assessment may include one or more of the following interventions: detoxification, short-term residential treatment, long-term residential treatment (such as a half-way house or therapeutic community), outpatient treatment, day or evening treatment, medications, and/or group treatment.

In Denise's case, the screening social worker identifies a substance abuse treatment agency with expertise in substance abuse treatment for pregnant women and arranges for an assessment appointment later that afternoon. The EI social worker is careful to ask Denise for written permission to communicate with the alcohol and drug program, so she can stay involved and informed. Assessment results indicate that Denise requires a medically supervised detoxification program, followed by a residential program for pregnant and parenting women. The EI social worker will have ongoing contact with Denise and her children through the provision of early intervention services.

## Conclusion

The SBIRT model has several advantages. It matches clients with the appropriate type and amount of services they require, avoiding under- or over-treatment. It also offers social workers a framework for how community-based services can interface with specialty alcohol and drug treatment programs. SBIRT has been identified as an "evidence based practice" by the Substance Abuse and Mental Health Services Administration with promising efficacy. Finally, SBIRT has been approved by the American Medical Association and the Centers for Medicare and Medicaid Services as a reimbursable service, meaning that social workers and agencies can be reimbursed for providing SBIRT services.

Please visit the following websites for more information on SBIRT:

- http://www.integration.samhsa.gov/clinical-practice/sbirt
- http://www.bu.edu/bniart/
- http://www.nida.nih.gov/nidamed/resguide/

## References

National Drug Intelligence Center. (2011). *The economic impact of illicit drug use on American society.* Washington D.C.: United States Department of Justice. Retrieved online at *http://www.justice.gov/ndic* on October 7, 2013.

National Institute on Drug Abuse. (2012). *Medical consequences of drug abuse.* Retrieved online at *http://www.drugabuse.gov/related-topics/medical-consequences-drug-abuse/mortality* on October 15, 2013.

Substance Abuse and Mental Health Services Administration. (2007). *SBIRT glossary.* Retrieved from *http://sbirt.samhsa.gov/glossary.htm* on February 3, 2007.

Substance Abuse and Mental Health Services Administration. (2012). *Results from the 2011 National Survey on Drug Use and Health: Summary of National Findings, NSDUH Series H-44, HHS Publication No. (SMA) 12-4713.* Rockville, MD: Substance Abuse and Mental Health Services Administration.

*Shelley Steenrod, Ph.D., LICSW, is an associate professor of social work at Salem State University in Salem, Massachusetts. She received her Master of Social Work from Boston University and her Ph.D. from the Heller School at Brandeis University. Dr. Steenrod specializes in the treatment of substance use disorders.*

# Groups

# A Hostility Reduction Group
## by *Thomas A. Lachiusa, Ph.D., LICSW*

Over a period of 17 years at the Hampden County Correctional Center in Massachusetts, I have collected comments from violent offenders in my hostility reduction group.

Participant comments and personal reflections are presented here in free verse format. After reading them, you will have a glimpse of what working to change the thinking of violent men can be like. The struggle to control violent behavior is as old as humanity itself. As you will see, it's a process of moral development.

Hostility reduction programs can lower violent behavior in the facility, and, eventually, in the community. One violent person without treatment can create a significant number of victims in his or her lifetime. Individuals who become pro-violent thinkers need opportunities to process their experience, get new perspectives, and practice new behaviors. Hostility reduction groups focus on helping participants share the struggle and move in the direction of decisions that eliminate thinking errors that promote violence.

The following commentaries and reflections should give some insight into this group experience.

*In [a] state prison, a can of soda tipped into a*
*guy's cell from a cell above*
*The inmate who lived in the lower cell respond-*
*ed with an out-of-control rage*
*His anger must have gotten really worked up,*
*and he kept insulting the inmate who*
*accidentally dropped the soda,*
*demanding very loudly he clean it up.*
*Later the inmate who dropped the soda dealt*
*with the complainer*
*With the help of two friends, a metal shank*
*was jabbed into the inmate's eye*
*To kill him*
*The trigger was a dropped soda*
*That brought on a rage of anger and a verbal*
*reaction*
*That could not be tolerated in such a hostile*
*prison environment*
*Where a life is less important than a cultural*
*belief about public respect.*

This violent person understands right and wrong at the pre-conventional level

of moral development (Kohlberg, 1973), infused with a distorted view of what justice is. The moral belief is that winning the conflicts is the only proof they need to verify that they were correct. People who lose conflicts are losers, and losers can only be correct if they win. The price of winning is something you have to pay, so you can be correct and earn respect. A person may have to die; a family may have to continue without a member; a person's future may have to change direction.

*When I was in the military my friend killed*
*his wife*
*He was overseas for six months and his wife*
*was hiding an affair with a captain*
*This kind of thing happens and ends, but in*
*this case it continued after he returned*
*My friend was really stressed out at work,*
*One day at work he said, I know something is*
*wrong, I have to go home early*
*When he got there the captain jumped out the*
*window and ran away*
*My friend shot his wife in the stomach with a*
*shotgun*
*After this outburst, she died; he is eligible for*
*the death penalty,*
*and their children were put in state care.*
*The captain got five years' time in a military*
*brig.*

It is not uncommon to hear inmates state that if people knew the consequences of their actions, it would be a deterrent. In the above situation, if the woman had told her lover that the husband would kill her for cheating, would he really have believed it? Could the husband control his

emotions to a level that he could foresee his children growing up without parents? The greater the pain that people feel, the less they care about the results of their actions. This inmate's conventional level of moral development (Kohlberg, 1973) is further developed than that of his murderous friend. He thinks people should obey the law, because outside forces will hold them accountable. The children in this example lose both parents, and in a functional family, this would not happen. It is an outcome that conflicts with the storyteller's view of what is right and wrong.

Next is a reflection of a man who had the ability to think beyond his own emotional experience and tolerate a level of personal frustration, only because he put it in perspective.

*Minding my business*
*My roommate is 32 years old*
*He was upset with me because I did not wake*
*him in time for his class*
*So angry, that he threatened to fight me so I*
*would not get my parole release.*

*My first thought was to   pull him out of*
*his bunk and beat him up*
*My second thought was     if he gets out of his*
*bunk I will kick his ass*
*My next thought was     I am not going to miss*
*the chance to be with my*
*children in three weeks*
*because of this guy*
*I put in a request to move him to another cell*
*He isn't worth the risk*
*His problem*
*Isn't my*
*Problem*
*Now*

Interventions inmates share with each other are ideas they have heard before but have not put into action and practiced over time. The above comments show the way this individual kept readjusting his self-talk until he got it right. He was able to find a non-violent solution and meet his personal goal. Some inmates are so stuck in a mindset of violent solutions that their default setting seems to be pro-violent. Only a powerful thought can counter this pull.

Inmates who heard his story determined that his action was being a snitch, because he told an officer about the threat. Inmate culture is not helpful in terms of avoiding violence. The story teller was acting at the post-conventional level (Kohlberg, 1973). His perspective that being with his children is the right thing allowed him to break the social contract of dealing with problems by fighting inmates who are taking advantage of a situation.

*In the first eight-week group*
*he would make some comments,*
*but was guarded and only disclosed at the last*
*class of the cycle*
*that he was having some child custody problems.*

*He shared how he feels unable to choose between two choices,*
*and neither is in his best interest.*
*He feels that the unresolved anger of his ex-wife is the difficulty*
*in his ability to have regular if any contact*
*with the son he has not seen in three years.*

*At his best he maintained sobriety for five years*
*At his worst he admitted to holding a gun in his hand*
*with a plan to kill his wife and then himself.*
*The memory of how he felt when his father died*
*was all that stood between his weapon and his victims.*

*He was eight when his father died,*
*In his view he didn't deal with it,*
*He saw that most of his life problems*
*have a root in his father's death*

*To do the same to his son was wrong,*
*that important cognition, was able to break through,*
*the angry feelings that would accept murdering,*
*to keep the choice of life as a plan to act on*
*that day, was an act of grace*
*that he could give.*

As a person begins to think in terms of others, and how they are affected, controlling violence is more likely when we truly care about a person or a moral premise. When this inmate could envision the impact to the victim, he moved closer to seeing the whole picture. The goal is for the person to do the right thing because it is right, not simply because it is in his or her best interest. People can do this when they are open to processing the moral dilemma in front of them. At that point, they use a moral decision-making approach to help them face the most difficult challenges of human life. "Human nature is complex.

Even if we do have inclinations toward violence, we also have inclination to empathy, to cooperation, to self-control" (Steven Pinker, 2011).

Promoting thinking that will support a less hostile lifestyle and zero violence against women is our primary goal. The potential for a mutually loving relationship grows from an ability to develop mutual respect and conflict resolution skills. This is a theme we brainstorm on a regular basis in groups.

*Relationships require conflict*
   *to sort out     the acceptable*
                    *and the unacceptable*
                 *the inconvenient and*
                     *the destructive*
*what can be accepted*
   *in moderation     and what*
               *can never be*
               *accepted*
   *the trust*
           *can pass from one to the other*
*risking trust   can engage stability  and build*

*Intimacy*
   *The place where relationships grow*
                *healing*
        *and learning exists*
     *open to our     self &*
        *open to the other*
       *learning from peers*
    *learning from professionals*
  *building trust*
  *risking new behaviors*
        *trusting in the process*
    *making a commitment to do the work*
*If you are not passionate about your commitment*
     *Then there is no intimacy*

\*\*\*\*\*

*An Inmate List*

*Argue when you have time to solve the problem*
  *In a calm place*
    *With a clear head*
      *Without distractions*
        *After a meal*
          *Allow time to get more*
            *Information and ideas*
            *Get help when you*
            *Get stuck*
               *Make decisions that are*
               *good for*
               *The Relationship*
*When is a problem is solved?*
  *When the issue is resolved*
    *When the pattern of behavior is changed*
    *When the trust is intact*
    *When the future is predictable*

The question, "How can a person like you help me?" surfaces in every group. Who are you to presume you know anything about why men like me are violent? Developing a therapeutic environment in a group of violent men seems to take about five weeks and addresses the informational and emotional needs of the group. In these groups, the facilitator has to be prepared for the testing and the challenges. The process of group formation can challenge your ability to care about the group members, protect them, and treat them in a fair way. The same issues of control that get played out in their personal relationships will surface.

*We do not allow just anyone to challenge us*
  *only people we respect can play a part in really changing us*
    *How right is their thinking*
      *is less important than how much*
      *we think they are right about us*
      *respect needs time to develop*
        *and relationship testing experiences*
        *are fatal*
         *without the time invested*
         *for a strong tie to build*
*We question*
  *Do they have a genuine concern for our well-being?*
  *Do they help us feel needed and valuable, by them and others?*
  *Do they help us feel good about our self?*
  *Is this a person we will respond to*
*and follow through with    what they verbalize*
  *Can they motivate us to do the work*
  *to put forth an effort*
*to improve   our   self*

*Can we comfortably share*
  *positive and the negative*
    *about who we are*
    *decisions we make*
      *information we hide*

As inmates try new behaviors and see relationships start to improve, a new door in their life has opened. They begin to see the personal faults they were hiding behind a cloak of denial while they blamed others. The process of moral development requires the debate of moral issues. For some, violence and abuse is a primary tool to assure avoidance of hurt in the future, because they do not have to stop and think. "Violence is the last refuge of the incompetent" according to Isaac Asimov (1951). Moral development is how we become competent to accept hurt and pain without transforming it into anger.

# References

Asimov, I. (1951). *Foundation*. New York: Gnome Press.

Pinker, S. (2011). *The better angels of our nature: why violence has declined.* New York: Viking, Penguin Group.

Kohlberg, L. (1973). The claim to moral adequacy of a highest stage of moral judgment. *Journal of Philosophy, 70* (18): 630–646.

Wilson, D., & Klein, A. (2006). *A longitudinal study of a cohort of batterers arraigned in a Massachusetts district court; 1995 to 2004.* National Institute of Justice (Grant No. 2004WBGX0011) http://www.ncjrs.gov/pdffiles1/nij/grants/215346.pdf.

*In 1996 Dr. Thomas Lachiusa developed his curriculum and began facilitating groups to reduce the hostility levels of men incarcer-* ated for domestic violence, violent crimes, and restraining order violations. He works at the Hampden County Correctional Center and promotes the reduction of violence in a residential setting. Based on his work with violent men, he has progressed to believe that family violence is the tap root of the behaviors we define as social problems. On a regular basis, he makes presentations on clinical issues and group work, and he teaches corrections and rehabilitation classes. He received his social work training at the University of Connecticut and the University of Southern California.

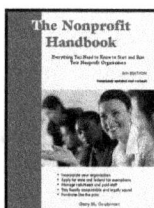

# The McSilver Awards

*by Courtney Kidd, LMSW*

On May 28, 2014, I had the honor of attending the second annual McSilver Awards–a day that "recognizes individuals and organizations that work toward addressing needs of children and families living in poverty." The theme was ending poverty; the message was hope. The day's events began with a series of panel discussions, first addressing the long-standing issues surrounding hunger.

Experts passionately advocated for the right for each individual, especially children, to have consistent and quality food. Later, the second panel switched gears and tackled homelessness, concluding that the right to affordable and livable homes is a basic, fundamental human right. The day radiated with forward movement, backed with the research showing that the demise of a strong support system, or "welfare state," led to increased poverty and only perpetuated the cycle in families. These factors were creating generations of individuals raised in sub-par conditions, suffering from high medical needs, obesity, and even traumatic disorders.

This charge to wage war on poverty has many heroes, as shown by this year's awardees: Pedro Antonio Noguera, Ph.D.; Commissioner Rosemonde Pierre-Louis; Hon. Ruben Diaz, Jr.; Jonathan Edwards; and Andrea Elliott. These men and women who have dedicated their lives to alter how we view the real causes of poverty. They create change through direct practice, community organiz- ing, and a hard hitting Pulitzer prize winning news series.

Yet, among these change agents you find a giant, the one who will hold together the pieces and shine the torch of hope leading the way. Those are the amazing individuals of the McSilver Institute for Poverty, Policy, and Research. Founded in 2007 by the generous and forward thinking Constance and Martin Silver, the McSilver Institute strives to use applied research and policy along with the far reaching collaborative partners within the community, in order to understand root causes of poverty. Together, they lead innovative and organizational efforts with front line workers, institutions, and policy makers to address what we must do to eliminate the problem.

We're honored at Social Justice Solutions to be one of those partners. Linked together with the dynamic and gifted team at McSilver, we have no doubt that change is coming. Poverty is not some far, outsourced problem to theorize about. It occurs within our very walls. Shifting the public's attitude toward the problem of poverty must be done with the combination of research, education, and action. Most importantly, we must have hope, and those at McSilver work tirelessly to provide that.

To read more about the McSilver Institute, visit: *http://www.mcsilver.org/*

*This article is provided as part of a collaboration between The New Social Worker and Social Justice Solutions. You can find Social Justice Solutions online at http://www.socialjusticesolutions.org.*

To know their world,
step into ours.

**Master of Social Work**

Improve the lives of children and families.

Gain a deep understanding of social work enriched
with a child development perspective.

Grow your professional identity with the support
of top social work faculty.

www.erikson.edu/NewSocialWorker

erikson
graduate school in child development
Chicago, Illinois

## STUDENT SOCIAL WORK ORGANIZATIONS

Please send us a short **news** article about your group's activities. Also, send us **photos** of your club in action–we may even feature you on our front cover!

It's easy to share your club's activities with our readers. Send your news/photos to:

Linda Grobman, ACSW, LSW, Editor/Publisher
THE NEW SOCIAL WORKER
P.O. Box 5390, Harrisburg, PA 17110-0390
or to *lindagrobman@socialworker.com*

## Greetings From the Phi Alpha Honor Society for Social Work

Phi Alpha supports chapters that actively recruit Phi Alpha members by providing them with a FREE Phi Alpha tabletop banner. Please contact the Phi Alpha office at PhiAlphaInfo@etsu.edu to receive your complimentary tabletop banner. Phi Alpha will offer double knotted blue and gold Phi Alpha honor cords for purchase in the fall.

Please visit the Phi Alpha website at http://www.PhiAlpha.org and check out the Phi Alpha tabletop banner and honor cords.

Kind regards,
Tammy Hamilton
Executive Secretary
*PhiAlphaInfo@etsu.edu*

## Pinwheel Garden at North Carolina Central University

A pinwheel garden was sponsored by the Undergraduate Social Work Society at North Carolina Central University in support of National Child Abuse Prevention Month. It was the brainchild of one of the junior members, Jennifer A. West, who organized the project and spearheaded the fundraising. As a result, the group raised more than $170 for NC Child Abuse Prevention.

*The pinwheel garden.*

# Social Work Students Graduate!

*Shown below: Marietta J. Smith, Master of Social Work (MSW), Cleveland State University, Cleveland, Ohio, Class of 2014.*

*From left to right: Jennifer R. James, Brittney E. Davis, and Tabbatha J. Woolwine. All three graduated from Indiana University East of Richmond, Indiana, on Friday, May 16, 2014.. They became best friends during the BSW program. "Our journey brought us together, and we are certain we will be lifelong friends."*

*Shown above: May 2014 MSW grads from Youngstown State University. They are wearing red shoes as part of the national red shoe movement to support women (and nurturing men) in professional roles. The names of the graduates are: Brittney N. Averhart, Elizabeth T. Ayana, Cynthia M. Bauer, Melissa S. Colon, Jeffrey A. Cook, Monica L. Ellis, Debra J. Felder, Diana L. Hartwig, Samantha M. Heller, Crystal R. Johnson, Caroline M. Jones, Griffin T. Long, Megan M. Martin, Davina L. McPheron, Angela Miller-Parker, Erinn Parnell, Michael C. Santilli, Alicia M. White, Susan E. Williams, and Ruby M. Wright.*

# Social Work Students Graduate!

*Appalachian State University MSW 2014 Off-Campus Cohort. From left to right: Kao Vang, Carmen McNeil, Ashley White, Jana Brown, and Alicia Coleman.*

*"I have no idea what I am doing." Congrats, class of 2014! Bachelor of Social Work grads in yellow Hoods and Bachelor of Arts in white hoods. In this photo: funny face in center is Tapiwa Kwenda, Bachelor of Social Work. Sitting left to right: Booth University College Chancellor, Vice Chancellor, and Vice President and Student Academic Dean. Photo taken at Booth University College, Winnipeg, Manitoba, Canada on April 27, 2014. Photo credit: Sarah Kwenda.*

*In the photo: Kaley Rhoden, University of Central Florida, Orlando, May 2, 2014, MSW graduation, with Niko. "He has been one of my biggest supporters since he was there during all of my late night study sessions. Also, he looks very cute with his bowtie." Photo credit: Diane Rhoden.*

*I am a new graduate! Kendra Beck (right), received her BSW from University of Texas at Arlington on May 9, 2014. Shown with her brother, Korrey Alexander.*

*Natalie Landry, Louisiana State University, Baton Rouge, LA, May 16, 2014, MSW. What's your superpower?*

**Congratulations, new social workers! Watch our website for a slideshow of 2014 graduates (coming soon).**

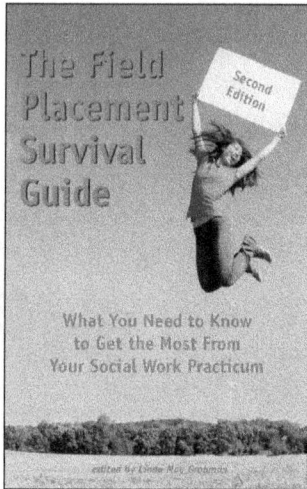

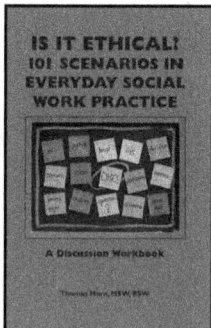

*Whitney Sewell continued from page 3*

the 2014 UNC Diversity Award (hers was in the Graduate Student category). In general, Sewell is interested in people in the community with marginalized identities, and she has a strong commitment to sexual health and other social issues.

"Early intervention is important with vulnerable populations," she says. "Do we want to help them now or four years from now, when they need social services?"

Also at UNC, Sewell was inducted into the Order of the Golden Fleece Honors Society, considered the university's highest honor. The society selects its members based on service to the university as reflected in scholarship, leadership, and other qualities in academic and extracurricular pursuits.

Sewell was inducted into the Franklin Porter Graham Graduate and Professional Student Honor Society, recognizing outstanding service to the university. Sewell serves as a board member for the Adolescent Pregnancy Prevention Council of North Carolina, is a member of Delta Sigma Theta public service

sorority, and is a troop leader for the Girl Scouts of North Carolina Coastal Pines. Her many professional affiliations include the International Association for Social Work with Groups; American Association of Sexuality Educators, Counselors, and Therapists; National Association of Social Workers; and NAACP.

When not involved in a whirlwind of academic and community service activity, Sewell relaxes through dancing, a great love. "I took a lot of classes," she says. "I'd do modern, anything to get moving."

She also runs and works out–partly to compensate for one sedentary passion: baking.

"Chemistry is amazing, how you put ingredients together," Sewell explains. "I love to give away baked goods."

The MSW graduate enjoys talking on the phone and getting together with close friends, as well as karaoke.

Since childhood, through it all, her energy level hasn't waned.

*Freelance writer Barbara Trainin Blank, formerly of Harrisburg, PA, now lives in the greater Washington, DC, area.*

## Belle Challenges Viewers To Think
### by Addison Cooper, LCSW

If you live near any independent theaters, you might have a chance to catch a very thoughtful exploration of racism, romantic love, adoptive parental love, and the interplay among all three of them. Fox Searchlight's film *Belle* recently had its mainstream release in the United States.

Set in 1769 England, the film looks in on Lord Mansfield, the Lord Chief Justice and highest judge in all of England, who must rule on a case that threatens to disrupt the nation's vast slave-based economy. Bound by the codes of the aristocracy, Lord Mansfield is also raising two of his nieces, Elizabeth and Dido. Dido's inclusion in his household has caused a scandal, because Dido is the mixed-race daughter of Mansfield's nephew and a slave. All of England waits as Mansfield prepares to rule on what is legal and on what is right.

Some in Lord Mansfield's household initially object to taking in Dido, but Lord Mansfield himself accepts her as family. Later in life, he confesses to his wife that he loves Dido "as though she was created of you and me."

There's a lot that I enjoyed about this film as a social worker, including the following three things:

### 1. Lord Mansfield is committed to doing what's right, regardless of whether it is popular or advantageous.

Two characters are noted for their desire to not only enforce policy, but to create policy. As social workers, we are often in positions of authority (or at least influence), and we may find ourselves with similar desires. In the context of our profession, we are governed by the laws of the land, the ethical codes of our associations, the regulations of our contracts, and the policies of our agencies, but we are not bound to treat them with unquestioning awe. We are not only "followers" of codes; ideally, we are also questioners, analyzers, and shapers of the codes. At one point, Mansfield decrees

that something is "not legal, neither is it right." May our work result in increasing agreement between "legal" and "right."

### 2. Dido is unapologetic about her heritage.

One young man takes a fancy to her, saying that he can forgive her bloodline. Dido ultimately rejects him, saying that she wants a husband who does not see forgiveness of her heritage as necessary. She does not apologize for her race, heritage, or paternal history. One of the things I appreciate about social work is its desire to respect every individual and to celebrate rather than tolerate the traits, beliefs, and characteristics that make us unique.

### 3. *Belle* captures the inner thoughts and passions of several characters as they wrestle with major ethical and societal issues.

Part of what drew me to social work is a general affinity for other people, and part of that (at least for me) is a desire to understand folks. In *Belle,* one character notes that people often try to disregard each other. It made me think—sometimes, people are quick to differentiate and exclude each other. Whether the divide is along religious lines, racial lines, identity lines, or professional/educational lines, we often try to find the categories where

we fit, and we differentiate ourselves from those who don't fit. I can't help feeling we lose something by this proclivity toward exclusion, and *Belle* challenges it. As social workers, we can challenge it, too. The first step toward challenging it is an honest season of self-exploration. Who do I exclude? How do I justify it? What do others lose by my disregard of them? What am I losing?

*Belle* is a thoughtful, powerful, challenging, and beautiful film. As you watch it, think about why you became a social worker, and ask yourself two questions: *In five years, what change do I hope to have accomplished in my community?* and *What change do I need to accomplish in myself to make the macro-level change flow from a more genuine place?*

See the change that needs to happen; then be the change that needs to happen.

*Addison Cooper is a Licensed Clinical Social Worker in California and Missouri. He reviews films and writes movie discussion guides for foster and adoptive families at Adoption at the Movies (www. adoptionlcsw.com), and is a supervisor at a foster care and adoption agency in Southern California. His articles on adoption and film have also appeared in Adoptive Families and Foster Focus magazines. Find him on Twitter @AddisonCooper.*

# Impersonating a Social Worker

## *by Julie Claypool, MSW*

Have you ever told a lie so many times that you convinced yourself it was true? If I met you at a party or the grocery store, and you asked me what I did for a living, I would repeat my well-rehearsed lie. "I'm a social worker." I told myself that it was not really a lie, because I actually worked as a case manager in a social service agency. It was irrelevant that my undergraduate degree was in journalism. Eventually, my white lie caught up with me, and I found myself beginning graduate school in my 40s.

Getting a master's degree was not on my bucket list. I had children attending three different colleges, and I was content. I had successfully survived having three teenagers in high school at the same time and was prepared to continue with my job in social services until all my children graduated. My life was running smoothly. Then I hit a major career roadblock.

I worked for a service coordination agency that contracted with the Illinois Department of Human Services. However, after Illinois was mandated to convert its grant programs to Medicaid waiver to receive federal reimbursement, my degree in journalism/communications was called into question. The government didn't care that I had spent 20+ years working in human services. I was told that for my agency to continue to bill for my services, I needed to take a minimum of 15 credit hours in a human services-related field. It came down to five additional bachelor's-level courses in psychology, human behavior, or social work. If I successfully completed these courses, I would be qualified for the position I already held.

My agency appealed the decision and provided the state with proof of 752 hours of Continuing Education Units (CEUs) that I had completed since becoming their employee. After repeated denials, it became evident that I would need to return to school or take a non-degreed position. I love to clean, so I strongly considered giving the janitor a run for her money, but found out that I wasn't qualified for that, either. Who knew that handling toxic cleaning agents required HAZMAT training? I reluctantly agreed to return to the halls of academia, and my employer offered to pay for my classes.

I chose social work courses, because as a case manager, I already considered myself a social worker. Never mind that I didn't have the degree.

I initially considered the local junior college, where I believed I could knock out the 15 hours in one semester. When the school counselor found out I already had a bachelor's degree, she looked me dead in the eye and lied. She said I could attend my alma mater and earn my master's in a mere two semesters. The program was called Advanced Standing. I found this news outstanding. I believed that only an additional semester stood between me and an MSW.

I returned to the same college I had graduated from more than 20 years earlier and ran into the second roadblock. The junior college counselor had failed to mention that to be eligible for the MSW program with advanced standing, my bachelor's degree had to be in social work. I was now looking at 64 hours instead of 15. Not outstanding at all.

While I contemplated returning to the junior college and signing up for the HAZMAT course, I stumbled upon the perfect loophole. It began with two simple words in the graduate school brochure—life experience.

I believed I had found the yellow brick road. My beloved college, unlike the state and federal government, was going to give me credit for life experience. Forget all that nonsense about years of school ahead of me. I had discovered a shortcut. I excitedly explained to my new counselor that I had two decades of life experience. I waited for her to type that into her computer and transform my journalism degree into a social work degree.

She cheerfully pointed out that I didn't have life experience as a *social worker*. I showed her my trump card—752 hours of CEUs. She said she was impressed with all my hard work, but informed me that none of the hours were in social work. It was time to stop living a lie. I begrudgingly signed up for the MSW program and resigned myself to earning a degree in a field that I believed I knew everything about to keep a job I already had.

## Fast Forward Two Years

I could write a book about my social work education adventure, but I will keep it brief. I admit that I was not a willing participant in the beginning. I felt that I did not belong in a program with starry-eyed amateurs who wanted to change the world. I worked in the real world, and I was only here to satisfy everyone else. I was disappointed when I discovered that I had a lot to learn and that social work was hard work.

Yet, the hard work was also fascinating and rewarding and promised more than a career at its conclusion. I had phenomenal internships that provided me with experiences at the micro, mezzo, and macro levels. I developed a passion for policy and found myself drawn to the business side of social work—administrative practice.

My 20 years of life experience was essential to my growth as a social work professional, but it was not enough. Once I stopped resisting, I could see that my social services experience perfectly complemented a career in social work. The knowledge I gained in the classroom flowed seamlessly into the real world experiences of my internships. I began to appreciate how my journalism training would enhance my work as a social work practitioner.

As I utilized my social work knowledge from my courses during my internships, I felt I was no longer living a lie. What I initially viewed as a career detour had become an amazing opportunity.

In my social work journey, I learned about the history, ethics, theories, research, and the practice of social work. I learned how to think and even how to think about my thinking. I learned an invaluable life lesson about shortcuts. If you can avoid them and take the longer route, you often find yourself enjoying the ride.

Now, when anyone asks me what I do for a living, I can respond honestly, "I am a social worker."

*Julie Claypool is a May 2013 MSW graduate of the University of St. Francis and holds a B.A. in Journalism/Communications from the same university.*

# Foster Kids Are Strong: The Importance of Collaboration Between Social Workers and Foster Parents

*by Jordan Wilfong, MSW, LSW*

Social workers who have clients in the child welfare system are well aware of the unique challenges associated with living in foster care. The trauma related to being removed from a parent or guardian can have negative effects on the mental health of children, while also increasing their chances of developing life-altering behavioral problems (Scott, 2012). Although reunification with the original caregiver remains the rightful goal of most foster care placements, it only succeeds 35% of the time (Berrick, 2009). Consequently, the children who are left without their biological families need assistance in processing trauma and forming new attachment relationships. Their welfare usually becomes the responsibility of social workers and foster parents, and both must work together to ensure foster children are receiving positive support.

Research has shown that children who spend significant amounts of time in foster care are not only at risk for developing mental health issues, but also for having substance abuse problems, educational deficits, and criminal justice issues (Scott, 2012). Scott asserts that half of the children who age out of foster care do so without a high school diploma, and a quarter will spend time in jail at some point in their adult lives. Furthermore, foster care placements can create a constant sense of instability for chil-

dren, leading to feelings of hopelessness (Berrick, 2009). The good news is that when long-term foster children are given a steady and supportive placement, they are far better able to adjust to adulthood and independent living (Scott, 2012).

My clinical work over the last four years has included extensive experience providing therapy for foster children. I will share the story of one child who has found a new home after being permanently removed from his biological parents. Working with this child has significantly influenced my development as a social worker, and this story shows the impact we can have on clients through adhering to our core values of equality and respect (National Association of Social Workers, 2008). Moreover, I learned that foster children are capable of overcoming even the most adverse circumstances when social workers and foster parents form partnerships with them based on empowerment and growth (Cherry & Orme, 2013).

To protect confidentiality, all names and details in this article have been disguised. When I first began working with Austin, he was eight years old and had been in foster care for more than three years. During that time, he was moved to six different homes when the foster parents became overwhelmed with his aggression, anger, and communication difficulties. Austin's time in

the child welfare system began when the police arrived at his parents' home after a domestic violence incident. Austin was found wearing dirty clothes and looking as if he had not eaten in days. His parents were also physically abusive and did not provide consistent supervision.

Austin's parents experienced severe trauma during their own childhoods. His maternal grandfather was murdered when Austin's mother was a child, and his paternal grandmother died of a heroin overdose when Austin's father was a teenager. The difficulties Austin faced were likely a result of the multiple generations of trauma in his family. There was a history of poverty in the family, and Austin's problems were only exacerbated by the economic, social, and emotional struggles that can develop from growing up in disadvantaged communities (Lindsey, 2004).

## My Journey With Austin

During our first in-home therapy session, the far-reaching effects of Austin's traumatic childhood were apparent. While still living with his mother, he had been left home alone for long periods of time, putting him in an almost constant state of fear. Being in many different foster homes had disrupted Austin's attachment relationships, making him extremely defensive when interacting with others (Cohen, Mannarino, & Deblinger, 2012).

These factors made it difficult to establish rapport with him. Austin had been around dozens of child welfare professionals in his young life, and to him, we all blended into one. All he saw in me were the disappointments of a difficult childhood.

Through my experience working as a child and adolescent social worker, I have come to believe that children deserve the opportunity to play and have fun. Therefore, after several unsuccessful attempts at engaging with Austin during our first session, I suggested we go outside for a walk. The fresh air helped him to relax slightly, and Austin's eyes began to water when I asked him how he was feeling. Seeing those tears helped me better understand how difficult life had been for him. I proceeded to ask Austin to say two words for me: "I'm strong." He hesitated at first, but eventually complied. It was the loudest and clearest sentence I had heard Austin say all day. I asked him to repeat it, and his voice went up another notch as he bellowed, "I'm strong!"

That walk became the silver lining to an otherwise difficult opening session, for we established hope within the therapeutic relationship (Poulin, 2005). When I returned for our second session, Austin was in the living room with his foster mother. He had lived with Mrs. Jackson and her family once previously, before being returned to his biological parents in a failed reunification attempt. After Austin's parents had further legal issues, he was moved back to his placement with the Jackson family. When I approached Austin, I inquired about how he was feeling. He responded with a vibrant, "I'm strong! Remember that?" I was pleased to hear he had. It was an example of cognitive restructuring, a beneficial therapeutic technique for children who need to create more positive thoughts about themselves (Webb, 2006).

Because Austin had experienced such significant trauma, it would take time for him to make progress (Cohen et al., 2012). The next few months included considerable difficulties in the therapeutic relationship, as I began to help him process his traumatic experiences. We engaged in play therapy activities, and sometimes Austin would cry uncontrollably, or get angry and confrontational. Similar outbursts were frequent during his interactions with his foster family. It was during these times that I helped Austin recognize that he was safe, and also validated the pain he was feeling (Cohen et al., 2012).

Austin's family traumas and multiple foster home placements made it difficult for him to trust people, and an important treatment goal was helping to facilitate more trusting relationships (Lindsey, 2004). It is my belief that no matter how effective a therapist can be, a child needs security within the home environment to make progress. Unfortunately, Austin's parents still had personal issues and continued to cancel their supervised visits with him. Therefore, his foster parents and I helped Austin realize we would support him until the judge decided what happened with his custody situation (Berrick, 2009).

Despite the fact that Austin had had only sporadic contact with his parents over the previous few years, he still held out hope that the family would one day reunite. The work of John Bowlby and Margaret Ainsworth highlights the strong connection children feel to their parents and original caregivers (Lindsey, 2004). That is why Austin's life became extremely difficult about six months into our work together, when his father was charged with homicide and soon pleaded guilty to second-degree murder. Furthermore, Austin's mother returned to jail for a parole violation around the same time.

Along with the county psychologist, Austin's foster parents and I told him what had happened regarding his parents. It was an extremely difficult experience, but as usual, Austin was strong. The sadness of the situation brought on an immense amount of stress for him, though. Not only was it traumatic to learn about his father's crime, but Austin also struggled to cope with the fact that his dream of reuniting with his parents would never happen (Berrick, 2009). He went into an almost catatonic state for nearly two weeks, often being unable to talk or move–only to cry. Austin also began to isolate himself from his foster parents, and he was getting into violent confrontations with his foster siblings.

I was concerned about Austin's well-being at this time, and our treatment team considered hospitalizing him. The stress of the situation led the Jacksons to have second thoughts about keeping Austin. They had two adopted children with behavioral issues, and they were worried the situation would add too much stress to the family. I sat down with the Jacksons, and we made a plan in which we would all work together to support Austin. We decided to utilize the upcoming summer to help him integrate into the family and process his trauma. If Austin was making progress by September, and the household stress was reducing, the Jacksons would move forward with adopting him.

The Jacksons were the only people who had provided Austin with consistency in his life, and he loved them deeply for the respect they showed him. For Austin to integrate into the family, I had to help him express that love in a positive way. I worked alongside Austin's foster parents on helping him identify his emotions and feel more comfortable processing his feelings.

Because Austin had spent most of his life in a near-constant state of stress, his foster parents and I continually made sure that he knew he was truly safe in their home (Cohen et al., 2012). By engaging in play activities with Austin and his foster sisters, we improved their bond, which helped form an important trusting relationship.

Austin was making significant progress as the summer came to a close. He was processing his trauma about his parents and opening up about the bullying he had faced in previous foster homes. It was not always an easy therapeutic relationship, though.

I had seen Austin cry dozens of times from the confusion and pain of his traumatic childhood, but our alliance was always based upon a better future. We were now having complete 2-hour sessions in which Austin refrained from emotional outbursts, and every professional in the child welfare system working on his case agreed he was ready for adoption. The Jacksons were fully committed to keeping him, too. Our final task was to help Austin understand that his biological parents would not raise him. Although he already knew this on some level, there is a limit to how much a 9-year-old can process, and he needed closure.

About two months before the adoption date, I arrived at the foster home and was informed by Mrs. Jackson that Austin's father had just mailed them two letters from prison. In one, written to Austin's foster parents, he thanked them for adopting him and also spoke about his own difficult childhood. In the other letter, written directly to Austin, his father explained the mistakes he had made. He stated that his actions were completely wrong, and stated Austin's childhood with the Jackson family would be far different from his. He went on to write that, for the rest of his life, he would be dedicated to asking for forgiveness. He concluded the letter with a few playful jokes the two had shared before Austin went into foster care.

When Mrs. Jackson and I read the letter with Austin, we had tears in our eyes as we saw his positive reaction. Yet again, Austin was strong, telling us how he forgave his father for what he had done. None of us denied the wrongness of the crime, but Mrs. Jackson talked to Austin about the power of redemption and explained how lucky he was to have four parents who loved him.

It is important for foster children to have a continuing bond with their biological parents, when possible (Berrick & Skivenes, 2012). Austin's mother has since gotten out of jail and is trying to make progress in her life. Austin has occasional phone conversations with her, and she has also been supportive of his adoption.

Now that Austin had closure from the past, he was busy thinking about the future. He talked about his hopes of living a life filled with peace and happiness—some days saying he wanted to become a pastor who works in prisons, and other days a famous inventor. Most important, Austin was dreaming about a bright future. He engaged positively with his adoptive family, and was doing well in school.

The road ahead likely will present more challenges. The trauma Austin faced does not just go away, but when you see him jumping on a trampoline, smiling, and giggling with his sisters, you realize his chances of having a positive future are as good as any other.

## References

Berrick, J. D. (2009). Take me home: Protecting America's vulnerable families. New York: Oxford University Press.

Berrick, J., & Skivenes, M. (2012). Dimensions of high quality foster care: parenting plus. Children and Youth Services Review, 34 (9), 1956-1965.

Cherry, D. J., & Orme, J.G. (2013). The vital few foster mothers. Children and Youth Services Review, 35 (9), 1625-1633.

Cohen , J., Mannarino, A., & Deblinger, E. (2012). Trauma-focused cbt for children and adolescents. New York: The Guilford Press.

Lindsey, D. (2004). The welfare of children. (2nd ed.). New York: Oxford University Press.

National Association of Social Workers. (approved 1996, revised 2008). Code of Ethics of the National Association of Social Workers. Washington, DC: Author.

Poulin, J. (2005). Strengths-based generalist practice: A collaborative approach (2nd ed.). Belmont, CA: Wadsworth Cengage Learning.

Scott, T. (2012). Placement instability and risky behaviors of youth aging out of foster care. Child and Adolescent Social Work Journal, 29 (1), 6183.

Webb, N. B. (2006). Working with traumatized youth in child welfare. New York: Guilford Press.

Jordan Wilfong, MSW, LSW, currently practices social work in Pittsburgh, Pennsylvania. He specializes in child and family therapy. He would like to thank Heather M. Martin, LCSW, for her help with editing this article.

# Turn Up the Tech in Social Work

## Social (Work) Connections Through Social Media

### by Ellen Belluomini, LCSW

The social work profession thrives through connections with individuals and systems. Twenty years ago, I relied on my supervisor, co-workers, trainings, community meetings, and organizational newsletters to develop my networking with colleagues. These options still provide a good place to start building your contacts. Don't let the opportunities for professional growth end within this circle. Advances in technology offer global access to resources, enabling a richness and depth to relationships never before possible.

If you are reading this article in *The New Social Worker* or on its website, you have a taste of the possibilities offered online. The following list provides guidelines to foster growth of your online networking potential.

Start with the basics. Decide why connecting is important and how much time you can devote to discussions. Motivation for professional interaction varies. Friendship, diversity in colleagues, keeping up to date in the field, career potential, or collaboration opportunities are all valid reasons for networking. Free time is precious to dedicated social workers. One hour on Sundays is enough to start developing your network.

List each passion or interest. Internet options for connections can be overwhelming. Keeping up with reading e-mail can be a challenge. How do you cultivate online relationships and keep new connections manageable? Enthusiasm about a topic will increase your interest in making and keeping related social media connections. Begin by only exploring your top one or two passions. Be specific. Narrowing topics leads to an increase in efficiency of your time and efforts. There is a big difference between "social work in a skilled nursing center specializing in dementia care units" and "I love social work!"

Create a goal for connecting. A goal will help narrow your scope, providing direction in types of social networks to enter. Future employment contacts can be nurtured through Google +, LinkedIn, and Meetup groups. If you are looking for support, there are numerous online support groups available. Collaboration on programs or research can be started through your groups or sites such as Academia.edu. Social needs can be met through Facebook, YouTube, and Twitter. Almost every university or social media group has connections to the big three. Subscriptions to social work magazines, blogs, and relevant newsfeeds will help generate content to post within the group.

Develop a strategy. Depending on the area of interest, strategies will differ. LinkedIn offers many group connections but is at times impersonal. Sustained relationships are more likely in group forums like Google+ or Meetup.com. When you join a group, evaluate it to determine if it meets your needs. Go back through the posts and comments. Is this a community you want to be a part of? Identify how many posts you will make a week. Setting specific times for posting helps keep groups manageable. I go to social media the last 30 minutes I will be on my computer. I see it as a reward for hard work.

Be proactive in each community. Just as in person, impressions can be made online and will stay in the psyche of people. Discussions and impressions are developed through your posts. Posting information relative to the community is an opportunity. Be constructive and add to the quality of information, or be friendly and supportive. Help your followers to want to get to know the person behind the post.

Become global searching for linkages. Social work is worldwide. Australia, Canada, China, Great Britain, and other countries offer diverse insights about evidence-based practices, social justice issues, and alternative programming. Learning about other cultures and problem solving strategies develops empathy for our client populations. Through global relationships, we can challenge our ignorance, improve the accuracy of our knowledge, and build global solutions together.

Think toward future possibilities. No one likes when someone pops into a community only to ask for favors or promote themselves. Connections made now can lead to important relationships. Nurture your groups as you would a budding relationship. Nurture trust, support, and respect in your communication. Be consistent. These relationships need nurturing as plants need light and water. If you forget about a plant, it will wither away. Dedication to relationships creates endless possibilities.

My presence in social work groups has led to an increasing support network, educational opportunities, research

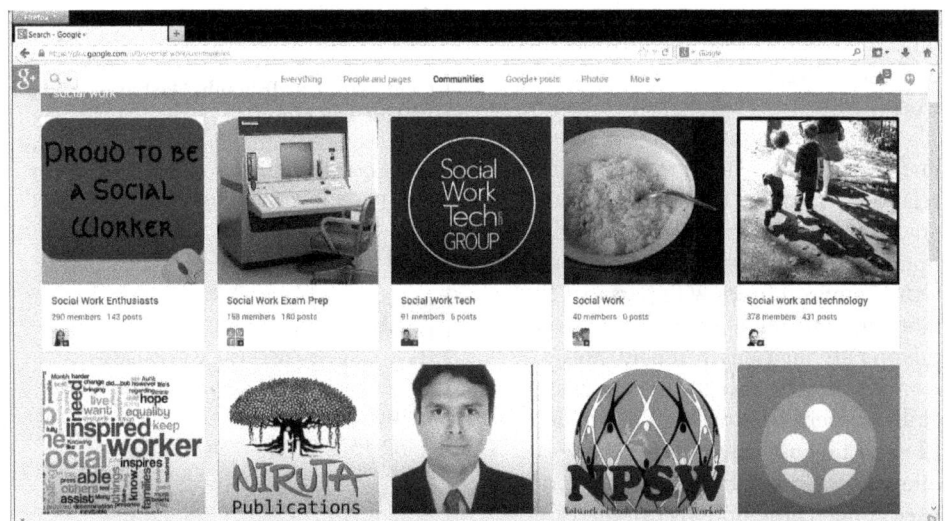

*Social workers connect through a variety of groups on Google+.*

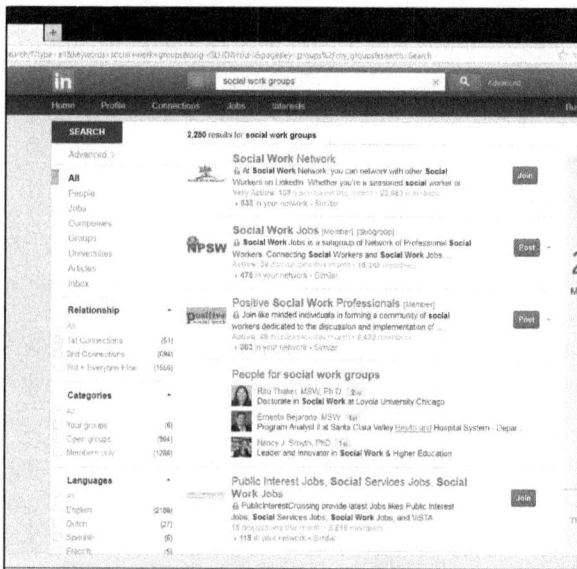

*LinkedIn is another good source of groups related to social work.*

collaboration, consulting, and speaking engagements. These groups meet personal and professional needs. *The New Social Worker, Social Justice Solutions, Social Work Helper,* and *GovLoop* are sites where I have found opportunities for education, networking, and advocacy efforts. Through a professional relationship I developed online, my crisis intervention class was able to join a Twitter debate on gun control with three other schools of social work. Students heard opinions from peers and other professors, and the experience opened them up to connections across the country. I posted to my social work and technology Google+ group about joining me in an ethics and technology course offered by Coursera. One of the members offered her participation. We are going to support each other through the course.

I enjoy finding new ways to play with these groups. My creativity is fed by others willing to experiment within the context of advancing the field of social work.

The future is promising for online connections. As communities and relationships move toward an online environment, the sophistication of digital options will increase. Second Life offers virtual environments with personal interaction through avatars. Avatars can manipulate their environment. Social workers may be able to participate in global experiences through this milieu. Low- or no-cost video conferencing is offered by Google Hangout, Skype, and FaceTime. These options can increase group cohesiveness of online groups. Nextt may be an option once a group

has been established. This new social media interface offers a private network for online coordination and in-person interactions. The platform uses a "blended" approach to track projects, ideas, and meetings of groups. Relationships, conferences, meetings, and think tanks can start online and manifest into face-to-face collaborations. Wherever the future is headed, one thing is certain—social media will be an intricate part of our personal and professional lives.

*Ellen M. Belluomini, LCSW, received her MSW from University of Illinois, Jane Addams School of Social Work and is currently a doctoral student at Walden University. She is a lecturer at Dominican University. She has developed online and blended curricula with an emphasis on integrating technology into human services practice. She writes a blog, "Bridging the Digital Divide in Social Work Practice," to increase awareness about technology's uses. She presents*

*and consults on various issues related to social services. Her clinical work has been in private practice, management of nonprofit agencies, and programming for vulnerable populations.*

## Accessing Apps: Networking Through Tech
*by Ellen Belluomini, LCSW*

### Apps to Facilitate Networking

**CamCard, CardMunch, Hashable, and WorldCard Mobile**
Turns business cards into contacts with notes about the person. No more card catalogs or piles of cards you can't remember why you kept.
Cost: Free to $6.99 for Android and Apple

**Bump**
Do you have an educational infographic about your agency? Did you develop an intake that could be helpful to disseminate at your next conference? This app can transfer files, videos, and photos, plus share contact information. Leave a lasting impression with a bump.
Cost: Free for Android and Apple

## Pamela Russo Receives Kristin Federici Bowser Award at Temple University Harrisburg

Temple University's MSW program at Harrisburg (TUH) celebrated graduation on May 17, 2014, at Whitaker Center for the Performing Arts. Graduate Pamela Russo received the Kristin Federici Bowser Award.

This award is in memory of graduate Kristin Federici Bowser, who died tragically at the hands of a drunk, texting driver. Kristin was an outstanding student, first president of the Student Alliance at TUH, established the first student mentoring program at TUH, and helped secure grant funding for the Baby Love program at Hamilton Health Center, a program for young single mothers. Kristin also served on the Board of Directors of NASW Pennsylvania Chapter as the Central Division Chair.

The award recognizes a graduating MSW student at Temple Harrisburg. Like Kristin, the recipient of the award must demonstrate academic excellence, outstanding commitment to the social work profession with a focus on community involvement, and service to the School of Social Work by leadership. Kristin's parents, Kathleen and Chris Federici, presented the award to Ms. Russo (pictured below).

# Reviews

*Children of Substance-Abusing Parents: Dynamics and Treatment, edited by Shulamith Lala Ashenberg Straussner and Christine Huff Fewell, Springer Publishing Company, New York, 2011, 288 pages, $41.66.*

This thorough and elegantly written book is a must-read for anyone who is involved with or teaches in the area of children of substance abusing parents. The book is divided into three parts that take the reader from an overview of the existing knowledge about children of substance abusing parents, to treatment issues in clinical settings, to possible interventions for these children. Although they remain "children" of substance abusing parents, the book delineates their story from newborns to adults. These 13 chapters are not simply well suited for academic audiences, but are also heartfelt and emotionally loaded for any interested reader. As one perceives the chaos, the problems, the tremendously difficult issues, and the consequences to their lives, one cannot help but feel outraged and heartbroken from the stories, shocked by the statistics, and compelled to do something for this population.

The reader becomes familiar with the dynamics of children of substance abusing parents and their chaotic attachment patterns in the first chapters. Once this background is established, one learns about the types of treatments that exist and their challenges. A number of treatments are discussed: from early interventions in alcohol and tobacco use by pregnant women, to evidence-based programs targeting children, to intervention strategies for adolescents and psychodrama as a form of intervention for adults who have grown up with substance abusing parents.

Psychodrama allows the body and the emotional memory to emerge through action and role-play, allowing adults to resolve previous conflicting situations in their lives. This type of therapy is well depicted in chapter seven. Other types of interventions and implications for social workers are further discussed in the third part of the book. Finally, issues of children of parents incarcerated for substance abuse are described, and practice implications are laid out for this extremely sensitive population. The book ends with five case studies that wonderfully weave together and illustrate all the discussions in previous chapters.

These five personal stories are heartwarming and make the entire book come alive.

I was positively impressed with the great emphasis on the social environment and its influences on children of substance abusing parents throughout these chapters. One can clearly notice how many emotional and behavioral problems of children are deeply rooted in family settings. Therefore, by preventing or intervening at the right time, social workers can and should make a crucial difference in the lives of these children. I wholeheartedly applaud the researchers who contributed to this collection and the editors who skillfully put this comprehensive book together.

*Reviewed by Bora Pajo, Ph.D., M.A., Assistant Professor, Mercyhurst University, Sociology and Social Work Department.*

---

*Sexual Health in Recovery: A Professional Counselor's Manual, by Douglas Braun-Harvey, MFT, CGP, Springer Publishing Company: New York, NY, 2011, 297 pages, $49.00.*

*Sexual Health in Recovery: A Professional Counselor's Manual* is a welcomed addition to the fields of addiction, sexology, sexual health, and sexual addiction. This book adds new knowledge and language to the discourse on sexual health and addiction. Doug Braun-Harvey utilizes the term *sex/drug linked behaviors* to describe clients who have drug and alcohol addictions and struggle with sexual behavior and sexual health issues that affect recovery. This book takes a holistic approach to recovery from drug and alcohol dependence that incorporates a sex positive lens to treatment that can focus on shame-based sex negative treatment and relapse prevention. Braun-Harvey also uses James Prochaska's work on behavior change to help reluctant clinicians and clients make the transitions to incorporate the sex positive approach to addiction interventions.

This book is divided into three sections. Section I, Counselor Readiness, focuses on elements such as the definition of sexual health; what sexual health looks like as a part of recovery; and understanding the counselor's values, attitudes, and beliefs about sexual health. Section 2, Sexual Health in Recovery Assessment, focuses on how to utilize the Sexual Health in Recovery Assessment Instrument, the instrument's limitations, and how to use it with clients to provide feedback. Section 3, Sexual Health in Recovery Counseling Skills, deals with skills counselors need to effectively help clients from a sex-positive paradigm.

As a clinician, sexologist, sex addictions therapist, and faculty member, I believe this book is truly a manual for all mental health practitioners who are interested in incorporating a sex positive approach into treatment of clients with high sex/drug linked behaviors. It allows the reader to examine and explore personal biases that they bring to this work and offers tools to make necessary change to help clients address their addictions from a holistic affirming paradigm. It does a thorough job of giving voice to what most counselors and therapists witness in practice working in drug and alcohol treatment centers—that is, how do we address addictions and sexual health in treatment? I would definitely recommend this book to students, faculty, and practitioners.

*Reviewed by Latoya Brooks, Ph.D., LCSW, CSAT-S, Assistant Professor, University of Mississippi.*

---

*Hungry for Ecstasy: Trauma, the Brain, and the Influence of the Sixties, by Sharon Klayman Farber, Ph.D., Lanham, Maryland, Jason Aronson, Inc., 2013, 413 pages, $90 hardcover, $56.99 e-book.*

Farber draws on her personal and professional experience, as well as her research, to explore the human desire for the ecstatic experience. She writes in a straightforward and engaging manner that would appeal to anyone who wishes to learn more about the cultural history, science, and psychology of the experience of ecstasy. She explores various ways, including religious ecstasies, cult-induced ecstasies, addiction, eating disorders, and body mutilation, in which individuals seek to fill a hunger for ecstasy. She weaves in concepts of how trauma is processed in the brain and is experienced in the body and describes what people are actually seeking when they engage in harmful behaviors. She illustrates altered states of consciousness and assists therapists in understanding dissociated communications from their clients.

Readers will come away with fascinating and thought-provoking perspectives of many different theorists, mental health practitioners, and individuals with their own stories of pain and a desire for an ecstatic experience, which will spark creativity in the therapist when working with individuals who are trying desperately to escape painful emotions. *Hungry for Ecstasy* is a must read for social workers who work with adults or adolescents who engage in self-mutilating, addictive, or other high-risk behavior, because it will spark the curiosity of the reader to further explore these concepts and to keep an open mind and be accepting when engaging with these individuals.

Farber provides rich examples of therapeutic dialogue and practical examples of how to be more self-aware, attuned, empathic, and caring in order to provide a safe and accepting space for these individuals to open up about painful aspects of their lives. She offers engaging ways to plant seeds and open the door to a discussion on how individuals can learn to manage difficult emotions without engaging in self-harm. Lastly, Farber provides countless references, giving the reader an opportunity for further exploration of captivating ideas and concepts.

*Reviewed by Danielle M. Willenborg, MSW, Veterans Village of San Diego.*

---

*What Is Your What? by Steve Olsher, 240 pages, Wiley, 2013, $17.00 hardcover.*

The back cover and initial pages of this book tout it to be a life-altering experience for every reader, claiming that anyone who completes the book and follows the steps as presented will walk away with a clear indication of their "what," which is how author Steve Olsher refers to a person's life purpose. As is often true with self-help books, the readers' results may vary, based on some key factors.

For example, this book asks the reader to consider personal life experiences and then to extrapolate on them. A reader (or a social worker's client) who lacks personal insight or who has not yet processed the effect of a trauma might seriously benefit from being required to baby-step through this portion of the book.

In another passage, the book instructs the reader to write about how she or he wants to be perceived versus how she or he believes others perceive her or him. For someone lacking self-awareness, this might be a great exercise. That said, it is also very possible that a client who has been working on personal growth might find this to be pedantic. Since those who would benefit most from these exercises might lack the ability to complete the exercises individually, a social worker may find that such tasks would be more helpful to complete as a discussion or with the social worker's immediate feedback during a session.

The author presupposes that every reader has at least one gift or major talent, something that may or may not be universally true and something that may be very difficult to process for someone in the midst of depression or who lacks self-esteem. In addition, folks who do not appreciate the implication that everyone is a sort of "special snowflake" may find this book pandering to a very different crowd than to be meant to reach those whose beliefs of self and others are more focused on the task than on the goal. Additionally, big-picture thinkers would be much more likely to find this book appealing than those who are short-term oriented.

With such disparity regarding the benefits of this book, it is possible that the guided self-reflection may benefit someone debating whether to pursue a career in social work. However, a practicing social worker would likely do better to keep this book in her or his office and utilize the exercises individually to encourage self-reflection rather than to recommend that a client purchase this book.

*Reviewed by Kristen Marie (Kryss) Shane, MSW, LSW, LMSW.*

---

*New Perspectives on Poverty: Policies, Programs, and Practice, by Elissa D. Giffords and Karen R. Garber (Eds.). Lyceum Books, Inc., Chicago, 2014, 539 pages, $59.95 softcover.*

Giffords and Garber, both associated with Long Island University, have edited a lengthy, detailed, and affordable first edition textbook to "challenge the old beliefs about people living in poverty" (p. xxi). With only 11 chapters, the 15 contributing authors were able to go into substantial depth and detail, and most of the chapters were single authored monographs of substance, despite the fact that more than a third of the contributors were junior faculty.

This textbook begins with two rather standard chapters that define poverty and summarize the history of social welfare programs in the United States since FDR. The first is stronger than the second, which tends to gloss over improvements in social welfare, such as the Earned Income Tax Credit, the Medicare Modernization Act, and the Americans with Disabilities Act, in an attempt to dichotomize social welfare trends within an ideological spectrum from liberal to conservative.

The third chapter is a thorough account of labor market policy, but many will find it difficult to follow the changing unemployment rates through the years.

This chapter is in desperate need of a graphic or table to help pull it together.

The seven chapters that follow focus on specific populations at risk of living in poverty: the homeless, single mothers, older adults, people with disabilities, people with mental illnesses or co-occurring substance use, immigrants and refugees, and military families. A standard outline is used that addresses demographics, historical perspectives, key issues, government policies and programs, social justice issues, micro/mezzo/macro interventions, and concluding case studies. The quality of these chapters is quite high with current references, up-to-date statistics, and clear writing, but sometimes poverty is overshadowed by the history and other issues discussed. Each chapter ends with discussion questions, an annotated list of Internet resources, and suggestions for further reading. A final concluding chapter by the editors summarizes the book and suggests 21 actions for readers to address poverty, ranging from volunteering at a soup kitchen to writing a member of Congress. The book concludes with a 19-page glossary, authors' biographies, and a detailed index.

In subsequent editions of this text, I suggest the addition of at least three chapters. The omission of Native Americans from a list of people at risk of poverty is unwarranted when so many reservations have unemployment rates over 50 percent. The labor market consequences associated with mass incarceration also calls out for chapter-length treatment in a book claiming to address new perspectives on poverty, and I am concerned that the most effective anti-poverty program—the Earned Income Tax Credit—is mentioned on only seven pages. The awareness of social welfare trends that the editors hope to cultivate among readers should also include more awareness of federal, state, and local tax policies. My final suggestion is for the editors to make it explicitly clear what is new about the perspectives shared in this textbook.

When selecting a textbook, I always look at the price first. Social welfare policy instructors who have sticker-shock over the escalating prices of many popular texts may want to peruse this one as an alternative. There is much to commend it, but I suspect that it will earn better reception among MSW students than BSW students.

*Reviewed by Peter A. Kindle, Ph.D., CPA, LMSW, Assistant Professor, University of South Dakota.*

*From Pariahs to Partners: How Parents and Their Allies Changed New York City's Child Welfare System, by David Tobis, Oxford University Press, 2013.*

In social work, we are often challenged to make a determination regarding the meritorious contributions a writer makes to the profession. This manuscript artfully commands the attention of child welfare professionals and academicians, alike. In his book, *From Pariahs to Partners: How Parents and Their Allies Changed New York City's Child Welfare System,* David Tobis captures the essence of perseverance in the wake of tremendous odds, with regard to New York City's Administration for Children's Services and the families affected by this system. In this book, Tobis offers a brief overview of the inner workings of a large bureaucratic system, the challenges that have saddled this organization and the city over time, and provides a guide to help everyday citizens implement fundamental changes at a grassroots level.

The author asserts his authority in writing this book by recounting his roles as a community organizer for a social movement, a consultant on an international level, and an administrator within the child welfare arena. Tobis' passion for effecting positive change began when he worked in the Deep South during the Civil Rights Movement, prior to working internationally with UNICEF and the World Bank. His commitment to helping underserved and under-represented populations led him to an administrative role with the Child Welfare Fund.

The book tells the story of micro and macro change, and it allows readers to immerse themselves in a system fraught with forces that leave children in precarious predicaments. Tobis profiles six parent advocates who, prior to their work as advocates, struggled to maintain stability in their lives. While in the throes of tumult and change, these parents were separated from their children. In the wake of this reality, they learned about what they did not know and used this information to form partnerships and help mobilize others who lacked knowledge about the system.

Tobis provides depth about the change agents who played major roles in shaping the environment that empowered parents to shift processes in a large bureaucracy. He discusses the influence of these organizations, which were committed to changing a system for the better, and, in turn, offers insight about how these processes could be adapted by others to change other child welfare service systems.

This book offers lessons for both the child welfare practitioner and the student who aspires to make a positive impact in the lives of children entangled in the child welfare system. Tobis opens wide the floodgates for helping others realize what is possible. This book promotes the idea that positive change is possible and probable when people are committed and willing to do the work it takes make it happen.

*Reviewed by Kenya Y. McKinley, Ph.D., Assistant Professor, Social Work Program, Department of Sociology, Mississippi State University.*

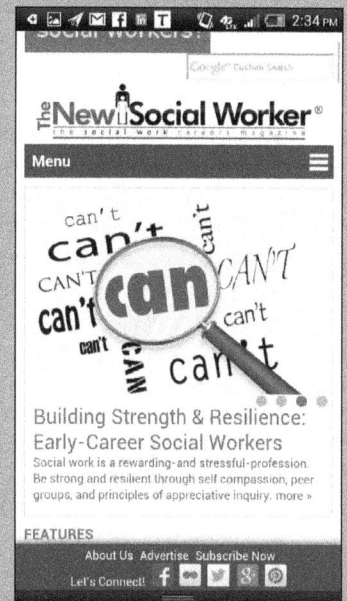

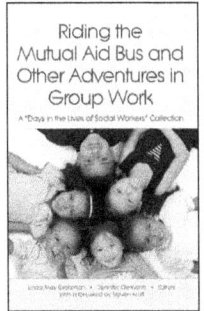

# Beginnings, Middles, & Ends
## *Sideways Stories on the Art & Soul of Social Work*
### Ogden W. Rogers, Ph.D., LCSW, ACSW

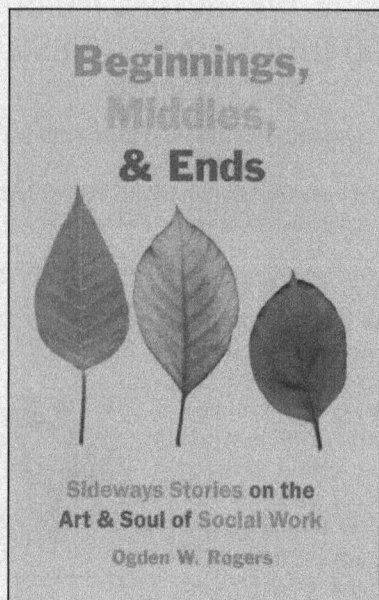

A sideways story is some moment in life when you thought you were doing one thing, but you ended up learning another. A sideways story can also be a poem, or prose, that, because of the way it is written, may not be all that direct in its meaning. What's nice about both clouds, and art, is that you can look at them and just resonate. That can be good for both the heart and the mind.

Many of the moments of this book have grown from experiences the author has had or stories he used in his lectures with students or told in his office with clients. Some of them have grown from essays written for others, for personal or professional reasons. They are moments on a path through the discovery of social work, a journey of beginnings, middles, and ends.

With just the right blend of humor and candor, each of these stories contains nuggets of wisdom that you will not find in a traditional textbook. They capture the essence and the art and soul of social work. In a world rushed with the illusion of technique and rank empiricism, it is the author's hope that some of the things here might make some moment in your thinking or feeling grow as a social worker. If they provoke a smile, or a tear, or a critical question, it's worth it. Everyone makes a different journey in a life of social work. These stories are one social worker's travelogue along the way.

## PRAISE FOR THE BOOK

*"As someone near the end of a long career in social work and social work education, I found the stories of Ogden Rogers in his collection,* Beginnings. Middles, and Ends, *to reflect so much of my own experience that I literally moved back and forth between tears of soulful recognition and laugh-out-loud moments of wonderful remembrances. There is something truthful and powerful about the artist who is willing to put a masterpiece together and leave the telltale signs of failed attempts. Too many who reflect on their past do so to minimize imperfection, setting standards unreachable by others. Ogden Rogers has charted a course of professionalism that encourages creativity, allowing for errors, and guided by honest reflection and dedication to those whom he would serve. This read is a gift to all, whether they are starting or ending their journey of service to others."*
    Terry L. Singer, Ph.D., Dean, Kent School of Social Work, University of Louisville

*"I found the stories humorous, sometimes painful, and incredibly honest and real. There is really nothing else out in our literature that is quite like this. It reminds me of when we teach the art and science of social work practice—this is the art."*
    Jennifer Clements, Ph.D., LCSW, Associate Professor, Shippensburg University

*"...a profound piece of creative literature that will reinstill idealism within senior social workers who are on the threshold of being cynical about their work."*
    Stephen M. Marson, Ph.D., Professor, University of North Carolina Pembroke

*"Recommended reading for new social workers, experienced social workers, friends and families of social workers, and future social workers because of the variety of anecdotal case presentations and personal perceptions. Truly open and honest portrayals of social work and the helping professions with touching, easy-to-read entries fit within the beginning, middle, and ending framework. This book is suggested for both public and academic libraries to support the career services and/or professional development collections."*
    Rebecca S. Traub, M.L.S., Library Specialist, Temple University Harrisburg

For the complete
Table of Contents of
Ogden Rogers'
***Beginnings, Middles, & Ends***

and other information
about this book, see:

***beginningsmiddlesandends.com***

Available directly from the publisher
now! Available in print and Kindle
editions at Amazon.com.

## ABOUT THE AUTHOR

*Ogden W. Rogers, Ph.D., LCSW, ACSW, is Professor and Chair of the Department of Social Work at The University of Wisconsin-River Falls. He has been a clinician, consultant, educator, and storyteller.*

ISBN: 978-1-929109-35-7 • 2013 • 5.5 x 8.5 • 249 pages • $19.95 plus shipping  Order from White Hat Communications, PO Box 5390, Harrisburg, PA 17110-0390
http://shop.whitehatcommunications.com  717-238-3787 (phone)  717-238-2090 (fax)

# The New Social Worker ®
## the social work careers magazine

Fall 2014
Volume 21, Number 4

*Abilene Christian University faculty member Dr. Stephanie Hamm is shown with then-BSW students Amanda Wallander and Alex Moran. The shirts were designed by students in a macro practice course. They had talked about the show* Whale Wars *in class and wondered why it is so much easier to get people on board with fighting for animal rights and conservation than fighting for human and civil rights.*

# FEATURES

NEW:

Achieving Racial Equity
Through Social Work

Turn Up the Tech in
Social Work

Social Work Goes
to the Movies

# In This Issue

· Ebola and the Ethics of Using Unproven Drugs
· The Importance of Agency Culture and
  Balanced Boundaries
· The "Social" Social Worker: 10 Tools for
  Successful Networking
· Burnout and Self Care: A Process in Helping
· Social Workers in Public Libraries

...and much more!

Student Role Model:
Cierra Kaler-Jones

# CONTENTS

THE NEW SOCIAL WORKER®
Fall 2014
Volume 21, Number 4

# Publisher's Thoughts

Dear Reader,

Fall is in the air! I want to welcome our new subscribers, including all new social work students and recent graduates.

In this issue, as we close out our twenty-first year of publication, I am happy to announce our newest columnists. Mary Pender Greene, Sandra Bernabei, and Lisa Blitz are social workers who are working every day to fight racial inequity and structural racism in our society. These are issues that are on my mind a lot. They are in the news, social media, and everyday life. It has been 50 years since "Freedom Summer," and racism still permeates our society.

*The publisher/editor*

Social workers, we must be at the forefront. When I heard Mary, Sandy, and Lisa speak at the National Association of Social Workers conference in Washington, DC, this past July, I decided right then that I had found the answer to making this conversation an ongoing part of *THE NEW SOCIAL WORKER*. I feel very fortunate that they have agreed to write a column and share their perspectives and ideas for action with our readers. Look for their column, "Achieving Racial Equity Through Social Work," on page 19 of this issue.

I have always loved libraries. They are places you can go and just get lost in books and information and discover things serindipitously. But they are also one of the few safe, public places where anyone can enter and find shelter for a while. I heard a few years ago about social workers in libraries, an idea I had thought and wondered about even before hearing that it was a reality. It makes sense to me. Apparently, the idea is catching on. I would love to see it become more widespread. Read about it in Barbara Trainin Blank's feature article on page 12.

As always, this issue is packed. Read articles on field placement, ethics, career networking, burnout and self care, agency culture, movies, technology, licensing, and more. Enjoy the articles, and then go to our website and share them with friends, colleagues, and classmates!

To subscribe to THE NEW SOCIAL WORKER's Social Work E-News and notifications of new issues of the magazine, go to the "Subscribe" link on our website at *http://www.socialworker.com*. (It's free!)

Until next time–happy reading!

*Linda M. Grobman*

## Write for The New Social Worker

We are looking for articles from social work practitioners, students, and educators. Some areas of particular interest are: social work ethics; student field placement; practice specialties; social work careers/job search; technology; "what every new social worker needs to know;" and news of unusual, creative, or nontraditional social work.

Feature articles run 1,500-2,000 words in length. News articles are typically 100-150 words. Our style is conversational, practical, and educational. Write as if you are having a conversation with a student or colleague. What do you want him or her to know about the topic? What would you want to know? Use examples.

The best articles have a specific focus. If you are writing an ethics article, focus on a particular aspect of ethics. For example, analyze a specific portion of the NASW *Code of Ethics* (including examples), or talk about ethical issues unique to a particular practice setting. When possible, include one or two resources at the end of your article–books, additional reading materials, and/or websites.

We also want photos of social workers and social work students "in action" for our cover, and photos to accompany your news articles!

Send submissions to lindagrobman@socialworker.com.

# The New Social Worker®
*the social work careers magazine*

## Fall 2014
## Vol. 21, Number 4

### Publisher/Editor
Linda May Grobman, MSW, ACSW, LSW

### Contributing Writers
Barbara Trainin Blank
Allan Barsky, JD, MSW, Ph.D.
Addison Cooper, LCSW
Ellen Belluomini, LCSW
Kathryn A. Krase, Ph.D., J.D., MSW

THE NEW SOCIAL WORKER® (ISSN 1073-7871) is published four times a year by White Hat Communications, P.O. Box 5390, Harrisburg, PA 17110-0390. Phone: (717) 238-3787. Fax: (717) 238-2090. Send address corrections to: lindagrobman@socialworker.com

Advertising rates available on request.

Photo/art credits: Image from BigStockPhoto.com © Sakkmesterke (page 4), Ra2studio (page 8), Pichelco (page 10), Sarantala Photo (page 12), Jorg Hackermann (page 13), Dvarg (page 16), Marmion (page 17), Afhunta (page 27), Mindscanner (page 28), Jam4travel (page 29), Sam2172 (page 29), and Wolterk (page 32).

### Editorial Advisory Board
Vivian Bergel, Ph.D., ACSW, LSW
Joseph Davenport, Ph.D.
Judith Davenport, Ph.D., LCSW
Brad Forenza, MSSW
Mozart Guerrier, MSW
Sam Hickman, MSW, ACSW, LCSW

Send all editorial, advertising, subscription, and other correspondence to:

**THE NEW SOCIAL WORKER**
**White Hat Communications**
**P.O. Box 5390**
**Harrisburg, PA 17110-0390**
**(717) 238-3787 Phone**
**(717) 238-2090 Fax**

lindagrobman@socialworker.com
http://www.socialworker.com
http://www.facebook.com/newsocialworker
http://www.twitter.com/newsocialworker

**Print Edition:**
http://newsocialworker.magcloud.com

# Cierra Kaler-Jones

## *by Barbara Trainin Blank*

Bubbly, energetic, driven. These words describe Cierra Kaler-Jones, a BSW student who not only competed for the Miss America title, but aims to someday become the U.S. Secretary of Education.

A schedule that normally could be described as hectic has become intense. In addition to her social work major at Rutgers University, where she has been earning a higher-than-3.9 GPA, the 21-year-old has a triple minor: women's and gender studies, critical and comparative race and ethnic studies, and criminology.

She spent part of the summer in India in a fellowship program and is now on the road a great deal of time as Miss New Jersey, representing her birth and home state. Kaler-Jones was away for two weeks in September with the 53 other Miss America contestants, for which she needed special permission to miss school.

On top of that, she is part of a Rutgers University dance team, which performs at football and basketball games. A lover of Broadway musicals, she was awed by the first performance she saw of the American Ballet Theatre.

Kaler-Jones thanks her parents—actually, her mother and the stepfather she considers her father—for giving her the confidence to achieve what she has. Kaler-Jones is the first person in her family to attend college, and her 17-year-old brother is following suit. "It's a big deal for my family," she says.

A lemon-makes-lemonade person, Kaler-Jones found a positive aspect of appearing in court in an attempt to have her biological father fulfill an obligation to pay for her education. "It shaped my desire to be an advocate," she said. "I was taken aback by the number of minority kids in the criminal justice system and the inequalities."

Not surprisingly, Kaler-Jones has always been a bookworm. "My parents took me to the bookstore every week," she says with a laugh.

She always has sought additional ways to learn and teach. Kaler-Jones earned a Certificate in Women's Leadership from the Institute for Women's Leadership; participated in the two-semester Human Rights Living-Learning Community, designed for students to research human rights policies, non-governmental organizations, and social justice movements around the world; and co-taught a course for the Barbara Voorhees Mentor Program at Douglass Residential College.

The BSW candidate was a U.S. Operations intern last summer for She's the First, an organization that sponsors girls' education in low-income countries to give them the chance to become the first in their families to graduate from secondary school.

Using technology and social media, She's the First is committed to connecting sponsors and scholars around the world in innovative, mutually beneficial ways to foster mentorship, philanthropy, equality, and leadership. Kaler-Jones developed the curriculum for She's the First's partnership with The Young Women's Leadership Schools of New York's Summer Camp.

"She's the First is so proud of Cierra," says the president and founder, Tammy Tibbetts. "She was named our 2014 Campus Leader of the Year, an honor given at our Leadership Summit each year (in August in New York City)."

What Tibbetts admires about Kaler-Jones is "how she inspires others around

*Cierra Kaler-Jones*

her to be part of her team, to take action that will not only create joy in her own community, but also create opportunities for girls around the world. When Cierra signs up to do something, she does it. She is one of the most authentic, persistent, and passionate young women I've ever met."

In addition to the social work degree she's completing, Kaler-Jones hopes to obtain a master's degree in education policy and then go to law school. In 2013, she was a summer intern in the Criminal Justice Division of the Office of the Attorney General of New Jersey.

The multifaceted young woman also has been an advocate for the arts. In fact, her platform for the Miss Jersey and Miss America pageants is "Empowering Today's Youth Through Arts Education." When arts programs were cut for lack of funding in her high school, she went to board of education meetings to voice her opinion about the benefits of such programs. "The arts taught me self-confidence and give a person cultural and personal capital," she told the officials. "For the first time, I felt my voice was important, that people really listened. That was a huge turning point

*Kaler-Jones continued on page 25*

# Ethics Alive!

# Ebola and the Ethics of Using Unproven Drugs
### by Allan Barsky, J.D., MSW, Ph.D.

*Editor's Note: This article was written in August 2014. As of October 1, 2014, the number of reported cases in West Africa has exceeded 6,000, with more than 3,000 deaths. Other developments have emerged, as well, including the first case of Ebola diagnosed in the U.S. in late September.*

By the first week of August 2014, more than 2,100 people in the west African countries of Liberia, Sierra Leone, Nigeria, and Guinea had contracted the Ebola virus. More than 1,100 of these people had died from Ebola.

In the midst of this epidemic, people with Ebola were told there was no cure. Although some pharmaceutical companies were in early stages of developing a curative treatment for Ebola, no medications had been tested on humans.

Frenzy erupted in American media when news broke that two American health workers who had contracted Ebola were being transported from Africa to Emory University Hospital in Atlanta, GA. Fear spread that these health workers could spread Ebola in the United States, putting this country at risk of an epidemic. Further news emerged that the two American health workers were provided with an untested medication, ZMapp, and that this medication had cured the Ebola.

The optics of the situation raised many concerns: Why were Africans told there was no medication for them, but "just enough" medication had been found for two White Americans? By what ethical standards is it okay to provide life-saving treatment to some people and withhold it from others? Was racism a motivating factor?

For social workers, this situation raises questions of social justice and respect for the dignity and worth of all people. Still, we must be careful to avoid a rush to judgment. When analyzing ethical issues, we need to consider not just what we know, but what we do not know:

## 1. What is the effectiveness of ZMapp, and what are its risks?

Even if two Americans seemed to recover from Ebola after taking ZMapp, we do not know whether ZMapp was the actual cause of their recovery, whether there were other intervening factors, and whether ZMapp would be equally effective for others who could take the medication. As we know from research courses, an "n" of 2 and a nonrandomized sample raise questions about the generalizability of the findings.

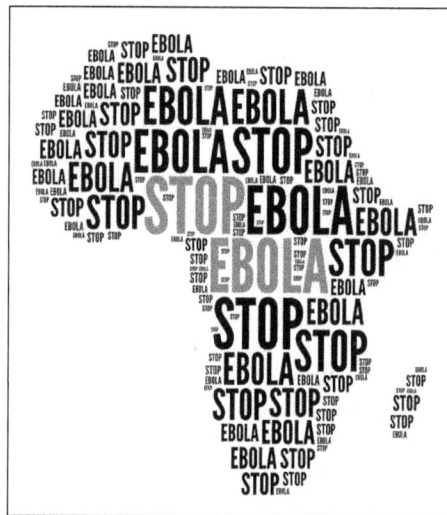

## 2. What were the motivating factors for providing ZMapp to Americans, while not providing it to Africans?

If the rationale was based on racist factors ("White American lives are worth more"), then the decisions violate ethical principles of social justice and respect. Alternatively, the World Health Organization and other decision-making bodies may have used other factors that are ethically justifiable.

Consider the history of using vulnerable populations to test new drugs and medical interventions. If the untested medications were provided to Africans and they suffered negative effects (e.g., hastening of death, greater pain), it may have appeared to some that American pharmaceutical companies or researchers were using Africans as "guinea pigs."

Another possible motivation relates to conditions in the west African countries. How did the financial, economic, political, health, and social challenges in these countries weigh in the decision not to provide Africans with the medications? If the issues were purely financial—the American government could pay for the medications and the African governments could not—then again, we have a violation of the principles of social justice.

On the other hand, perhaps the conditions on the ground made it difficult to administer and monitor the administration of the medications. Some African communities may have lacked basic necessities, such as water and electricity (e.g., if the medications needed to be refrigerated).

Likewise, we would need to know whether the African governments would have approved administration of the medications. The U.S. government (including the Centers for Disease Control) acted unusually quickly to allow administration of an untested drug. Were the African governments even asked?

## 3. What forms of help were provided to the Africans?

When considering whether it is ethical to withhold a certain type of help to a particular client or group, one should also consider what forms of help *were* offered. Although each person's life is deserving of dignity and respect, we may also need to consider the greater good. During the Ebola epidemic, controlling the spread of Ebola may be a greater need than treating those who have already contracted this disease. Given distrust of the medical professions in some African communities, many people may have resisted receiving "untested drugs." Ultimately, it may be more helpful to work with the community to help isolate those with Ebola, protecting the rest of the population.

## 4. What forms of treatment will be made available to Africans in the near future?

Even if ZMapp is an effective treatment, how much ZMapp is currently available, and how soon could it be made available, particularly to those in dire need? In ethics, the question is not simply what has been done, but what can be done. Thus, even if the initial choice to provide medications to two White Americans is questionable, the decisions of governments, pharmaceutical companies, and health care workers moving forward can make the situation ethically better—or worse.

If governments can work out reasonable protocols to make medications available, the benefits of the medications may be maximized and the risks reduced. ZMapp is not the only Ebola medication under development. At what stages of development and testing are the other medications, and what does early research suggest about their efficacy and risks? What type of encouragement or support do pharmaceutical companies need to develop treatments—not just to cure Ebola, but also to prevent its spread? And how can communities in west Africa and elsewhere act to reduce or eliminate further transmission of Ebola?

For social workers, the lessons of the Ebola epidemic extend beyond the use of unproven medications. Social work interventions comprise a range of talk therapies, counseling, advocacy, mediation, brokering, community organization, prevention campaigns, and other services. When we choose to offer clients particular models of intervention, we need to have sound rationale for using them. We should identify the best research evidence available, so we can help clients select the interventions that are most likely to be effective. We should be cautious about using untested interventions. We should involve our clients in making decisions about what interventions we are using—including whether we know the full extent of the risks and benefits of the interventions.

When we are working with ethnic minorities, people living in poverty, or other vulnerable populations, we should be particularly careful about the use of unproven interventions. On one hand, we do not want to exploit vulnerable populations to test these interventions. On the other hand, we do not want to withhold potentially helpful interventions simply because the client comes from a potentially vulnerable situation. We also need to work with communities, not just individuals, to promote good health and social functioning for all.

Finally, we should be careful about rushing to judgment. What might seem unethical at first may look different after we have gathered and assessed all the facts. In the midst of an urgent situation, it is difficult to assess all factors. Although we need to make ethical decisions in the moment, it is helpful to reflect back and evaluate the ethical implications when we have more information and the benefit of a longer-term perspective.

*Dr. Allan Barsky is Professor of Social Work at Florida Atlantic University and former Chair of the National Ethics Committee of the National Association of Social Workers. He is the author of* Ethics and Values in Social Work *(Oxford University Press),* Conflict Resolution for the Helping Professions *(Oxford University Press), and* Clinicians in Court *(Guilford Press). The views expressed in this article do not necessarily reflect the views of any of the organizations with which Dr. Barsky is affiliated.*

# Field Placement

## Social Work Experience
### by Danielle Carey

There is a lot to learn, through excitement
and through fear
Through hardships, stress, challenges, and
tears
The last 4 months have taught me a ton
But I'd say the journey has only begun...

During the first week, things were exciting
and new
But that was only because I didn't have a
clue
I began to learn how to balance my time
I utilized self care and I learned how to
rhyme.

I learned a lot of information and skills
But applying them practically was the true
thrill!
Information can only get you so far
Diving in to practice is what turns you into
a "social work superstar."

I learned the logistics of meeting face to face
Week two would prove to quicken the pace
I was armed with trainings and ethics galore
But my real skills were ready to be ex-
plored!

The third week arrived and I was finally
set free
On my own with clients, how hard could
it be?
I began to learn to engage and to plan
...Uh, oh. What now? Can you lend me a
hand?

What EBPs do I use, and how do they
apply?
Wait, it's been an hour already? Time truly
does fly
I survived my first client, now on to the
next one
Engagement of the client is important but
fun!

I struggled my way through the first few
But by week 4, I finally had a clue
I was learning to rely on instincts and self
To worry all the time would be bad for my
health.

Bias comes into the picture and it is not
always nice
To recognize it alone, is not enough to suffice
I had to learn to be honest and learn how
to work through it
It's good for my pride to be able to take
the hit.

I am a lot more biased than I would like to
admit
But Dr. Gallagher helped equip me to
handle it
It's important to recognize, to learn and to
grow
But it never truly goes away, the semester
goes to show.

Bias comes in waves like negative thoughts
Feelings of pride, apathy, and annoyance
had to be fought off
I think I am a stronger social worker than
before
Simply because of the biases I was able to
explore.

Values also came largely into play
Learn them, adopt them, they are here to
stay
Loving others unconditionally is easier said
than done
But as a social worker it comes second to
none.

I learned just how important relationships
can be
But it's all about them, not you, or not me
We should not give up if someone is demanding or hard,
To sabotage the relationship could leave
them emotionally scarred.

There were times of frustration I was ready
to walk
The hour was an hour, just 60 minutes on
the clock
I lost sight of the person, and their wants
and their needs
I just wanted the hour out of selfishness
and greed.

I reminded myself to take a step back
And remember that empathy should never
be lacked
The individual is frustrating, but that is not
an excuse
Unconditional positive regard should still
be produced.

I remembered values and that people need
love
Not only when it's easy but also when it's
tough
Relationships are fragile, and can be easy
to break
But I learned to push through, because it's
unfair to flake.

A natural flow came about by the 7th week
I felt as if I had hit my peak!
I had no complaints, things were going
pretty well
Weeks 8, 9, & 10 were also quite swell.

I was learning to maintain, and keep balance of time
Is being in a rut with some clients really a
crime?
I had to figure out a new style and approach
So that my clients could continue to grow
as I coached.

I learned that it's easy to get comfortable
and stuck
But easier to change things up, with any luck
My clients needed me to critically think
To avoid becoming stagnant, which was
right on the brink.

To change things up was the task at hand,
New approaches were needed to avoid
going bland
I learned new EBP skills to put to use
To knock us right out of our stagnant,
"stuck in a rut" blues.

IMR and DBT were the lifelines I called
upon
It was everything we've learned in class,
and quite the phenomenon!
The knowledge I've acquired is proving to
work!
"Who would have thought," I was able to
smirk.

The next few weeks elicited personal
growth and pride
My fear of confrontation was nullified
I handled conflict with strength I didn't
know I had
To put this fear in the past, I was actually
glad.

I doubted myself and my ability to handle
difficult staff
But now that is something I can put in the
past
I learned how to remain professional and
strong
Whether or not I was the one who was
wrong.

As far as future development, I have a long
way to go
This 16-week learning experience is just
the beginning of the show

It's okay to be unsure and it's okay to be scared
But exploring the unknown is the only way to be prepared.

Book knowledge and training can only get us so far
It's the experience under our belt that will really raise the bar
I plan to turn the unknown into "tried"
Even if I don't like it, I can uphold my pride.

I will push myself to continue to explore new avenues
To let something get the best of me, well, I just refuse
Professional development is an ongoing thing
We can think of it like, marriage...only without the ring.

We cannot give up on it, we must continue to learn
To work, and to struggle, and to inward turn
We're never done learning, it's sad but it's true
But we will always have co-workers and supervisors to help us through.

We are just starting out, we have a long way to go
But this last 16 weeks is only Act 1 of the show
It's not over yet, it's exciting yet scary
I know I've learned a lot through experiences that vary.

My ultimate goal is to graduate and use my newfound skills
And obtain a job that helps pay all my school bills
I want to help people to learn and to grow just the same
And to remember all the obstacles that they overcame.

I have not decided one direction to go
But there's plenty of areas, as it goes to show
I will wait to see what the next year brings
But for now, I'll continue to explore new things.

To sum it all up, I've come a long way
I can go to bed proud at the end of the day
And I feel a little more prepared to graduate next May!

*Danielle Carey is an MSW student at Indiana University-South Bend.*

# Poetry

# Tired of Societal Apathy
*by Pauline McCollough, LMSW*

As a young social worker seeking to bring awareness regarding issues of society, it is frustrating to me to witness lawmakers, politicians, people in higher positions, and even the average layman, all of whom know the issues within society but either do nothing to relieve the suffering or commit actions to bring further strife. I wrote the following as a wake-up call for action from myself and others who strive for change.

## "Tired"

*"Do not put your trust in princes, in human beings, who cannot save." – Psalms 146:3 (NIV)*

At 29 years old, the world says that I still have a long ways
to go before I've learned an ounce of what needs to be
learned. And by some people's standards, I am still young with
some battles yet to be fought, wars remaining that need to be won,
or, at the very least, maintaining the willingness to remain standing
and at first, those were my intentions, my plan to etch myself into the
forefront of history, to mark my place in society,
simply by diving into the recesses of my mind of lost childhood dreams
i.e. that of wanting to save the world, to be a superhero.

Speaking literally, of course, because as a child, that was all I knew and
22 years later into the future, fumbling along the path of a social worker, I find
there was a reason dreams remained in the recesses of the mind and
there comes a time when childish ways need to be left behind for
in my age of adulthood I find that society has a long way to go.

And I know that's no excuse for a superhero but as a mere social worker at 29 years old,
simply put: I'm tired.

I'm tired of a system that's constantly broken
I'm tired of the lies spoken from the lips of politicians and people in
higher positions

I'm tired of policies that lie by means of omission.

I'm tired that the only way our leaders know to run things is into the ground
I'm tired of the little guys, the nobodies, the hasbeens getting stuck and trampled on at the bottom time and time again.

I'm tired that the ones at the bottom know something needs to be done but
don't have enough will and drive to pull themselves from themselves long
enough to get along, to work together to pull themselves further up on the rungs.

I'm tired of them striking each other instead of raising a fist to the ones who assisted in
their disposition and insist nothing is wrong.

I'm tired of the politicians
I'm tired of the politicians
I am tired of the politicians
I am tired of politically motivated conservatives and liberals
Democrats or Republicans,
frankly, it makes no difference because no matter which side of
the fence the grass lies, on both sides, the money is always green.

I'm tired of their greed
I'm tired of their need to pit one against the other and placing their focus
on the growth of their wallets, giving in to distractions, leaving their
people to suffer.

I'm tired of a childhood dream deferred, one marred by a continually broken society created by the ones in charge...
and the rest of us.

I'm tired
of hearing people say they're tired of the way things are
yet take no action,
myself included.

*Pauline McCollough, LMSW, is a 2010 MSW graduate of Winthrop University. She resides in South Carolina, where she works as a Medicaid eligibility caseworker specializing in long-term care Medicaid for people who need nursing home Medicaid assistance.*

# The Importance of Agency Culture and Balanced Boundaries

*by Alyssa Lotmore, LMSW*

Imagine being 23 years old and fresh out of the social welfare program. You have just passed the licensure exam. You land your ideal job and are thrilled. Then, when you begin your job, you realize that your boss is severely burned out, and the staff is under heightened stress from negative leadership, which is causing poor worker-client relationships.

That is what happened to me a few years ago as a brand new social worker. My boss, who had a counseling background, created a tense environment. Within my first two months, I could see the emotional toll having a negative workplace culture was taking on both the staff and youth being served in the agency. One day, a staff member broke down in my office after being reprimanded for a menial task, and I witnessed a power struggle between staff and youth that left both angry and frustrated.

I went home that night and was at a loss as to what to do. *Do I stay in an environment that is far from the therapeutic culture that I felt was needed?* I knew I was not ready to leave. I had started to build relationships with the youth, and I honestly would have felt bad leaving them in such an environment. I decided I was going to get a good night's sleep and go to work the next day thinking about ideas to make the culture better.

As I looked at my boss and saw the impact she had on staff, I began to wonder how a person with a counseling background could end up in such a state. I also saw how her leadership had had a negative impact on the staff. Poor leadership yields unhappy staff, which can be felt by the population being served. In the end, the organization itself will stray from its mission and fail.

In my coursework, I had learned a lot about boundaries. The focus was always on how to avoid entangled boundaries, which could lead to burnout. *Entangled* meant that the worker was over-involved and investing time and emotional energy into a client in a way that was not helpful to the client.

However, I knew that was not what I was observing. This was more of a rigid boundary between staff and youth, in which a significant distance within the relationship was noticeably felt. This type of boundary failure could result in client neglect, client abandonment, and uninformed assessments.

The relationship between the worker and client is very important for the therapeutic process. With boundaries placed on a continuum, with rigidity at one extreme and entanglement at the other, how do I help the staff fall somewhere in the middle and be considered "balanced"? I began to learn that the professional setting can influence where the worker lies on the boundary continuum. For example, a setting where the staff has high caseloads, is unsupported, deals with resistant clients, or is under pressure from administration can lead to more boundary rigidity. I realized that having an environment in which staff feel appreciated, valued, and respected is critical in having a positive outcome for the client population.

Over the next few months, I began having youth create motivational pieces that I displayed around the workplace. Hand-made posters and original artwork allowed staff to connect more and be reminded of what the youth needed. I made sure to check in each morning with staff, just offering a friendly, "Hello, how is everything going this morning?"

I realized that as professionals, we all have a home life and, at times, it can be stressful. When we enter the workplace, especially a demanding work environment, we need to check ourselves and not bring the stress of personal issues into the work environment. I created a comment box where staff could anonymously make suggestions and leave feedback that I would discuss at the administrative meetings. These changes on my part did not make the workplace culture perfect, but they did make it more bearable until more major changes could be made.

My boss was replaced mid-year. A new leader came in and did a complete overhaul of the workplace culture. Some staff were let go, new rules and policies were made, intensive trainings that had a strong social work basis were given to all staff, and the agency transformed into a thriving, inspiring environment where staff and youth knew that they were cared about. Over the next three years, I witnessed a shift from rigid boundaries caused by poor organizational leadership and a weak workplace culture, to balanced boundaries with a workplace environment that made staff glad to be employed there.

Many individuals in society see social workers as powerful, as they can report abuse, evaluate mental health, and make community-wide changes through advocacy. Yet, many social workers see themselves as powerless. They feel caught in the formalities and regulations of their own bureaucracies and are troubled by the lack of resources available to address the many issues that arise. These feelings of powerlessness can cause emotional stress for workers, causing them to develop more rigid boundaries. In instances such as these, having strong leadership to create a positive workplace culture is critical.

A healthy workplace culture also entails professional development and resources that promote self care. Professionals, especially in the field of social work, are exposed to not only their own personal trauma, but also the trauma of others. A more balanced workplace environment can lead to more balanced boundaries. With balanced boundaries, staff will use their authority fittingly, use professional judgment and self-reflection skills in their assessments, not exploit their clients' vulnerabilities, nor infringe on their clients' rights. Every professional is susceptible to moving outside of the ideal balanced range, depending on the situation, but with the guidance and support of the agency and its leadership, the worker has a better chance to remain in the center of the boundaries continuum.

Despite completing all my requirements for my MSW, I plan on going back to school to take courses on agency management and leadership. Even though I may never be in that role, I feel that as a staff member, I should have the knowledge and background to make positive suggestions and/or interventions if I see the workplace culture breaking down in my agency. If someone had asked me during graduate school the importance of workplace culture, I would have said it was important—but I never realized how critical it is until now. I recommend that both current social work students and those who are in the field take a class or two on organizational leadership. Even if you are not directly in the leadership role, there are certain ways that you can help to add to a positive workplace culture.

## References

Davidson, J. C. (2005). Professional relationship boundaries: A social work teaching module. *Social Work Education, 24* (5), 511-533.

Nelson-Gardell, D., & Harris, D. (2003). Childhood abuse history, secondary traumatic stress, and child welfare workers. *Child Welfare, 82* (1), p 5-26.

*Alyssa Lotmore, LMSW, is a graduate of the State University of New York at Albany. She is currently employed at her alma mater, serving as the Assistant Director and Coordinator of Baccalaureate Field Education. She is also the co-host of UAlbany's* The Social Workers Radio Talk Show.

# Social Work Career Connect

## The "Social" Social Worker: 10 Tools for Successful Networking
### by Valerie Arendt, MSW, MPP

*70-80% of job seekers find their jobs through contacts. As few as 20% land their jobs through the traditional "reactive" job search method, namely, applying for posted positions on job boards or want ads.*
*Simmons College Career Education Center*

I never appreciated the importance of a professional network more than when I moved from Minnesota to North Carolina in 2010. Through graduate school, internships, and jobs, I built a beautiful network of social workers and nonprofit professionals in Minnesota who knew my professional history and competencies. I tried to do some research and networking before I moved to North Carolina, but I didn't know which organizations to target and didn't have connections to ask. I was starting from scratch. Even though I had plenty of professional experience, I had to work hard to connect with social work and nonprofit professionals in North Carolina to help me land a job I love.

Networking isn't about being in a secret club, and it's not just for business professionals. It is for all professionals. Social workers are great at building relationships and trust with their clients. Networking really isn't that different. It is about nurturing relationships over time, gathering information, and expanding your knowledge about career opportunities. Networking is not about using people to help you find your next job. It is a two-way street and should be an on-going, mutually beneficial relationship.

Whether you are just starting to build your network or have been at it for years, here are some indispensable networking tools you should always keep in your toolbox, not just when you are looking for a job.

## 1. Your Elevator Speech

Tell me about yourself. The elevator speech is like a commercial to sell yourself in 90 seconds or less. It's an invaluable part of networking that can be used for job interviews, informational interviews, and anytime you meet someone new. In the same way that you should practice for your job interviews, you need to practice your elevator speech so it seems natural and genuine.

What should you say? You should provide an overview of who you are, what you have done, and what you are seeking. It is an opportunity to articulate your career goals clearly while creating a positive impression on your listener. If you are unemployed, don't be embarrassed. Swallow your pride and let people know you are actively seeking work. How else are people to know they should contact you with job opportunities if you don't tell them?

## 2. Social Media

Research is a big part of job search, but beyond looking at an organization's website, where can you actually meet people to network? By joining groups on LinkedIn, Facebook pages, and Twitter, you can start following organizations and be apprised of the latest job openings. This is where I learned which organizations to target and when they were holding events and conferences I could attend to network in person.

*LinkedIn:* If you are currently job searching, you should have a LinkedIn profile. Period. LinkedIn is the best online networking tool. This is a place for your professional network to recommend you and for potential employers to find you. Join groups that are relevant to your geographical location and area of practice. Post engaging questions and relevant information, so folks see you as a source of information. Don't flood group feeds with your unemployment woes, but do let people know you are searching. Be respectful when asking people to connect with you on LinkedIn. Remind them of how you know them and that you would enjoy being their professional connection. Make sure your information is up to date and don't be shy about asking

appropriate connections to recommend your work.

*Twitter:* Believe it or not, Twitter is an excellent way to connect with organizations and other professionals in the field. There are several Twitter accounts that provide daily job Tweets and many, many accounts that will give you tips for job search success. I have made many professional connections on Twitter, and I believe it has strengthened my professional network nationally. Don't just retweet. Tweet content that is original and provides valuable information about your area of practice.

*Facebook:* Some social workers are wary of joining the world of Facebook, but this can be a great tool. It allows you to follow your target organizations and find out when their events are and when they are hiring. Some organizations work hard to reach out to their followers by posting relevant information on their Facebook feeds. Commenting and liking appropriate posts shows the organization you are an engaged member. You never know if this will make a difference. Also, if you are job searching, you should let your personal network know on Facebook! You never know who your great-aunt from Kansas might know in the social work field in Massachusetts.

*Google+:* GooglePlus is definitely useful for professional networking. Your posts can be picked up in Google searches, and you can show off a public profile full of information about what you do. You can share content and post links to your website or blog.

## 3. Professional Memberships

When alone in a new state, my professional association was my most valuable networking tool. Reach out to your NASW chapter, alumni association, or other groups in which you can network with others to get your name out there and learn what opportunities might be available. Even when I was unemployed, I found my memberships to be the best investment in my career, and this helped me land my current job. Conferences and association memberships that are relevant to your profession and the job you do may be tax deductible (see *http://www.irs.gov/publications/p17/ch28.html*). Always remember to consult your tax professional about your personal tax situation.

## 4. Volunteering

Nothing shows organizations that you are committed to their mission more than volunteering for them. I have been a volunteer at three organizations that eventually hired me. Find volunteer opportunities that are in line with your professional passions and career goals. Even if the organization isn't able to hire you, it will be able to provide a reference for you or help connect you to other organizations in the community. However, don't jump ship as soon as you find another opportunity. Volunteer commitments should be taken seriously, and you should honor your obligation.

## 5. Networking Cards

It is not really feasible to take your résumé with you every place you go. Whether you are job searching or just want folks to be able to contact you outside of your current job, a networking business card is an excellent tool to get your name out there and for people to remember how to get in touch with you. There are several sites that will print your networking cards for free, and you

Your Name, MSW, LCSWA
SOCIAL WORK PROFESSIONAL

HOSPICE/PALLIATIVE CARE
INDIVIDUAL AND GROUP THERAPY
CASE MANAGEMENT
NASW MEMBER

(321) 555-6741
YOUR.NAME@GMAIL.COM

WWW.LINKEDIN.COM/IN/YOURNAME

pay for shipping. Be sure to include the following information:
- Your name and credentials
- A title: Social Work Professional, School Social Worker, Nonprofit Professional, Grief Counselor, Licensed Clinical Social Worker–whatever you think best defines you professionally.
- A professional summary or a few lines on your area of expertise to

help the reader know what type of work you may be looking for: e.g., Hospice and Palliative Care, Individual and Group Therapy, Case Management, Addictions Specialist, Conference Presenter, Adjunct Faculty, Volunteer Management.
- Phone number and e-mail address. Let folks know how to get in touch with you.
- Your personal website or LinkedIn profile website. This is important. You want a place where someone can see your résumé virtually. When I was job searching and passing out my card with my LinkedIn profile listed, I was amazed by how many people actually connected with me via LinkedIn instead of by e-mail or phone.

## 6. Continuing Education

Conferences and workshops are not just a place to sit back and learn. They are the best places to network with other professionals. Talk to the folks sitting around you, engage the speakers, and visit the exhibitor tables. *THE NEW SOCIAL WORKER* published a great post (see *http://bit.ly/1rnUYNw*) about the informal in-between moments at conferences that can create the most value and provide constructive networking opportunities. Don't forget to take your networking cards!

## 7. Informational Interviews

A skill you should have as a social worker is the ability to interview someone for information. Use this skill in your professional networking. Informational interviewing is one of your most important networking tools. An informational interview is a 30-minute meeting that you set up with an individual, preferably in-person, to gain career advice and information. It is not a time to inquire about specific employment opportunities. Again, networking is about building relationships, not burning bridges. Come prepared by researching the individual and the company where he or she works, and have questions ready to ask, but let him or her do most of the talking.

## 8. Thank You Notes

If someone has taken the time to do something for you regarding your professional career and aspirations, a handwritten thank you note will go a long way in letting this person know you appreciate the time and effort he or she put in to whatever you requested. Don't just save your handwritten notes for after job interviews. Use them in all aspects of your professional networking. I guarantee the person will remember you and your professional courtesy and will most likely remember you for future opportunities.

## 9. The Follow-Up

Yes, this is a tool. I am on the board of a nonprofit professional networking group. We work very hard to provide networking opportunities and professional development to young professionals in our community. Our goal is to help folks build their networks! It is disappointing when we spend our time offering advice and are willing to meet with individuals to provide more information, and yet they never follow up. I have contacts! I can help you out! And still, nothing. Make sure you follow up with every person who has offered to help you, even if their help isn't the right fit for you. Follow up with an e-mail or call and let them know you appreciate their valuable time.

## 10. Stay in touch

Your professional network needs tending. Don't drop off the face of the earth while you are in the process of interviewing or after you find a job. Let your network know you landed a position, and thank them for their support. Occasionally, reach out to maintain that relationship you worked so hard to build. They will no longer be in your network if they only hear from you when you need another job.

You will find success with your professional networking if you are genuine and respectful. Be honest, open, and do your homework.

*Valerie Arendt, MSW, MPP, is the Associate Executive Director for the National Association of Social Workers, North Carolina Chapter (NASW-NC). She received her dual degree in social work and public policy from the University of Minnesota and currently provides membership support, including résumé review, to the members of NASW-NC.*

# Public Libraries Add Social Workers and Social Programs
## *by Barbara Trainin Blank*

Public libraries have always been democratic, serving a cross-section of the population. After all, they are public, often easily accessible, and free.

As these populations have shifted to include more of the disadvantaged population, including people who are homeless, there is a small but growing trend for libraries to include social workers—not as patrons, but as helping professionals on staff.

It's not surprising that libraries have become hubs for homeless people or even the equivalent of day shelters. In addition to their other assets, libraries have plenty of bathrooms and no security checks.

They are also safe, which is an important consideration. According to the National Coalition for the Homeless, as of July 17, 2014, 337 homeless people have been killed in hate crimes in 15 years.

The trend toward providing social services in libraries began at the San Francisco Public Library (SFPL), which hired a licensed marriage and family therapist, not an MSW.

"Many of my clients have told me that they consider the library a sanctuary, and many of them utilize and truly enjoy the library resources," says Leah Esguerra, LMFT, hired through a partnership between the San Francisco Public Library and the San Francisco Department of Health/San Francisco Homeless Outreach Team.

But in addition, the library's goal is to connect its homeless and indigent patrons to available community resources, where their basic needs for food, shelter, hygiene, and medical attention can be addressed. Esguerra spends her day roaming the library floors, keeping an eye out for regulars who might need help.

At first, Esguerra's primary responsibilities were to provide direct services to patrons and training to the library staff on issues of homelessness, mental health, and substance abuse. But because of the interest the program has aroused among libraries and social service agencies, she also communicates with institutions that are considering hiring a social worker.

Esguerra supervises six health and safety associates and two team leaders to do further outreach at the main library and some of the branches. "The associates are formerly homeless people who have first-hand experience with San Francisco social services," she says.

Elsewhere in California, the Pima County Library became the first in the nation to hire public health nurses in its branches. The San Jose Public Library sent a caseworker to SFPL for training and consultation and now has a case manager on staff in a program entitled "Social Workers in the Library."

Begun by Deborah Estreicher (a librarian on staff who has worked with outreach programs), Peter Lee, Glenn Thomas, and Cyndy Thomas, the program brings volunteer social workers into the library twice a month for free 20-minute referrals. Members of the National Association of Social Workers, North California Chapter, staff the program.

The social workers can help with such issues as education; emergency services (food, clothing, housing, and crisis support); employment; family matters; health improvement (including health insurance); immigration; and support groups for men, women, and teens.

The Encinitas Library in San Diego may soon have free access to social workers. It has been exploring a partnership with San Diego State University's School of Social Work.

The Edmonton Public Library in Canada also hired a social worker, modeled after the San Francisco program. David MacMain, BSW, formerly of the Edmonton Library, was the first social worker in the program, which started in August 2011.

He called it the "brainchild" of Virginia Clavette, manager of programming at the main downtown branch, which has become "very much a hub of activity and community center, in the proximity of homeless shelters and frontline agencies."

The Edmonton Library applied to the provisional government and won a Safer Community Initiative grant. Part of the grant was to pay for three social workers and to provide IDs for patrons. "It's a huge barrier when they cannot pay for their own," MacMain notes.

Edmonton aimed to serve both diagnosed and undiagnosed individuals with mental health issues who have fallen between the cracks. "Many libraries serve the middle class, but this one has a different demographic, and we decided to embrace it and make a difference in the community," he adds. "A big part of the outreach worker's job is to connect people with resources and do community building."

The library social worker trend is too uncommon for the National Association of Social Workers to track—yet. Neither does the American Library Association, although the ALA provided examples of its member branches with these or similar programs.

The Denver Public Library's Community Technology Center team pays regular visits to the area day shelter for homeless and low-income women. The women receive instruction in job interviewing techniques and technology skills, and once class is over, receive bus tokens to tour the main library and get library cards.

Even in the absence of such formal programs, librarians often feel they must help users find shelter, food, and other public services, as more and more people seem to fall between the cracks. Partly, this is because they get to know patrons, especially those who come in on a regular basis.

Sari Feldman, director of the Cuyahoga Community Public Library (Ohio) and incoming president of the ALA (as of 2015-2016), noted that today's libraries "play a huge role in serving all people, in particular, the neediest. We have a great opportunity to create equity and to change lives."

Some libraries work one-on-one, or help people who want to go back to school or work, through adult basic education, GED classes, and career counseling workshops. "Computers in a library make a big difference, as a lifeline to dislocated persons," Feldman says.

Although the rate of homelessness has been growing for decades, today's society is witnessing more homeless youth and more homeless people with mental illnesses in the community after deinstitutionalization.

"During the day, the homeless are looking for free, safe places without recrimination or discrimination. The library has always been that place, but now it embraces the role," Feldman adds.

There would probably be more social workers in libraries, she says, except libraries have faced extreme budget cuts in recent years, and adding positions is a challenge. Staff training in dealing with homeless or mentally ill patrons is also needed.

Mary Olive Thompson, MSW, MLS, has been hired by the Kansas City Library as Director of Library Outreach and Community Engagement. She works out of the Bluford Branch, which she calls an "epicenter" for a library health and wellness initiative.

Thompson, who has master's degrees in social work and library science, says, "Increasingly, the public library is a community site, not just a repository of books and tapes. We can make referrals for needed services."

Thompson stays informed about services in the community, information she shares with branch staff. She gets calls from them periodically about how to help patrons, like the ex-offender who had trouble finding housing. "There are resources out there," she says.

In addition, staff go out to transitional housing sites and day care centers and help individuals meet with social service agencies.

Public libraries can also help patrons with applications for public assistance—as this often has to be done online, and many people either don't have computers or don't know how to use them.

The nation's capital has been no exception to the trend. The Martin Luther King branch of the DC Library hired Jean Badalamenti, an MSW, who is the health and human services coordinator of the office of programs and partnerships of the DC Library.

Badalamenti, on the job only since May, said the hiring of a social worker at the library is part of an "intentional focusing" on the homeless population of the area, in partnership with government and non-government agencies. In addition, the DC Library is in the process of obtaining funding to provide library services as of 2015 for the DC jail. "Hospice also wants to do a program with us," she says.

Although the staff at the library don't ask questions or assume anything about who is coming in, they are aware that at MLK, the homeless population makes up a large percentage of the patrons. Most of the homeless patrons are male and single, although there are also some women and families.

Badalamenti doesn't do case management. Her goals for the library are to create partnerships with service providers, connect people and services, and maybe provide some of these services in the library. Another aim is to find places for people to rest or have meal services—sleeping in the library is a "no-no" at most (but not all) libraries.

Badalamenti would like to develop a comprehensive list of community resources for homeless patrons, and provide more staff training about this population and how to deescalate the situation if someone is in crisis.

The DC library allows anyone to come in and check e-mail, look for a job, or go on Facebook. Badalamenti is also looking to create daytime programming for people experiencing homelessness. One such program already in place off site is Story Time at the DC Homeless Family Shelter, the only such facility in the capital.

"My long-range plan is to bring providers into the library and maybe do a coordinated assessment of individuals to get them to the right services," she says. "Some need a lot of help or a little, or they might need permanent supportive housing. No coordinated assessment [of these needs] has been done in DC."

There is evidence that the shift in populations served by libraries isn't really new—only the awareness of it is. The media aren't full of coverage of library social work, but some, including National Public Radio, governing.com, and Reuters, among others, have written about it. *The Washington Post* ran an article about Badalamenti's work at the DC Library in August of this year. *Health Day,* an online publication, questioned how librarians can protect themselves from troubled or violent patrons—a darker side of the democratization of libraries to include those who fall through the cracks.

Libraries, says DC's Badalamenti, are becoming "real places of the community, and embracing diversity." Her MLK library, for example, partners with

*The New York Public Library*

the DC Fringe Festival and welcomes musicians and entertainers in the great hall. Undergoing renovation now, it will include a café within a few years.

The HOME Page Café, opened in 2008, is a coffee bar owned and operated by Project HOME in the Parkway Central Branch of the Free Library of Philadelphia. At the café, four formerly homeless individuals serve more than 150 customers daily. A total of 17 formerly homeless people have been trained and gone on to other employment—often going back to school and reuniting with family.

The café offers extensive training in customer service, coffee preparation, and workplace skills to staff, who also pass the Serve Safe Food safety exam.

The ALA notes other examples of social service type programs. The New York Public Library is reaching out to at-risk youth. BridgeUp, an educational and antipoverty program, provides academic and social support to at-risk New York City youth in an effort to prepare them for success. Supported by a $15 million grant from the Helen Gurley Brown Trust, the five-year program offers services to more than 250 New York City eighth to 12th graders each year at NYPL branches in underserved neighborhoods.

"Libraries are on the front line, whether they want to or not," says Jeremy Rosen, director of advocacy at the National Law Center on Homelessness and Poverty.

In cooperation with the Baltimore County Communities for the Homeless—a network of volunteers formed to eliminate homelessness through education, government relations, advocacy, and community development—the Baltimore County Public Library created the Street Card program. Services include employment, food and other emergency assistance, health, financial support, legal help, shelters, and others.

The Sacramento Public Library's Central Library has partnered with the Downtown Sacramento Partnership, dedicated to the improvement of the city's central business district, and beginning in 2011, contracted for the services of one of its Homeless Outreach Workers (Navigator). The Navigator works in the library Tuesday through Friday, interacting with patrons she believes may have homelessness or mental illness issues. As she gains their trust, she helps them "navigate" through social service programs to find the help they need with housing, substance abuse, income assistance, and more. She also provides staff with in-house expertise in reference, information, and referral for vulnerable populations.

For sure, the quiet library of the past is not the library of today. Initiatives such as hiring library social workers live up to the public library's tradition as the "first social justice initiative of Western society," adds MacMain, formerly of Edmonton. "Access to information is power, and the library gave people that access."

The ways that access is being given may change, but it's all part of an honored tradition.

*Barbara Trainin Blank is a freelance writer based in the Washington, DC, area.*

# 8 Key Areas of Support for Guiding Court Appointed Special Advocates

*by Ernesto Che Tabasa, M.A., Trisha Kajioka, B.S., and Eleanor Willemsen, Ph.D.*

When volunteer mentors work with youth at risk, they can be assisted to facilitate the healthy development of these youth by training and regular reporting on their cases that emphasizes key components of healthy development. Here we illustrate how such assistance works in practice at one agency with the view that this approach might be adapted for use in the fieldwork portion of the training of new social workers, and for training other volunteers who mentor youth.

## The National Court Appointed Special Advocate (CASA) Program

Court Appointed Special Advocates (CASAs) are volunteers who receive appointments in dependency court to testify

about the best interests of foster children at the periodic hearings regarding their placements and needed services. CASAs typically have one case at a time and can spend time mentoring their assigned child in the course of activities, as well as investigating the child's school, medical, mental health, and biological family situations. Ideally, the CASA works collaboratively with the child's social worker to investigate the child's life and work with the foster parents, school, therapist, doctor, and biological parents seeking to reunify. However, CASAs are specifically charged with the duty to enter an independent opinion about issues in the child's case, including placement, in court.

## The Eight Strengths Framework Used by Child Advocates of Silicon Valley

Child Advocates of Silicon Valley (CASV) is affiliated with the National CASA program, but places a more equal emphasis on the mentoring role and the court representation role. The staff supervisors of the CASA volunteers guide them to engage their children in activities that will promote their healthy development. CASA volunteers make monthly reports of their progress, their concerns, and current situations that need focus.

In the past several years, staff members at CASV have worked to develop a reporting system that is easy for busy advocates to use but will still provide good information about how the children and youth in foster care who have advocates are doing. This reporting system centers on eight key areas of support. These key areas were repeatedly occurring in the longer reports used earlier. The key areas overlap closely with the 41 "Developmental Assets" identified by researchers of risk and resilience. The Developmental Assets are derived from extensive reviews of the literature showing which characteristics of children and youth, their families, schools, and communities are systematically associated with the youth being resilient to the risk factors in their personalities and, especially, in their life situations (Benson, 2003).

The eight key areas of support are:

1. self esteem building
2. trust and relationship building
3. experiencing cultural and community events
4. having new experiences
5. education support
6. doing extra-curricular activities
7. help with making healthy choices, and
8. reaching developmental milestones, including skills for independent living for older youth.

Research shows the importance of a positive relationship with a caring adult, such as an advocate, for reducing the incidence of violence, substance abuse, and early sexual behavior (Fergus

& Zimmerman, 2005). Because children in the welfare system have a higher risk of behavioral, emotional, and substance abuse problems than the average youth (Casanueva et. al., 2012), an advocate who provides mentoring is especially important. These relationships are associated with higher self esteem, one of the eight key areas of support (Resnick, 2000) and with greater emotional and cognitive competence (Catalano, Berglund, Ryan, Lonczak, & Hawkins, 2004). In turn, these competencies can lead to greater educational success and healthy decision making, outcomes related to two of the eight key areas of support.

The eight key areas of support form a framework that is the basis for the newer monthly reporting form used by CASV. Advocates briefly describe their activities with the child each month (as well as concerns and immediate goals) and check which of the eight key areas of support were addressed.

## Studying the Eight Key Areas of Support in Action

In 2012, staff members at CASV reviewed between 39 and 109 reports for each month of 2011, tabulating the frequency of occurrence of the eight key areas. These quantitative data were of a summary nature and indicate that the key areas of support are each reported with high frequency. This has encouraged the staff to view the reporting system and the training given on the framework as a coaching tool directing advocates to productive activities with their children.

More useful to readers of this article are qualitative illustrations of the eight key areas of support in action. To get a systematic sample of these, Ernesto provided the other two authors with a complete year of monthly reports (2011-2012) for 12 cases varying in age, ethnicity, and gender. Eleanor devised a method for selecting two months to examine for each case, so months were represented equally. This produced 24 reports to examine, looking for the best examples of the key areas of support. Trisha and an assistant selected the two best examples of each key area, first independently, and then through a consensus achieved by discussion with each other and the third author. We present those here.

References to *self esteem building* include the advocate of a 16-year-old Caucasian male saying, "X's unwillingness to conform to the rules and behavior expectations may have something to do with his anxiety toward moving into public high school as he may not have the confidence that he can do the work," and another advocate describing her 11-year-old African American girl reporting on awards: "She wanted to tell me that she had earned two awards at school, one for perfect attendance and the other for an English essay about her life...."

Descriptions of *trust and relationship building* include this comment from one advocate of a 7-year-old Hispanic girl: "X looks forward to my visits. She asks her grandmother how many days until she sees me...," and this one from the advocate of an 11-year-old African American girl: "She was not feeling well, but had insisted on going to school because she wanted to see me."

Examples of *cultural and community events* included one about an 11-year-old African American girl: "Went to eat, then to Prush Farm for Harvest Festival. X is very confident approaching various people, asks about exhibits, motivated by the give-aways but still, she listened to what various 4H stands had to say...," and another about a 7-year-old Hispanic girl: "We saw the musical *Mary Poppins* at the San Jose Performing Arts [Center]. Went to the library and out for Gelato, went to the CASA picnic."

Examples of *new experiences* advocates provide for their youth were (for an 18-year-old Hispanic girl) "Guided hike at Ano Nueva State Park to see elephant seals," and for a 9-year-old bi-racial girl, "I took X to Shoreline so we could fly the Barbie kite that I had bought for her a while back. She had never flown a kite before (neither have I), and I wanted to be sure and do this before she moves...."

*Providing education support* is a staple of the work of child advocates as seen in these report quotes: " I do keep in touch with the school about X's behavior and academics on a regular basis" (for a 16-year-old Caucasian boy), and for a 5-year-old Hispanic boy, "We practiced counting numbers and practiced with number sense...we also practiced sounding out words."

Advocates provide varied *extra-curricular activities,* but often these are sports

activities. For example, the advocate of a 9-year-old bi-racial girl reports, "X's last soccer class for the season was this month. X wants to continue taking soccer, and has even asked if she can play soccer through the league at her school." Another advocate, working with a 7-year-old Hispanic girl reports, "X made a lot of progress with her swimming this summer, and we will continue working on her new skills. The first time she was fearful of putting her face in the water. She loves going swimming and asks, 'Can we spend five hours at the pool today?'"

*Healthy choices and behaviors* are often supported through exercise and diet as seen in these examples: For a 15-year-old Hispanic boy, "X's participation in MMA and gym workouts has resulted in lost weight and increased muscle tone... we discussed strategies to continue funding for this program for him," and for a 9-year-old bi-racial girl, "We attended the Healthy Cooking and Zumba CASA class."

*Supporting developmental milestones* can mean very different things for different ages. For a 19-year-old African American male, it means, "X continues his progress toward high school graduation, additional applications for post high school programs, and [I am] supporting X in completing his independent living goals, applying for jobs, and figuring out housing options." For a 5-year-old Hispanic boy, his advocate reports, "He has shown improvement as far as sharing. He used to take other peoples' toys away, but this time he didn't."

These varied illustrations show that the framework of eight key areas of support can make advocates more conscious of how they are helping and point them to good activities to do and conversations to have.

## Conclusion

The framework of eight key areas of support provides a reporting tool that also guides mentors. In our case, they are Court Appointed Special Advocates for children in dependency. However, this flexible tool can be adapted for use by fieldwork supervisors of social work students and by those who supervise mentors of children.

## References

Benson, P. L. (2003). *Developmental assets and asset-building community: Conceptual and empirical foundations.* In R. M. Lerner & P. L. Benson (Eds.) *Developmental Assets and Asset Building Communities* (pp. 19-43). New York: Kluwer Academic.

Casanueva, C., Wilson, E., Smith, K., Dolan, M., Ringeisen, H., & Home, B. (2012). *NSCAW II wave 2 report: Child well-being. National survey a/child and adolescent well-being. OPRE Report #2012-38,* Washington, DC: Office of Planning, Research and Evaluation, Administration for Children and Families, U.S. Department of Health and Human Services.

Catalano, R. F., Berglund, M. L., Ryan, J. A. M., Lonczak, H. S., & Hawkins, J. D. (2004). Positive youth development in the United States: Research findings on evaluations of positive youth development programs. *The Annals of the American Academy of Political and Social Science, 591 (1), 98-124.*

Fergus, S., & Zimmerman, M. A. (2005). Adolescent resilience: A framework for understanding healthy development in the face of risk. *Annual Review of Public Health, 26,* 399-419.

Resnick, M. D. (2000). Protective factors, resiliency, and healthy youth development. *Adolescent Medicine: State of the Art Reviews, 11* (1), 157-164.

*Ernesto Che Tabasa, M.A., is a lead advocate supervisor at Child Advocates of Silicon Valley (CASV) in Milpitas, CA, where he supervises and trains volunteers who serve as CASAs (Court Appointed Special Advocates) for Santa Clara County foster youth.*

*Trisha Kajioka graduated from Santa Clara University with a Bachelor of Science in psychology. She now works as a behavioral interventionist at Easter Seals.*

*Eleanor Willemsen, Ph.D., is Professor Emerita of Psychology at Santa Clara University. She specializes in developmental psychology and serves as a Court Appointed Special Advocate for youth in dependency.*

To know their world,
step into ours.

**Master of Social Work**

Improve the lives of children and families.

Gain a deep understanding of social work enriched
with a child development perspective.

Grow your professional identity with the support
of top social work faculty.

www.erikson.edu/NewSocialWorker

erikson

graduate school in child development
Chicago, Illinois

# Achieving Racial Equity Through Social Work

## by Mary Pender Greene, LCSW-R, CGP, Sandra Bernabei, LCSW, and Lisa V. Blitz, Ph.D., LCSW-R

Welcome to our new column on racial equity. We represent an alliance of thousands of antiracist social workers in the Northeast United States, connected to a national effort to undo structural racism. Why this column? Why is achieving racial equity still an important focus for social work? We will be here in each issue to explore this question together and to give you tools to create change in yourself, your organization, and your community. First, we want to share a bit about ourselves and why racial equity is important to us.

**Mary:** I used to think of racism as individual, intentional acts of meanness, which inhibited my ability to talk about privilege or racism in my organization. When I tried, White people took offense, as if I was criticizing them or our agency, and I feared backlash and isolation. Without a structural understanding of racism, I had no way to talk about what I saw and experienced. I was painfully silent, often the only Person of Color in social work settings, surrounded by talented, caring people who did not understand that structural racism impacts the lives of all people of color. I found my voice, and my ability to create transformative change, when I learned how to intervene with the systems that carried oppression. We need to grapple with racial equity because racism has an impact on us daily. I look forward to sharing my journey of finding my voice and becoming my best professional self.

**Sandy:** When I started my career, my vision was to help people create lives of their own design. I graduated from social work school and worked as a clinician for many years. My work was fulfilling, but it became clear that helping people find personal power within adversity was not addressing root problems. I needed to do more. Graduating from the *Undoing Racism®* workshop provided by the People's Institute for Survival and Beyond taught me what I needed to do. I learned to use a power analysis to help people locate themselves within our social, economic, and politi-cal landscape and to grasp the external social forces that have an impact on their lives. Beyond my clinical work, I became an agent of social change and a community organizer practicing struc-tural social work. I see this column as an honest discussion that supports others in their transformational work, providing a foundation to organize for change.

**Lisa:** My MSW program taught me to be a better racist. I went to a prestigious school—one that enjoys an international reputation for pushing the envelope of progressive thought. I got a great education. I learned how to see my clients, see their community, see how they received and responded to services. I learned to think systemically, to under-stand the interplay between person and environment, and to target my interven-tions to improve the fit. I learned about organizational systems and power, and how to see myself in the context of that power. I was also taught to be colorblind, to see poverty as the overarching op-pression. I did not learn about structural racism, nor did I learn to see myself as a gatekeeper with the power to either maintain or change that structure. I wish I had. Since learning this, everything about my practice has improved.

We want to make clear from the onset that our broader focus is on social justice for each individual and each com-munity. Eliminating the many manifesta-tions of oppression—homophobia and transphobia, sexism and misogyny, Is-lamophobia and anti-Semitism, classism—and all the rest too numerous to list—is urgent. We have come to understand, however, that although all of these "isms and obias" are shared among many coun-tries throughout the world as remnants of patriarchy, what distinguishes the United States is that our country was constructed as a race-based society. So this is where the conversation must begin. To see our nation through the lens of race shifts ev-erything about how you see everything. At least it did for us. And once you see it, you have to act. At least that is what hap-pened for us.

In the next issue, we'll focus on how structural racism plays out in our lives and our work. If you're ready to act now, here are a few ideas:

- Review the *www.AntiRacistAlliance.com* website.
- Watch this 20-minute video of Michelle Alexander speaking on *The New Jim Crow in the Age of Color-blindness: https://www.youtube.com/watch?v=U_HEu4Lnewg*
- Read a book, *The New Jim Crow: Mass Incarceration in the Age of Color-blindness.*

## About the columnists

*Mary Pender Greene, LCSW-R, CGP, is an organizational consultant, psy-chotherapist in private practice, career/executive coach, professional speaker, and co-founder of the AntiRacist Alliance. She has a passion for assisting organizations in addressing structural racism and is committed to the advancement of women and People of Color in leadership roles. Her background also includes executive and management responsi-bility for America's largest nonprofit—the Jew-ish Board of Family and Children's Services. Mary is the author of* Creative Mentorship and Career Building Strategies: How to Build Your Virtual Board of Directors.

*Sandra Bernabei, LCSW, is President of the National Association of Social Workers—New York City Chapter. She is a metro area community organizer and private practitioner. Sandy is a founding member of the AntiRacist*

*Racial equity continued on page 21*

# The Decision
## *by Karla Garcia, MSW*

It has always been my dream to be a social worker, so I looked into a program near my home. It seemed perfect for me, because it was part-time and classes were offered in the evening. The program seemed geared toward adults with busy schedules who worked full time.

I was living with my boyfriend, so I had a serious conversation with him and told him that this was my dream and would greatly advance my career. He was supportive from the start and encouraged me to apply.

I was accepted to the program, and my employer also offered a scholarship program that would pay for graduate school as long as I would commit to work for them for as long as it took to complete the program. That meant they would pay for three years in the part-time master's program, and then I would work for them for an additional three years. It seemed like a good deal. I realize that this may seem very simple, and it was. I never really thought all that much about it. I decided I wanted to do it, and I just applied and was granted the scholarship.

## The Breakdown

Although I was warned that it was hard working full time and going to school, I decided that I could do both and still maintain a social life. I definitely underestimated the amount of time that school work would require. I quickly learned that every day was a new struggle in prioritizing my life events, whether school, work, or personal. I immersed myself in school and work, because I didn't want to fail at either.

It wasn't long before I was completely overwhelmed and having symptoms of anxiety. I found myself worrying excessively about everything, and it was extremely difficult for me to control the worry. I was consistently on edge, tense, and irritable. My boyfriend and family felt they had to walk on eggshells when they were near me. I would yell for no reason and really get extremely angry over little things. I would wake up in the middle of the night worrying about a variety of things.

I also experienced a few panic attacks that scared me, because I felt so out of control of my emotions to the point that I was having physical reactions. I felt as if I couldn't breathe. I would have to get up and go outside. It seemed that my heart was beating so fast that I was going to have a heart attack. I felt light headed and almost in a daze. My body would shake uncontrollably, and my mind would race. I think what made it worse was that I worked with people who had mental health problems, and the last thing I wanted to do was end up in a psychiatric hospital, so that worry would intensify all of the physical reactions that I was having.

At first, I had no idea what was happening. I didn't realize I was experiencing panic attacks and that the symptoms I was feeling were the exact criteria for Generalized Anxiety Disorder. I couldn't explain what I was feeling, so I just kept going. I kept trying to be perfect in school, work, and in my personal life. I wasn't taking care of myself. I began to isolate myself, because I didn't like who I was and really didn't know what to do about it. I had lost touch with all my friends, who were my main support system other than my boyfriend. I rarely saw my boyfriend, even though we lived together. A whole month could pass without me even realizing that I hadn't talked to a family member.

It wasn't until I became this person that I didn't even recognize that I decided to get help. I knew that my true self was not this monster I was acting out. I couldn't control myself. I knew that I was a happy, outgoing, and energetic person, and I needed to find her again, but I was afraid that I never would.

## Working Toward Help

I felt as though I would be stigmatized if I went to a therapist. I felt that I should be able to manage my own emotions, given my career choice. My thoughts were that as a social worker, I should know how to intervene in my own life and be the master of my own emotions. I felt that if I couldn't control my own emotions and figure out what was going on with me, then how could I become an effective social worker? I felt like a failure in needing to get help.

One of my classmates was having a similar experience. When we were working on a school project, the conversation about our situations came up. She talked about what she had been going through, and I finally felt relief just knowing that I wasn't alone. She talked about going to get help and being afraid of the stigma that is associated with getting help from a mental health specialist. After talking for a long time, we decided that we would seek help so we would be able to manage our emotions and continue in our master's program.

The first therapist I saw was not very helpful. She was focused on trying to get me to see a psychiatrist for medication. I knew that I didn't want that to be the first route I took, so I decided to look for another therapist. I found out that I could get free therapy at school from the social worker there. The very first session was so much better than the others I had experienced at the community mental health center. This social worker understood exactly what I was going through. She believed that I could feel better without medication, and even shared some of her story. This empowered me and gave me hope, because I knew she understood what it was like to live with the emotions I was experiencing. She also was the first to mention that there is no shame in seeking help. It was then that I understood and learned that social workers seek help all the time. It is even encouraged for us to seek out mental health professionals to work through our issues.

## The Breakthrough

I'm so glad I sought out professional help. I was diagnosed with anxiety, which made so much sense. At the time when I was feeling all of these emotions, I had not yet taken the course on diagnostic criteria, so I had no idea what I was feeling, which was extremely scary. What was interesting, though, is that the semester I decided to get help was the same semester I had that course (on diagnostic criteria), and the week after I was diagnosed, I learned about anxiety.

Fueled with the power of knowledge (thanks to my class and my therapist), I was able to work past my life altering symptoms and learn how to manage my emotions. The key was self-care. Now that may sound simple, but it was (and is) a bumpy ride (to put it lightly). I learned that living with anxiety is a constant battle, but it was a challenge I was ready to take on if it meant getting my life (and really myself) back. The therapist gave me a lot of homework that helped me take control of my emotions. She helped me realize that I was in control of my anxiety and that I had the power to change my emotions. Through breathing techniques, visualizing techniques, and mini experiments (such as eating in public by myself), I was able to make great strides in managing my anxiety.

## The Learning Experience

I realize that you (the reader) may be wondering what this has to do with going to school while working full time. I feel that my experience can be used as a learning experience for others. Clearly, the decision to go back to school as a busy adult should not be made as lightly as I made it. It is a lot of work, and before the decision is made, you must think about how you are going to emotionally and physically take care of yourself.

I wouldn't change anything, because I feel that I have grown and realized what is truly important in life. I realize that I don't have to be the stellar employee and student. I just have to have a balance of all things in my life. I won't lie and say that I have it all figured out, but I do believe that the following is decent advice for those working full time and entering a graduate program.

- Acknowledge when you are overwhelmed, and take time for yourself.
- Stay connected with your support system or build a stronger one if you need, because those people will help you get through the hard days.
- Don't ignore emotions or physical symptoms that are abnormal for you.

- Don't be afraid or ashamed to get professional help, if needed.
- Don't be afraid or ashamed to talk to professors. Don't underestimate how much they can help or guide you in the right direction, or maybe they can just be venting sources. I have found professors understand the struggle of students, especially those with jobs, families, and other responsibilities. Most professors will also understand if life or work is pulling you away from school responsibilities. Just explain it to them, and you may be given some kind of extension on school work.
- Listen to your heart and instincts.
- Find something that you love and that takes you away from what overwhelms you, and allow yourself to do that once or twice a month, as it fits your schedule.
- If it's possible, re-examine your situation and see if there are any changes you can make to help you feel less overwhelmed.

## The Re-Examination

This last point was very helpful for me during my last year in my graduate program. I decided to stop working full time for my last year of graduate school. I even stopped the monetary help from the scholarship, because I realized that my full-time job was not my future career. My passion was in a completely different concentration, so I decided that focusing on learning skills for my career was more important. I was able to survive on student loans and financial assistance from family. I realize that this is not a possibility for all; however, just re-examining your options may help you come up with your own unique way to restructure your life. Life will always be stressful, but there are times when you can do things that will decrease that stress with just a little assessment of your life and goals.

At first, I would schedule every minute of my day and still would not find time for myself. After I re-examined my life (even before I left my job), I was able to make sure I had time for myself. I would allow myself to have some time every week to do something that I love, such as going for a jog, or spending time with friends or family, because I know now that this is what helps me be a better student and eventually will help me be a better social worker.

I can't stress enough how important it is to always be mindful of taking time for yourself, because as I stated earlier, dealing with these emotions is a daily struggle. To this day, I feel the rush of nervousness that has become the landmark of when my anxiety is trying to get the better of me, along with the irritability and constant worry. Sometimes I get overwhelmed again and need to take a break and mindfully go through the techniques (breathing and visualizing) that I learned in therapy to help me calm down.

Some days are harder than others. I realize that this is only my experience, and it will be different for everyone, but I think it is key to know yourself and learn what works to help you feel less stressed and to manage the inevitable stress in a positive manner.

This may all seem so simple for some people, but for people who suffer from anxiety, dealing with stress can be a real struggle. I hope my experience and tips can help some people take control of their lives and emotions again.

*Karla Garcia, MSW, received her Master of Social Work from Indiana University Northwest in May 2013 and her Bachelor of Arts in sociology from Northern Illinois University in 2007.*

---

*Racial equity continued from page 19*

*Alliance, an antiracist organizing collective of New York City area human service practitioners. ARA is building a movement to undo structural racism in our lifetime and to bring an analysis of structural racism as outlined by the People's Institute for Survival and Beyond to social work education and practice.*

*Lisa V. Blitz, PhD, LCSW-R, is a social worker, researcher, and educator with 25 years of experience in mental health and social justice centering on culturally responsive trauma-informed practice and organizational development. Lisa is currently engaged in community based participatory research with K-12 schools developing practice approaches to eliminate disproportionally negative outcomes for students of color and those who are economically disadvantaged.*

## Greetings From the Phi Alpha Honor Society for Social Work

Free Phi Alpha table top banners are available to chapters that recruit! Please contact Tammy at PhiAlphaInfo@etsu.edu with your mailing address. Phi Alpha double knotted blue and gold honor cords are available for resale at the International Office for $12.00.

Please visit the Phi Alpha website to view the banner and cords at PhiAlpha.org.  Join the Phi Alpha listserv at: Phialpha-subscribe-request@listserv.etsu.edu.

Please stop by the Phi Alpha booth (#201) at CSWE-APM in Tampa, Florida and pick up a media kit.

Kind regards,
Tammy Hamilton
Executive Secretary

*Social work students at California State University-Long Beach at NASW Lobby Day in Sacramento, CA.*

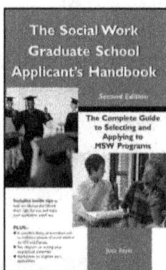

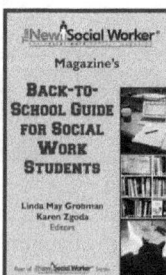

# Social Work Students Wear T-Shirts!

Hayley Booker, a senior in the social work program at Eastern New Mexico University, takes a selfie.

Officers of the University of North Carolina-Greensboro BSW social work student organization show off their Peace, Love, and Social Work t-shirts. From left to right: Quanya Eaton, Treasurer; Alex Moseley, Chair Coordinator; Beth Russell, Secretary; Candice Foreman, Public Relations; Joe Barker, President; Lena Younger, Vice President; and Jack Register, BSW Program Director and student organization advisor.

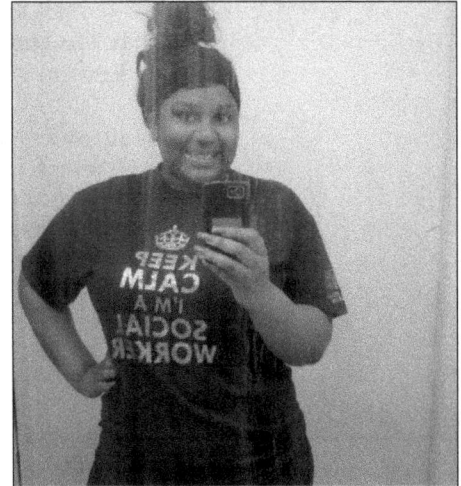

Joseph Clark, BSW Class of 2017, University of Louisville, Kent School of Social Work

Social work students from St. Catherine University-University of St. Thomas are shown at Minnesota's Social Work Day at the Capitol. The t-shirts were designed by MSW student Nicole Dahl and won "best t-shirt" of the day.

University of Southern Mississippi BSW Club members show off their "The Power of Social Work" t-shirts.

View our social work t-shirt slide show:
http://www.socialworker.com/extras/creative-work/social-work-students-wear-t-shirts/

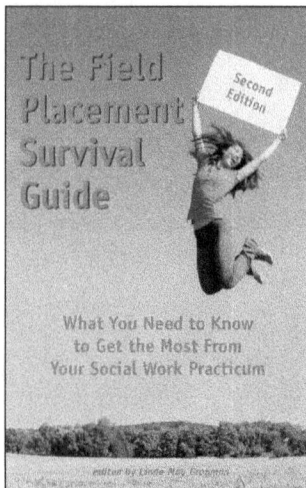

# THE FIELD PLACEMENT SURVIVAL GUIDE
## What You Need To Know To Get the Most From Your Social Work Practicum
## 2nd Edition

Field placement is one of the most exciting and exhilarating parts of a formal social work education. It is also one of the most challenging. This collection addresses the multitude of issues that social work students in field placement encounter, including choosing a placement, getting prepared, using supervision effectively, working with clients, coping with challenges, and moving on to a successful social work career.

This collection is a goldmine of practical information that will help social work students take advantage of all the field placement experience has to offer. Each chapter (many written by seasoned experts in field education; others by students) presents a different aspect of the practicum and offers students insight into the importance of both the challenges and the joys of this unique learning experience.

This book brings together in one volume the best field placement articles from THE NEW SOCIAL WORKER. Packed with practical, essential information for every student in field placement!

*"As an older (52), non-traditional student working my internship for my B.A. in social work, I ordered your book. It was so reassuring that others had survived and gone on to successful careers!"*

*Linda Chamberlain*

Edited by Linda May Grobman, ACSW, LSW
Founder, publisher, and editor of *THE NEW SOCIAL WORKER*.

ISBN: 978-1-929109-26-5  2011  Price: $22.95  284 pages          Shipping/Handling: add $8.50/first book, $1.50/each additional book in U.S.
Canadian orders: add $14.00 first book, $4 each add'l book. Other orders: contact us. If ordering from Pennsylvania, add 6% sales tax.
Order from White Hat Communications, PO Box 5390, Harrisburg, PA 17110-0390
http://shop.whitehatcommunications.com  717-238-3787 (phone)  717-238-2090 (fax)

# IS IT ETHICAL? 101 Scenarios In Everyday Social Work Practice
## A Discussion Workbook
### by Thomas Horn, MSW, RSW

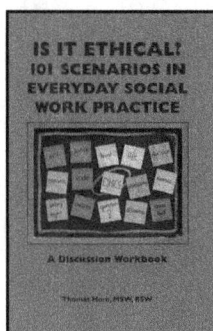

What would you do if you were asked to be your hairdresser's social worker? How about if you developed a crush on a client? Or if you unexpectedly received a $100 check in the mail from an agency to whom you had referred a client?

Social work is filled with these kinds of questions. They come up every day in professional life. Will your students be prepared to make the ethical decision?

Very few social workers go to work looking for ways to exploit, manipulate, or mislead the people with whom they work—clients, colleagues, managers, the government, or the general public. Yet, it is possible to cross into unethical behavior unintentionally, often as a result of poor decisions that are misguided. The line between ethical and unethical can become blurred.

This workbook provides students with 101 different everyday scenarios and challenges them to think about what the ethical and unethical choices might be in each situation. Through examining these scenarios on their own and in discussion with classmates and others, they will become more familiar with how to apply the ethical guidelines and standards that they will be required to follow as professional social workers.

Space is provided after each scenario for readers to write their own responses as they prepare to discuss the scenario with classmates, supervisors, and others. There is space for students to write their own scenarios, as well.

Resources are listed, including Code of Ethics Web addresses for nine different social work associations, as well as ethics journals.

*"...if you need a resource to begin a discussion of ethics in a classroom or agency in-service, this workbook qualifies for Social Work Ethics 101."* Paul Dovyak, ACSW, LISW-S, University of Rio Grande, Journal of Social Work Values and Ethics

## ABOUT THE AUTHOR

Thomas Horn, MSW, RSW, is a Registered Social Worker (RSW) with both the Ontario College of Social Workers and Social Service Workers (OCSWSSW) in Ontario, Canada, and the General Social Care Council (GSCC) in England. Tom is also a graduate member of the British Psychological Society. He has worked in the social services field for more than 20 years in a variety of settings, including residential developmental care, residential and outpatient child and adolescent mental health, residential drug/alcohol treatment, and inpatient psychiatry. Currently, Tom works with an inpatient forensic mental health team at a large psychiatric hospital in Ontario. He routinely provides field supervision to social work students at the undergraduate and graduate levels.

2011 • ISBN: 978-1-929109-29-6 • 118 pages, 5½ by 8½ • $14.95 plus shipping
White Hat Communications, P.O. Box 5390, Harrisburg, PA 17110-0390 Phone: 717-238-3787 Fax: 717-238-2090  shop.whitehatcommunications.com

*Kaler-Jones continued from page 3*

for me." Eventually, the arts programs were reinstated. Being Miss Jersey gives Kaler-Jones the opportunity to continue such advocacy.

Once she makes a decision, Kaler-Jones moves fast. She told her mother a week before the Miss Atlantic County Pageant that she was entering, and then scrambled successfully to get together the different pieces she needed.

Four years later, she was named Miss New Jersey and caught the bug. "The position gives you the power to spread a message," she said. "I've also found my very best friends in the competition."

Sharing New Jersey roots, Tibbetts says she is very proud that the young woman is representing the state and "our generation." She continues, "I'd be thrilled if Cierra wins Miss America, but regardless, she is a true global citizen, and that's the best anyone can really ever be."

Many of her friends were "perplexed" that as a self-described feminist, Kaler-Jones was drawn to beauty contests. She herself saw a contradiction at first. But Kaler-Jones, who lives close to Atlantic City, was impressed by an earlier Miss New Jersey who visited her school and spoke of being a role model. "Feminism is also about empowering women to feel comfortable in our own skin," says Kaler-Jones.

Even the swimsuit competition–now renamed "Lifestyle and Fitness"–is a positive for Kaler-Jones, who grew up "very overweight" and not comfortable in her skin. "Since then, I've learned about fitness and wellness and have taught my family. If you can go onstage in a swimsuit, you can do anything."

Kaler-Jones spends non-competition time in a swimsuit, as well. As much as she loves to read, do research, and public speaking, she also enjoys the beaches of her native state. She enjoys journaling and blogging and once played piano, saxophone, and a self-taught guitar.

The one thing Kaler-Jones wishes she had more time for is talking to friends. "I'm very much a people person," she says.

*Freelance writer Barbara Trainin Blank, formerly of Harrisburg, PA, now lives in the greater Washington, DC, area.*

# From Jane Addams to the Yurt Slums of Mongolia
## *by Ann McLaughlin, MSW, ACSW*

When I travel and speak in Africa, I encounter this notion that money grows on trees in America. I emphatically tell the people I meet there that what has made America great is that we are a nation of immigrants. I tell them that my Irish ancestors came to America because they were hungry. That usually is new information—that Europeans were starving and getting on boats looking for a better future.

In Tanzania, my social work colleagues are pushing to get a bore hole dug in a remote village. As it stands now, women get up before dawn to walk to the nearest water hole about three to four hours away. They usually get back at noon. Wow...it would be nice to live a life of ease. It would be nice to have indoor plumbing and water come out the faucet instead of walking half the day.

When I was in Ghana, a teenage school girl walking home from school with her friends said to me, "American, American...take me home with you! I want to go to America." I spun on my heels to face her and said, "If you really want to go to America, then study very hard...and be one of the smartest in your country, so that you can get a scholarship to one of our best schools."

That is the promise of America that Barack Obama talked so much about at the Democratic Convention in 2004, when he said, "I stand here knowing that my story is part of the larger American story, that I owe a debt to all of those who came before me, and that, in no other country on earth, is my story even possible."

I would say in these discussions in Africa, "If you want to imitate or emulate anything from America, the most relevant is how we learned to 'make somethin' outa nothin.'"

One of my favorite books on this subject is Napolean Hill's book called *Think and Grow Rich*. Andrew Carnegie charged Hill with the task of interviewing all the Rags to Riches moguls at the turn of the century: Henry Ford, Rockefeller, JP Morgan.

I emphasize that we are just a few generations ahead of Africa. We had slums with poor sanitation, and our barefoot kids had worms in their feet.

The swamps of Louisiana bred malaria until the Army Corps of Engineers filled in those swamps.

At the turn of the century, America was flooded with wave upon wave of immigrants, mostly from Europe. From 1880 to 1914, immigrants from Southern and Eastern Europe came to Chicago hoping to find work in the stock yards and steel mills. It was in these tenements of Chicago that Jane Addams worked.

## Why Jane Addams Is So Important to the Social Work Tradition

Why is every social worker in the United States, and Canada for that matter, obliged to study Jane Addams' work at Hull House and the tenements of Chicago? Because social work has a proud tradition of caring about what happens to the poor of this world. This emphasis on tackling poverty is what makes social work one of the most important and required credentials in international development and humanitarian work.

Psychology emphasizes the intrapsychic. Social work teaches that the *context* that someone lives in affects well being.

Thus, when I get requests for international volunteers, my contacts in Mongolia ask for social workers to help with improving the lives of the people in their capital's yurt slums.

Social work teaches an attitude. As Jane Addams said. "The good we secure for ourselves is precarious and uncertain until it is secured for all of us and incorporated into our common life."

I do understand and truly appreciate why we study Jane Addams and Hull House and the English Poor Laws. My only regret is that the emphasis is on the past, rather than what is going on in the world today. This is why I submit occasional articles to *The New Social Worker*. I would like to see the social work profession tackle the challenges of the present and future.

## What Is Different About the Slums of Today? From Rural to Urban

In Jane Addams' Chicago, the poor came from other countries. Read Oscar Handlin's *The Uprooted* about what political or economic events pushed people from their homeland to America, whether it was the pogroms in the shtetls in the Ukraine or poverty in Poland.

In the slums of today—whether it is Kibera slum in Nairobi, Kenya, or Cochabamba, Bolivia, or Lima, Peru—the influx of people is not from other countries but people moving from the rural areas to the city hoping to find a better life.

In Bolivia, the Altiplano—the plane of the Andes—is very dry. All the rain drops in the Amazon, so there is not much rain in the Andes. The high Andes of Bolivia are sparsely populated, because there is not water to grow crops. It is hard to make a living in the highlands. Whereas women walk for miles in Africa for water, women walk for miles to find wood for the fire to cook meals.

So people migrate from the highlands to the cities, hoping to find work. There is none. Often mom and dad are unemployed, and the family is supported by the son who shines shoes.

When I was in Cape Town, South Africa, I met a young woman in the townships who definitely thought she had made a step up in the world after leaving the Xhosa countryside near where Nelson Mandela grew up. Why did she think life was better? Because there was a spigot with running water. Like the Tanzanians, she had had to walk miles for water in the countryside.

## Helping in the Slums of Mongolia

In Mongolia, where our colleagues ask for social workers to help in the slums, the nomads lived for generations in their yurts in the countryside.

Mongolia, the land of Genghis Khan and nomadic herders, is in the midst of a remarkable transition. Rich in coal, gold, and copper, this country of fewer than three million people is riding a mineral boom that is expected to more than double its GDP within a decade. Some now call Mongolia "Mine-golia."

Nomads are flooding into Ulaan Baatar, hoping to get a piece of the action. Just like the peasants flooding into Lima, there are not the jobs that they thought there would be. They are finding that the Canadian mining companies require that their Mongolian workers know how to speak English.

So just as in Africa, where people bring their style of housing to the city, there is a yurt slum at the edge of Ulaan Baatar.

There are one million people in Ulaan Baatar, and 60% of the people live in the slums. As in the countryside, it is cold. Ulaan Baatar sits just south of Lake Baikal in Siberia. So the people in the yurts burn wood or coal for heat. Thus, Ulaan Baatar now has the second worst air pollution in the world. So another initiative is to help get solar cookers into the yurts in the capital.

As with Jane Addams in Chicago, the social work challenges are similar in the slums of Mongolia—helping the people improve their housing, sanitation, and water; set up schools; create livelihoods or a way to "get by" if they do not get a job in the mines.

So are you up for the challenge in Mongolia? Jane Addams would be proud.

*Ann McLaughlin, MSW, ACSW, directs NGOabroad, a service that helps people enter or advance in international humanitarian work and provides frugal, customized volunteer opportunities.*

# Comprehending the Social Work Licensing Exams: A Brief Intro
## by Susan Mankita, LCSW

There is nothing that frustrates me more than when a good social worker can't pass the licensure exam. I am a firm believer that every good social worker *can* earn his or her professional license, once he or she has the appropriate tools.

According to the website of the Association of Social Work Boards (ASWB), the developer and administrator of the exams, in 2013, 77.9% of first time test takers passed the clinical exam, 82.3% passed the master's exam, 77.8% passed the bachelor's exam, and 75.3% of those who took the advanced generalist exam passed.

Clearly, only a percentage of social workers who take a licensure test will pass it on the first try. In 2013, 2,309 master's level and 2,289 clinical level exam takers did not.

For many of these social workers, this is the beginning of a frustrating process involving more study, self-doubt, and anxiety. Many assume that purchasing expensive study guides, making more flashcards, or memorizing more of the DSM is the key to their licensure success.

Although that's possible, it is likely that what they need *first* are Exam Question Comprehension Skills. Once trained to understand the anatomy of an ASWB test question, it becomes possible for social workers to successfully apply all the knowledge, skills, and abilities they regularly use in their day-to-day practices.

ASWB doesn't list statistics on how many pass on their *next* try. The good news is that some will be able to do so simply by increasing their preparation efforts.

## Exam question comprehension skills

Every test question can be dissected and understood. Even better, ANYONE can learn to do this, even if it doesn't come naturally. If you are someone whose head starts to swim every time you see a complex scenario, this may be exactly the skillset that you are missing.

ALL high stakes professional exams have certain things in common, or they wouldn't be able to call themselves valid and reliable. A "good" item (not all are in the form of a question) MUST be constructed in a certain way in order to meet these criteria. That means there is both a formula for writing them AND a process for understanding them. Once you recognize that the exam is testing to insure that we have the knowledge, and the capability of applying it, even in challenging situations, it's easier to recognize what is being tested. In a nutshell, the exam is testing to see if a social worker can:

- recognize, understand, and apply the values and standards of the social work profession
- use best practices with clients
- prioritize well
- pick the best intervention for the given situation
- communicate the effective "social work" way
- focus on what is most important at a given point in time
- critically evaluate a series of options and choose the best one from a pool of good ones
- act ethically and in the clients' best interest

Dissecting a test question to see which of the above is being tested is critical to success.

*Susan Mankita, LCSW, teaches licensure prep courses for social workers. In the past eight years, she has helped more than 170 individual social workers around the country, including more than 100 re-takers, pass the social work licensure exams. Look for more detailed articles on the licensing exam from Susan in future issues of* The New Social Worker.

# Burnout and SELF CARE: A Process in Helping

by David M. Papia, LCSW

Is burnout an endpoint or a process? If it is an endpoint, are professional helpers at risk for that outcome while having limited ability to do anything about it? If it is a process, doesn't that suggest we can have control over burnout?

What is this notion of self care? Is it a New Age term that we have yet to embrace collectively? Or is self care an established notion in the helping professions? Furthermore, as professionals, we want to know what burnout and self care have to do with being a good professional helper and where our responsibilities lie in relation to these issues.

## Introduction

The words "burnout" and "self care" have been catchy and useful but might need linguistic assistance. We sometimes say we are burned out. This term is static and suggests immobility. The best term may be "burning out." When we are aware that we are burning out, when we can step back and see our situation more objectively, we begin to see how burning out truly is a process. Often, we say we need to take better care of our selves. The process a professional helper undergoes may simply be referred to as "caring for our selves."

When viewed this way, we can begin to understand that burnout and self care are fluid experiences, hardly ever static, and for the professional helper this implies we can have control over these processes. As professionals, we need to address these terms and the issues sur-

rounding them. My intention is to produce clarity and support for the sake of the professional helper and, in particular, the profession of social work—a profession in which I have been intimately involved for 30 years. I have come to realize how very important it is to be knowledgeable, preventive, and proactive regarding burnout and self care.

## The Literature on Burnout and Self care

The literature on burnout has spanned nearly 40 years. Freudenberger is widely credited to be the first to apply the term (Thompson, 2009; Smullens, 2012; DeSilva, Hewage, & Fonseka, 2009; Waugh & Judd, 2003). He referred to burnout as having the experiences of feeling like a failure, feeling worn out, and becoming exhausted (Thompson, 2009).

Other early authors have had similar views on the subject of helping and burnout. In Edelwich and Brodsky's study (as cited in DeSilva, Hewage, & Fonseka, 2009), the authors state that the professional feels "a progressive loss of idealism, energy, and purpose." In Pines and Aronson's study (as cited in Waugh and Judd, 2003), the authors state the professional feels "a state of physical, emotional, and mental exhaustion." Maslach seems to be the most widely acknowledged contributor to thinking about burnout. In her work and research (as cited in the National Association of Social Workers NASW–Professional Self Care policy, 2009), she states that

burnout is "a syndrome of emotional exhaustion, depersonalization, and reduced personal accomplishment that can occur among individuals who do 'people-work' of some kind."

With this historical view of burnout, we could easily be led to the sense that burnout is a downward spiraling experience that brings us to an unfortunate end. What I see in these descriptions is that burnout equates, in functional terms, to the professional having less capacity to sustain and less capacity to give.

Self care is not new to our profession. In Poulin and Walter's study about burnout and self care (as cited in Smullens, 2012), they address how burnout can be reversed and that self care is "a process that can be engaged to restore balance in our personal and professional lives." Maran Dale (2008, November), in her article, "The Profession Must Prioritize Self Care," addresses the individual social worker's responsibility and the responsibility of educational settings and agencies to provide healthy work environments. Tracy Whitaker (as cited in Dale, 2008), said, "We learned that it was not the clients themselves who were causing the major portion of the stress, but the work environment itself," and, "The primary stress social workers face is that they don't have enough time to do their jobs, and related to that, have too heavy a workload," and "This was true across practice areas."

The NASW Policy Statement on Professional Self Care, approved by the NASW Delegate Assembly in August 2008, is a gift to our social work profession, as well as to other helping professions. This Policy Statement addresses how "the practice of self care" is not only the way to respond to our occupational stressors, but it is also "a core essential component" to our competent and effective ongoing professional practice (2009). As this policy statement describes self care and articulates the case for the vital importance that self care has for the professional and the profession of social work, and as this statement describes burnout and its effect on the professional, it challenges all of us to respond and to move forward.

## Burnout in Social Work

Our social work profession is noble. This is a very special career path. We get to participate in important matters in people's lives. We learn about ourselves, about others, and about humanity. We

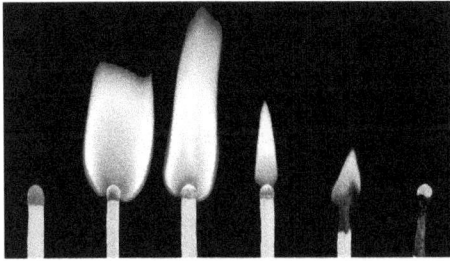

engage in giving and receiving, and we engage in relationships that further who we are and further those to whom we attend. However, our profession comes with many significant challenges and occupational hazards that threaten to weaken our profession and the resolve of the professional social worker.

We know that our profession has become deeply entrenched in managed care practices, bureaucracies and governing bodies determining our daily work conditions, very high caseloads, low salaries, and a profound amount of accountability expectations. These realities and conditions can and sometimes do weigh very heavily. It is easy to recognize the feelings and sentiment of doubt and questioning: *Should I continue in this profession? Am I enjoying my job? How can I sustain?* We might even wonder if someone should consider entering our profession. As a father whose daughter has recently gone off to college and has an interest in social work, I notice myself being "on the fence" about her interest in our field.

We also have the stressors and realities of doing clinical work day after day. Smullens (2012) articulates the stressors, psychological issues, and "sheer exhaustion" associated with clinical work in describing and defining burnout. Smullens expands her discussion about burnout when she addresses the "attendant syndromes" of vicarious traumatization, compassion fatigue, and secondary traumatic stress—and their resulting effect on the social worker. It is commonly known that doing clinical work, and especially work with very challenging and traumatized populations, presents risks for experiencing burnout. Suffice it to say, the experience of burnout as an occupational hazard in our profession has its roots in clinical, organizational, and systematic experiences we face daily.

## Self Care in Social Work

There are literally hundreds of self care practices available to the professional helper. *A Self Care Assessment,* provided by Saakvitne, Pearlman, & Staff (adapted by Lisa D. Butler, Ph.D., University of Buffalo School of Social Work) details a self care worksheet that is divided into six life areas: physical, psychological, emotional, spiritual, relationships, and workplace or professional. This helps us to see how ideas about self care can be presented in various forms, giving us a number of ways to view and consider different practices.

The Columbia University School of Social Work, as discussed in its "News and Events" in November 2012, offered two experiential self care days for social work students, meant to enhance the lives of the students and help them to define

what self care is for them and to learn to practice self care. As a result, the school's students began to better understand self care and then include that in their daily functioning.

When self care practices are examined, understood, and put into practice, we see they all—no matter what form they come in—essentially give us the same outcomes: we become rejuvenated, energized, inspired, healed, restored, and happier. In so doing, we become increasingly capable to continue to serve others, to give to others, to engage in giving and receiving in a manner and to the degree that honors our profession and the role of a professional helper. Self care practices improve and enhance our human being-ness and our human performance. They help our heart to remain open, our mind to remain clear, and our compassion to come forth. The social work profession, as with other helping professions, requires us to know our selves and effectively use our selves in our professional capacities. Caring for our selves will help us to become more of our selves closer to our fullest potential.

## Our Challenge: The Time Has Come

Victor Hugo has been widely quoted as saying, "There is one thing stronger than all the armies in the world and that is an idea whose time has come" (Kolsbun & Sweeney 2008, pp. 20-21). The idea I wish to put forth is the following: Because burnout (burning out) and self care (caring for our self) are two of the most significant issues we will encounter during our careers, it is imperative that we be well informed, that we do respond, and that our response is wise and effective. I believe that by changing our *viewing* and changing our *doing* relative to burnout and self care, this will open up immeasurable possibilities for growth and will support our response that is needed.

*Viewing:* When we are viewing burnout (burning out) and self care (caring for our selves) as ongoing processes, this offers us a real sensibility that these issues are under our control; something we can manage and develop mastery over. Additionally, defining these terms in a way that captures their functional nature is also to our advantage. Burning out and caring for our self are active and dynamic entities that do not exist in isolation. Their definitions need to make sense in our world of social work, where our primary mode of functioning is through the relationship. To that end, I offer the following definitions.

*Burnout:* Whereas burnout (burning out) happens in relationships, and it is influenced by conditions, situations, experiences, and our attitudes, the process of burning out leaves us feeling depleted and having less capacity to give to and connect with others.

*Self care:* The effects and outcomes of self care (caring for our selves) are what we bring to our relationships. The process of caring for our selves leaves us feeling enriched and having more capacity to give to and connect with others. I believe that viewing burnout and self care in these ways guides us to become ready to act accordingly, and differently, when needed.

*Doing:* As professional helpers, we want the situations and outcomes to improve for those we serve. We want this for ourselves, as well. To be effective and to make these improvements, we need to be conscious and active participants in the ongoing processes of burning out and caring for our self. We know we will continue to be confronted with risks for burning out. And we know that caring for our self will help us to overcome those situations. I firmly believe that with understanding burning out and caring for our self to be ongoing processes, and with knowing we can effectively participate in these processes, we can bring about positive change. Participating in these ongoing processes will be a matter of choices we make during our careers. To engage in properly addressing the challenges we face is to become wise and learned professionals. And to engage in caring for our selves is a vitally important career decision—one that will benefit us every step along our journeys as helping professionals.

## References

Columbia University School of Social Work. (2012, November 9, 21). Retrieved from *http://socialwork.columbia.edu/news-events/how-social-work-students-define-and-practice-self-care*.

Dale, M. (2008, November). The profession must prioritize self care. *NASW News,* National Association of Social Workers.

DeSilva, P. V., Hewage, C. G., & Fonseka, P. (2009, September). Burnout: an emerging occupational health problem. *Galle Medical Journal, 14* (1), 52-55.

Kolsbun, K., & Sweeney, M. (2008). *Peace: the biography of a symbol*. Washington, DC.: National Geographic Society.

National Association of Social Workers. (2009). *Professional self care policy*. In *Social work speaks: National Association of Social Workers policy statements 2009-2012* (8th ed., pp. 268-272). Washington, DC.: NASW Press.

Saakvitne, Pearlman, & staff of TSI/CAAP. (1996). *Transforming the Pain: A workbook on vicarious traumatization*. Norton. Retrieved from *http://www.ballarat.edu.au/aasp/student/sds/self_care_assess.shtml* and adapted by Lisa D. Butler, Ph.D.

Smullens, S. (2012). What I wish I had known: Burnout and self care in our social work profession. *The New Social Worker, 19* (4), 6-9.

Thompson, B. (2009, February 16). *Burnout: definition and risks*. Retrieved from *http://biznik.com/articles*.

Waugh, C., & Judd, M. (2003, Spring). Trainer burnout: the syndrome explored. *Journal of Career and Technical Education, 19* (2), 47-57.

*David M. Papia, LCSW, earned his master's degree in social work at the University of Buffalo. He is employed at Child and Family Services, a large human service agency in Buffalo, New York, whose roots trace back to the first Charity Organization Society in the United States.*

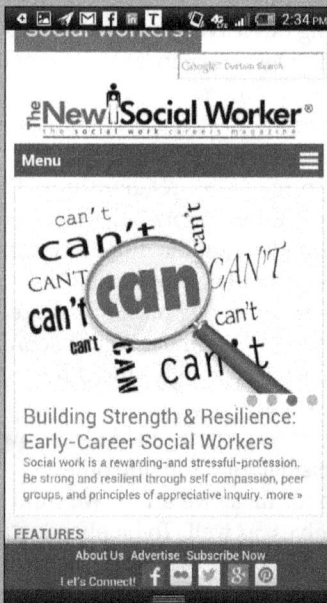

# Social Work Goes to the Movies

## How Movies Can Help in Working With Kids
### by Addison Cooper, LCSW

I recently reviewed the new Disney film, *Planes: Fire and Rescue.* One of the things I liked best about the film was the protagonist's torque meter. Maybe I should explain that. *Planes: Fire and Rescue* is the sequel to Disney's 2013 film *Planes.* In the first film, humble workaday plane Dusty Crophopper becomes a famous racing plane. A year later, Dusty is still enjoying his celebrity status; however, he finds that he is having difficulty performing at the level his fans are used to. A mechanic explains the problem: Dusty's machinery is breaking down and cannot be replaced. Too much torque will cause Dusty to break. To help him avoid disaster, the mechanic installs a meter that will help Dusty assess how much stress he is under. The mechanic even includes a warning light to let Dusty know when he is being over-taxed.

This reminded me of a tool introduced in Karyn Purvis' Trust-Based Parenting video curriculum, in which kids are asked to indicate the level of emotional energy they're feeling by using a simple, home-crafted indicator. I suggested something similar on my site, *Adoption at the Movies,* and a reader sent in photos of a very interesting emotional tachometer. A colorful needle can be moved around to point to a range of faces, each illustrating, and labeled with, a different emotion.

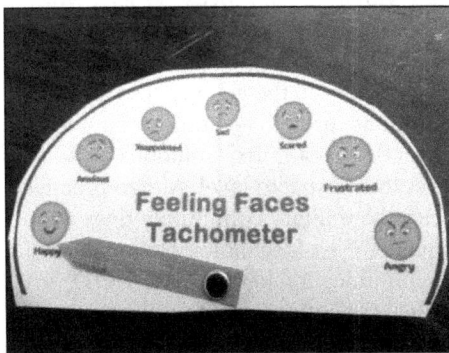

*Image credit: Her at Parents of Color Seek Newborn to Adopt*

This could certainly be a helpful tool for families and professionals to use in helping kids identify their difficult emotions, and it might be more palatable to kids, since it can be tied into the story of a beloved film hero.

Here are some other ideas of how movies can tie into exercises that families can use to help their kids talk about their feelings.

In *Frozen,* Elsa has struggled with others' expectations that she hide her feelings and other truths about herself. She finally faces the pressure of these expectations and decides to "let it go." She embraces herself, but still expects that others will not accept her. She later finds that others do accept her for who she is. A video of the song could be an invitation (or a celebration) for a child to work toward releasing shame. A simple question could be asked: "What would you let go, if you could?"

In the delightful French film *Ernest and Celestine,* a bear and a mouse become friends—and ultimately become family—even though their respective cultures expect them to be incompatible enemies. This could be suggested viewing for kids who are struggling with membership in a blended or multicultural family. Little Celestine draws pictures to convey her impression of her relationship with Ernest, and parents could invite children, after watching the film, to be like Celestine and draw family pictures.

Disney's *Meet the Robinsons* focuses on Lewis, an orphan who mourns a loss from his past until he is confronted with a hopeful future. This film could be used to encourage children to optimistically imagine the future while also examining the past. Lewis is an inventor; after watching the movie, parents could ask children to use Legos to design an imaginary invention that will make the world better. Once it's built, parents can ask children what it does, how it works, and how it makes the world better.

In *The Tigger Movie,* the "bouncy, trouncy, pouncy, flouncy, fun, fun, fun, fun" tiger conveys his loneliness at being the only tiger among his group of friends. He wonders where the other tigers must be, and although he does not find them, he finds comfort and belonging in his group of friends. He also carries a locket, which holds a picture of the thing closest to him. A child could be asked to design a similar locket to identify the things that are most important. It can be opened, to share what is important, or closed, to provide security that you can keep your thoughts confidential for a time. The child can choose when to open or close the locket (and also, when to change the picture, and what to change it to).

In *Rise of the Guardians,* a character uses nesting dolls to illustrate that people have many layers to their identities. Children could be invited to see the film and then complete a similar craft to express the different aspects of how they perceive themselves and how they wish to be perceived. Parents could provide a series of small jewelry boxes, and on the outside of each box, in sequence, children can draw how they want to be seen by strangers, friends, and family, with each smaller box representing how the child wishes to be seen by the more intimate group of people. On the inside of the smallest box, children can draw representations of who they believe they are, or of who they wish to be.

This is a small list of suggestions. Many films are released each year, and many kids are often excited about the newest film. Why not make the cinema part of your professional development? With a clinical eye, movies can provide an excellent and easy way to connect with clients, to provide them with understandable analogies, and possibly even provide exercises to use at home!

*Addison Cooper is a Licensed Clinical Social Worker in California and Missouri. He reviews films and writes movie discussion guides for foster and adoptive families at Adoption at the Movies (www.adoptionlcsw. com), and is a supervisor at a foster care and adoption agency in Southern California. His articles on adoption and film have also appeared in Adoptive Families and Foster Focus magazines. Find him on Twitter @AddisonCooper.*

# Turn Up the Tech in Social Work

## Solving the Veterans' Crisis With Technology and Advocacy

### *by Ellen Belluomini, LCSW*

Technology in systems is only as good as the planning behind it. An example of needing a systems plan integrating technology is the current crisis in Veterans' mental health and health care. The U.S. Department of Veterans Affairs (2011) estimated there were almost 23 million veterans in the United States. Yet only 7.8 million veterans use their health care benefits. The VA's current access audit uncovered the need for 90,000 veterans to be contacted because of their long wait times. Over the past 10 years 64,869 veterans never saw a clinician after being enrolled. The United States surpasses the world in technology, yet large government systems such as the VA and the Affordable Care Act remain rife with technology problems. Social workers can advocate for systems changes with technology solutions.

The Department of Veterans Affairs (VA) and Department of Defense (DOD) excel in implementing programs for micro systems. The VA is innovative in development of health and mental health phone applications. The DOD provides free training and information for mental health and health providers. The U.S. Department of Health and Human Services Health Resources and Services Administration (HRSA), the Center for Deployment Psychology, the National Council for Behavioral Health, and the Defense Centers of Excellence for Psychological Health and Traumatic Brain Injury offer an introduction of education toward effective care for military populations. The only issue with these services is how the information is disseminated.

Unless providers are willing to surf the Internet for education and training, they may inappropriately treat military clientele.

I worked as a Family Advocacy Prevention Specialist on the Great Lakes Naval Base and as the director of an emergency shelter program on a VA campus. These experiences trained me to provide services to military members and their families. The manner of my practice with these military populations differs significantly from that with civilian populations. Common issues addressed include military values, power issues, trauma reactions, conflict resolution practices, and reintegration problems. These differences create a culture friction between military families and civilian lifestyles.

Here are some troubling statistics from the U.S. Department of Veterans Affairs:

- Veterans with Post Traumatic Stress Disorder
  » Almost 31% of Vietnam veterans
  » As many as 10% of Gulf War (Desert Storm) veterans
  » 11% of veterans of the war in Afghanistan
  » 20% of Iraqi war veterans
- 22 veterans commit suicide each day, the highest percent between the ages of 50 and 59.
- 57,849 veterans are homeless on any given night, and 1.4 million veterans are at risk of being homeless.
- The rate of depression is five times higher in soldiers than civilians.
- 55% of women and 38% of men report being victims of sexual harassment in the military.
- 20% of Iraq and Afghanistan veterans have substance abuse addictions after returning home.
- Of reported domestic violence situations in the U.S., 21% of these include combat veterans.

Military values and practices are not the same as in the civilian sector, but how are social workers addressing these variations? I informally asked several colleagues in the community who regularly work with military families. Not one of the 10 professionals I surveyed had ever taken any type of online or in-person training in the cultural literacy of military populations. Only one professional had taken a course on a treatment (EMDR) that specifically addressed military members as a subpopulation. Although all of the professionals "knew a veteran" from their extended family or friends list, they had never had a conversation with them about their military experience. Education is a gap within treatment of this population.

Higher education is responding to the need for specialization in working with military populations by providing training for social workers. The University of Southern California (USC) is breaking ground with research and education on military populations. USC developed a technology simulation to help social work students. The Motivational Interviewing Learning Environment and Simulation (MILES) allows students to practice therapy with a military member simulation. MILES is groundbreaking in its approach to supporting military studies. Some social work schools are offering concentrations and certificates in military social work. The Council on Social Work Education provides a full list of universities with a military focused social work degree or certificate program. (See *http://www.cswe.org/default.aspx?id=17491.*)

How well the government creates solutions through technology on a micro level does not mirror solutions on a mezzo and macro level. Mezzo practice with the military community does not include use of technology to enhance communication between the DOD, VA, veterans support programs, and community services. Each agency has separate electronic medical records and its own approach to mental health services. One community is not aware of the interventions of the other unless by self-report. The government is responding on a macro level with an increase in VA medical services, but it is not including mental health alternatives in this package. Societal solutions need to include the entire continuum of care.

Technology provides a bridge to services and communication. The Department of Housing and Urban Development financially supports each community's Continuums of Care planning body for people experiencing homelessness to develop a single point of access to its system. This coordinated entry system moves people more quickly through services, provides communication of care between agencies, minimizes duplication of services, and increases the data collection accuracy on client needs for future services. This is a government system easily replicated for military communities. The system is effective for urban, suburban, and rural areas.

Social workers do not have to recreate the wheel in addressing needs of the military community. Awareness of this population's cultural differences coupled with a collaborated voice of advocacy can make a difference. Military members and their families have made sacrifices for the stability of our nation. We need to work toward stabilization of their family systems.

*Ellen M. Belluomini, LCSW, received her MSW from the University of Illinois, Jane Addams School of Social Work and is currently a doctoral student at Walden University. She is a lecturer at Dominican University. She has developed online and blended curricula with an emphasis on integrating technology into human services practice. She writes a blog, Bridging the Digital Divide in Social Work Practice, to increase awareness about technology's uses. She presents and consults on various issues related to social services. Her clinical work has been in private practice, management of nonprofit agencies, and programming for vulnerable populations.*

**Share this issue of THE NEW SOCIAL WORKER with your friends, colleagues, and classmates!**

# Accessing Apps: Veterans
*by Ellen Belluomini, LCSW*

These apps are not only specific to veterans, but can help a wide range of clients with similar mental health issues. Mostly government funded, these apps can be used at no cost. Access the applications by placing the name of the app in a web browser.

**BioZen**
This is a portable biofeedback app created by the Department of Defense. It monitors electroencephalogram (EEG), electromyography (EMG), galvanic skin response (GSR), electrocardiogram (ECG or EKG), respiratory rate, and skin temperature. It also displays Delta, Theta, Alpha, Beta, and Gamma brain waves. It does need a biosensing device (BioPatch, BrainAthlete, NeuroSky), which can be pricey.
Android Free

**Breath2Relax**
This app develops a person's diaphragmatic breathing to help with anxiety and anger control. The screen is visually appealing and tracks information.
Android and Apple Free

**LifeArmor**
This is an education app for military members. Seventeen different topic areas include education, assessment tools, tools to improve mental health, and videos from military members on how they manage different problems.
Android and Apple Free

**mTBI Pocket Guide**
The Mild Traumatic Brain Injury Pocket Guide is an educational app for up-to-date clinical and medical care. It helps with assessment, diagnosis, and treatment of brain injuries. Coding is also a feature of this app.
Android and Apple Free

**MyHealtheVet**
This app helps veterans track their personal health records. Prescriptions can be filled online from the app. When seeing VA doctors, patients can pull up their records for immediate education of medical personnel. Since veterans will be able to see outside providers more easily now, this app can act as communication between the VA system and the civilian world without the red tape.
Android and Apple Free

**PE Coach**
Prolonged exposure treatment is an evidence-based treatment to decrease distress caused by trauma. Therapy sessions are recorded for later use by the client. The app tracks homework and symptoms for the clinician. The client is provided psychoeducation, homework forms, breathing retraining, and scheduling of their practice sessions.
Android and Apple Free

**Positive Activity Jackpot**
This is one of my favorites. This app schedules "pleasant events" to decrease depression. Local activities and invites increase the ability for people to reach out to others. I use this as a supplement and reinforcement for exploring activities in session.
Android and Apple Free

**Provider Resilience**
Working with veterans' issues can be intense for therapists. Compassion fatigue is addressed through this app. Burnout surveys and resilience tools help clinicians be aware of their level of stress and provide mechanisms for renewal. This tool is a nice reminder of how we can use technology for ourselves.
Android and Apple Free

**Virtual Hope Box**
This supplement to treatment addresses behavior from a positive psychology route. Tools for this app include relaxation, positive thinking options, distraction games, and coping education. I especially like the ability to create your own affirmations on virtual cards. I use Louise Hay's cards as supplements.
Android and Apple Free

# Reviews

*Pleading Insanity, by Andrew James Archer, Archway Publishing, Bloomington, IN, 2013, 275 pages, $18.*

*Pleading Insanity* is a personal account of the author's early struggles with bipolar disorder. The author, Andrew Archer, introduces the topic discussing his genetic link for the disorder, as the child of a parent who was also diagnosed with bipolar disorder. He states, "I never wanted to turn out like him," yet points out that even early on, there were symptoms of his own struggles from infancy, through childhood, adolescence, and young adulthood.

Archer discusses his symptoms and experiences as they begin to escalate during his freshman year in college. What is remarkable is the amount of detail Archer is able to recall and the painful emotions the retelling of his story must surely invoke. He describes his thoughts and behavior in such a way that the reader is often laughing and similarly wanting to cry as he describes his mania and his depression.

What sets this book apart from others about this topic is Archer's honesty and firsthand accounts of his thought processes, as faulty as they may be, and his behaviors, which do not seem so farfetched once they are paired with his thinking. Especially helpful to the reader are parenthetical diagnostic criteria to provide a link between his symptomatology and that described in the terminology of the DSM IV. This link adds clarity for any reader, whether mental health professional, family member, friend, or someone diagnosed with bipolar disorder.

Archer also describes his struggles with alcohol and drugs, which initially appeared to be a method of self-regulation/self-medication that soon escalated out of control. He describes how family and friends tried to help him, but they either didn't know what do to or, because of legalities, were unable to intervene. He makes an important observation that sometimes the very system that is in place to help those experiencing mental illnesses are also the systems preventing timely intervention by loved ones.

Given the media coverage of the past several years and the correlation being created between acts of "random" violence and the mental health of those perpetrating the violence, perhaps avenues of intervention need tweaking.

The author, after experiencing a disruption in his education, getting involved in the legal system, experiencing cycles of mania and depression, is able to ultimately get his MSW and LICSW. Through his struggles, Archer learns the approach that has helped him to live a healthy life and reduce recurring episodes, which he describes using the image of a "carpenter triangle"–medication, support, and mindfulness.

*Pleading Insanity* should be required reading for anyone going into the fields of social work, psychology, or mental health. Additionally, the book is helpful for anyone who has a family member or friend who has to live with bipolar disorder, as well as anyone who wants to gain a better understanding of mental illness. I thoroughly enjoyed reading the book and highly recommend it.

*Reviewed by Nancy Anderson, MSW, Social Work Field Education Director at Warner University.*

---

*Gender-Inclusive Treatment of Intimate Partner Abuse, Second Edition, by John Hamel, 2014, New York: Springer Publishing Company, $56.*

John Hamel, LCSW, has written a well-designed and possibly controversial 376-page book in regard to evidence-based approaches for gender-inclusive treatment of intimate partner abuse.

The book consists of three main components, including research, assessment, and treatment. The research component focuses specifically on partner abuse today and details the prevalence of partner abuse, its impact on partners and families, and an in-depth summary of research regarding prevalence/context/risk factors/impact on victims and families.

The assessment component focuses explicitly on diagnostic issues and conducting partner abuse assessments. Specifically, the diagnostic issues focus on categorizing partner abuse, partner abuse in the DSM-5, dominant aggressor assessment, anger and coercion, assessing victims, and why partner abuse is under-detected by therapists. The conducting of assessments focuses on general guidelines/protocol, considerations for LGBT and ethnic minorities, and substance and partner abuse.

The treatment aspect is especially detailed in regard to developing the treatment plan, group work, family systems, couple interventions, working with families, and partner abuse in disputed child custody cases.

*Gender-Inclusive Treatment of Intimate Partner Abuse* is essential to a social worker's literary collection. Often, social workers overlook the macro level of social work practice. "Do we want to be politically correct or do we want to reduce domestic violence in our communities?" (Hamel, p. xxiii) Sadly, most funding for domestic violence is appropriated to the majority of domestic violence victims (e.g., women). However, Hamel provides thorough evidence to suggest that we are forgetting a population: men. His research reveals a disturbing report of 302 male victims who contacted the domestic abuse helpline, in which half of them were not taken seriously.

Hamel is clearly drawing a line to stand up for all genders and emphasizing taking male victims more seriously, especially in regard to emotional abuse and control (coercive behavior) in which he says men and women have nearly identical rates. The traditional domestic violence treatment, which typically focuses on a feminine perspective, is colliding with a more evidence-based approach of gender equality through a psychotherapeutic type of treatment.

Whether you are a traditionalist or progressive in regard to domestic violence, there is no denying Hamel addresses the concept of "bridging the gap" between social workers and domestic violence counselors with evidence-based concepts found within the text.

The *NASW Code of Ethics* demands that we adhere to ethical principles such as service, social justice, dignity and worth of a person, importance of human relationships, integrity, and competence. Hamel is clearly demonstrating a knowledge and application of all of these principles, which can be evidenced through his text. This is a must-have text for social workers who strive for excellence within our field and want to see progress within the domestic violence treatment field.

*Reviewed by Craig Carpenter, LCSW, Associate Licensee,Clinical Social Worker, U.S. Military.*

---

*Trans Bodies, Trans Selves, Laura Erickson-Schroth, Editor, Oxford University Press, 2014, 672 pages, $35 paperback, $15 Kindle.*

At a time when the first transgender woman on the cover of *Time* magazine is also nominated for an Emmy Award, and at a time when the frequent and brutal murders of transgender people are becoming increasingly reported about in local and national news media, it can be difficult for anyone to tell whether trans equality is moving forward or backward. Add in that there are so many terms and phrases, as well as so much question for social workers about what is and isn't appropriate, and this book clearly comes at the perfect time.

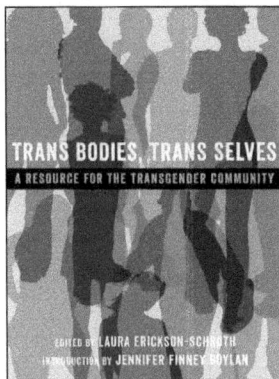

Social workers and other professionals certainly need to know every bit of what is contained within, but it is certainly more realistic to think of this book instead as more of a reference book.

Bridging the gap between being understandable to the newest of readers and being helpful to those more versed in transgender issues, the vastness of topics covered includes everything from sex work to sexual safety, from romantic relationships to personal feelings about one's changing body. The mix of personal stories and professional guidance from doctors and therapists allows the reader to have a well-rounded learning experience about each of the topics.

In addition, a great deal of transgender history is discussed, something crucial to the transgender experience, yet so often not considered. This allows every reader to see the full and colorful history of transgender issues, the trans equality movement as it has been occurring and continues to occur, and what may be happening in the lives of individual trans people.

In addition, this book may or may not be a great recommendation for clients and requires a clinician to know each's personality and situation. Whereas one client may feel inspired or calmed by having access to the stories of those who have previously walked the transgender path, others may feel overwhelmed by the depth of the information. One parent of a trans person may feel comforted in knowing his or her own child isn't alone in this process, and another parent may feel the information is too much, too soon and do better learning about the process as the child (or adult child) goes through the experience.

As previously said, it is understandably unlikely that a non-specialized professional would read this book cover to cover at one time. Certainly, every clinician should read through the index, familiarize him/herself with the proper terminology, and begin to review the history and future of the transgender population. As much as we have come to learn about the uniqueness of the story of other minority groups, this is no less important and, though the population is hidden from most school texts, it certainly deserves to be known.

It is worth mentioning that this book contains discussions related to gender as being non-binary, as well as how or why a person identifies outside of the binary norms. Professionals and clients may question and struggle with these concepts, as they are not necessarily mainstream opinions. Others may struggle with some of the discussions related to medical interventions and transitions because of their religious beliefs. This note is not to discourage anyone from reading this book. Certainly, everyone is entitled to his or her own value system. However, it is encouraged that the reader approach this book with a willingness to learn and to listen.

*Reviewed by Kristen Marie (Kryss) Shane, MSW, LSW, LMSW.*

---

*Practical Supervision, by Penny Henderson, Jim Holloway, Anthea Millar, 2014, Jessica Kingsley Publishers, 160 pages, $22.42.*

*Practical Supervision* is a comprehensive and well outlined examination of the process and content of solid supervision. Early in the book, the authors examine the fact that clinicians often are thrown into supervision roles without any training or guidance. Their goal in presenting this material is to "orient people new to supervision in various helping professions to possibilities and practicalities" (p. 13.) The authors deliver exactly as promised; the book teaches practical supervision.

The authors approach supervision from an experienced and well-read perspective, which examines the supervisor's internal process while also studying the supervisor's actions and the supervisee's response to supervision and to the client.

With just the right combination of practical wisdom and an understanding of the need for new supervisors to learn specific supervision skills, the authors present a useable guide to effective supervision. Readers will come away with practical ideas for the development of the clinical relationship and for exploring tasks, skills, and the dynamic process of supervision, as opposed to management. The book discusses how to handle clinical elements that occur in supervision, such as creativity, unconscious processes, and ethics.

Lastly, special modalities are discussed, such as the use of technology, group supervision, and other different contexts and roles of supervision. Throughout, the authors provide an outline for supervision that includes specific exercises and resources that can further the reader's understanding of these topics. *Practical Supervision* provides resources and further education for the more seasoned supervisor who wants to improve his or her supervision sessions.

As a clinician and experienced clinical supervisor, I believe this book is truly a manual for all new supervisors who are interested in improving the effectiveness of their supervision. It allows readers to identify their supervisees' supervision needs and respond to them effectively and efficiently. I would recommend this book to new supervisors and others who wish to improve their effectiveness in supervision.

*Reviewed by Michelle Evans, LCSW, LSOTP, CADC, Clinical Supervisor, Cobra Clinical Services, Aurora, IL.*

## NON-PERSONNEL

### HTTP://SOCIALWORKEXAM.COM

Social Work Exam Prep Review. Prepare right on the Internet!! Multiple choice exam banks, Timed Questions, Secrets to Passing, DSM-IV Terms, Notables, all Online and Interactive. Reveal strengths and weaknesses so you can map your study strategy. Check out our FREE QUESTION SAMPLER!!
Licensure Exams, Inc.

**I TRANSLATE INTO SPANISH** books, articles, essays, blogs, websites, newsletters. Luis Baudry-Simon, Spanish translator luisbaudrysimon@gmail.com (815) 694-0713 www.lbmcm.com

Join **Peeradigm** and meet with your peers in live, online meetings. Bring a case to review or come with a professional/practice question. Get feedback from the first session. Share and learn new approaches to therapy and assessment for ongoing professional support and development. For all licensed mental health professionals. www.peeradigm.com info7@peeradigm.com

---

Social Work Employers • Publishers
Schools • Continuing Ed Providers
Please contact Linda Grobman for information on advertising in our publications and on our websites.
lindagrobman@socialworker.com

---

## The New Social Worker® in Print!

Back by popular demand! We are pleased to announce that *The New Social Worker* magazine is available in print. If you love the feeling of curling up with a hard copy of your favorite magazine, head over to *http://newsocialworker.magcloud.com* today! Several back issues are now available in this full-color, high quality print format.

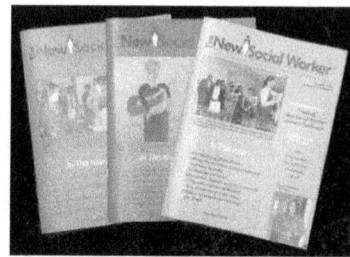

*http://newsocialworker.magcloud.com*
Contact lindagrobman@socialworker.com
for details on bulk orders.

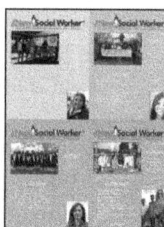

Annual volumes of *The New Social Worker* are available at Amazon.com—a whole year (4 issues) in one beautiful bound volume for each year since 2010. You can find these bound volumes at: *http://www.amazon.com/author/lindagrobman*

---

## Network With *The New Social Worker!*

As of October 1, 2014, we have reached 82,974 fans (or "likers") of our page on Facebook at *http://www.facebook.com/newsocialworker*.

Besides providing information about *The New Social Worker* magazine, the page has features of a typical Facebook timeline. We list upcoming events and send updates to our "likers" when there is something interesting happening!

Are you on Facebook? Do you love *The New Social Worker?* Show us how much you care! Be one of our Facebook "likers" and help us reach 100,000 (and beyond)!

We also have a Facebook page for our SocialWorkJobBank.com site! Go to *http://www.facebook.com/socialworkjobbank* to "like" this page. New job postings at *http://www.socialworkjobbank.com*

are now automatically posted to the Facebook page, as well.

Finally, stay up-to-date on our latest books at *http://www.facebook.com/whitehatcommunications*.

In addition, we'd like to know how *you* are using Facebook. Have you found it a useful tool for networking with social work colleagues, searching for a job, or fundraising for your agency? Write to lindagrobman@socialworker.com and let us know.

Facebook address: *http://www.facebook.com/newsocialworker*
**Also check out our other pages:**
http://www.facebook.com/socialworkjobbank
http://www.facebook.com/newsocialworkerbookclub
http://www.facebook.com/whitehatcommunications

AND...look for The New Social Worker's group on LinkedIn.com:
**http://www.linkedin.com/groups?gid=3041069**

Twitter: **http://www.twitter.com/newsocialworker**

Google+: **https://plus.google.com/+Socialworkermag/posts**

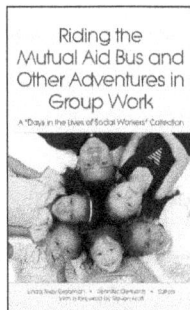

# Beginnings, Middles, & Ends
## Sideways Stories on the Art & Soul of Social Work
Ogden W. Rogers, Ph.D., LCSW, ACSW

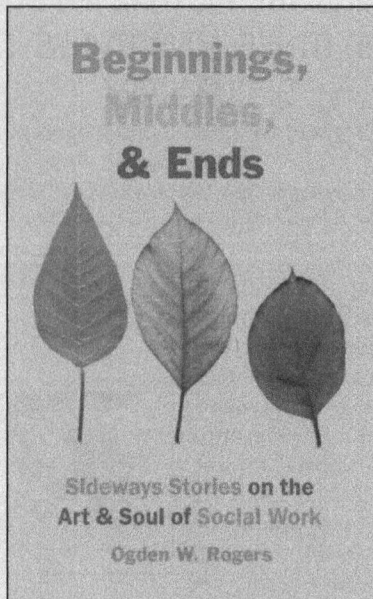

A sideways story is some moment in life when you thought you were doing one thing, but you ended up learning another. A sideways story can also be a poem, or prose, that, because of the way it is written, may not be all that direct in its meaning. What's nice about both clouds, and art, is that you can look at them and just resonate. That can be good for both the heart and the mind.

Many of the moments of this book have grown from experiences the author has had or stories he used in his lectures with students or told in his office with clients. Some of them have grown from essays written for others, for personal or professional reasons. They are moments on a path through the discovery of social work, a journey of beginnings, middles, and ends.

With just the right blend of humor and candor, each of these stories contains nuggets of wisdom that you will not find in a traditional textbook. They capture the essence and the art and soul of social work. In a world rushed with the illusion of technique and rank empiricism, it is the author's hope that some of the things here might make some moment in your thinking or feeling grow as a social worker. If they provoke a smile, or a tear, or a critical question, it's worth it. Everyone makes a different journey in a life of social work. These stories are one social worker's travelogue along the way.

## PRAISE FOR THE BOOK

"As someone near the end of a long career in social work and social work education, I found the stories of Ogden Rogers in his collection, Beginnings. Middles, and Ends, to reflect so much of my own experience that I literally moved back and forth between tears of soulful recognition and laugh-out-loud moments of wonderful remembrances. There is something truthful and powerful about the artist who is willing to put a masterpiece together and leave the telltale signs of failed attempts. Too many who reflect on their past do so to minimize imperfection, setting standards unreachable by others. Ogden Rogers has charted a course of professionalism that encourages creativity, allowing for errors, and guided by honest reflection and dedication to those whom he would serve. This read is a gift to all, whether they are starting or ending their journey of service to others."
　　Terry L. Singer, Ph.D., Dean, Kent School of Social Work, University of Louisville

"I found the stories humorous, sometimes painful, and incredibly honest and real. There is really nothing else out in our literature that is quite like this. It reminds me of when we teach the art and science of social work practice—this is the art."
　　Jennifer Clements, Ph.D., LCSW, Associate Professor, Shippensburg University

"...a profound piece of creative literature that will reinstill idealism within senior social workers who are on the threshold of being cynical about their work."
　　Stephen M. Marson, Ph.D., Professor, University of North Carolina Pembroke

"Recommended reading for new social workers, experienced social workers, friends and families of social workers, and future social workers because of the variety of anecdotal case presentations and personal perceptions. Truly open and honest portrayals of social work and the helping professions with touching, easy-to-read entries fit within the beginning, middle, and ending framework. This book is suggested for both public and academic libraries to support the career services and/or professional development collections."
　　Rebecca S. Traub, M.L.S., Library Specialist, Temple University Harrisburg

## ABOUT THE AUTHOR

**Ogden W. Rogers, Ph.D., LCSW, ACSW,** is Professor and Chair of the Department of Social Work at The University of Wisconsin-River Falls. He has been a clinician, consultant, educator, and storyteller.

ISBN: 978-1-929109-35-7 • 2013 • 5.5 x 8.5 • 249 pages • $19.95 plus shipping Order from White Hat Communications, PO Box 5390, Harrisburg, PA 17110-0390
http://shop.whitehatcommunications.com  717-238-3787 (phone)  717-238-2090 (fax)

www.ingramcontent.com/pod-product-compliance
Lightning Source LLC
Chambersburg PA
CBHW081416270326
41931CB00015B/3290